BEYOND *WRITING CULTURE*

BEYOND *WRITING CULTURE*

*Current Intersections of Epistemologies
and Representational Practices*

Olaf Zenker and Karsten Kumoll

berghahn
NEW YORK · OXFORD
www.berghahnbooks.com

First published in 2010 by

Berghahn Books

www.berghahnbooks.com

©2010, 2013 Olaf Zenker and Karsten Kumoll
First paperback edition published in 2013

Library of Congress Cataloging-in-Publication Data

Zenker, Olaf.
  Beyond writing culture : current intersections of epistemologies and representational practices / Olaf Zenker and Karsten Kumoll.
    p. cm.
  Includes bibliographical references and index.
  ISBN 978-1-84545-675-7 (hardback) -- ISBN 978-1-84545-817-1 (institutional ebook) -- ISBN 978-1-78238-333-8 (paperback) -- ISBN 978-1-78238-334-5 (retail ebook)
  1. Ethnology–Authorship. 2. Ethnology–Methodology. I. Kumoll, Karsten. II. Title.
  GN307.7.Z46 2010
  306.01–dc22

                                                                    2010007284

British Library Cataloguing in Publication Data

A catalogue record for this book is available from the British Library

ISBN: 978-1-78238-333-8 paperback
ISBN: 978-1-78238-334-5 retail ebook

Contents

Preface

This is a book about anthropological thinking and anthropological writing in general. It addresses problems of knowledge, of the validity of knowledge, and of representation. What, for example, is the relationship between a description and what is described? Who writes about whose 'culture' (or who writes whose culture) and on which grounds, with which credentials, which legitimation?

All this is not conflict theory but 'general anthropology', at least in the sense of a library classification. Or is it? There are at least three reasons why this book fits into the research programme of my department 'Integration and Conflict' at the Max Planck Institute for Social Anthropology in Halle, Germany. The first concerns the interests of particular researchers in the field of conflict studies. The contributions on which the chapters in this book are based were first delivered in a workshop that was organized by members of my department. The organizers had come to the conclusion that the issues addressed in *Writing Culture* were relevant for their work on conflict; therefore, they wanted to explore these issues with a select group of colleagues and to draw new conclusions for contemporary research. So, general anthropology or not, the issues discussed in these chapters are also of interest to conflict analysts.

The second reason has to do with the history of the particular type of anthropology that it addresses. One of the roots of the *Writing Culture* approach to anthropology is critical anthropology, a tradition that goes back to two volumes dealing with the relationship between anthropology and colonialism (Hymes 1969; Asad 1973). This relationship has implicated anthropology in a very conflictual, often violent history and has, therefore, remained a bone of contention among anthropologists.

The third reason is not historical but may be derived instead from contemporary debates. Problems of representation – for example, determining whose views of society get promulgated, who speaks about whom and who speaks for whom – are *always* political, always conflictual, though, fortunately, they are not always resolved by resorting to violent means.

In all of these senses, the issues addressed in this book are not just matters of general anthropology but also of conflict studies. In fact, the problems addressed in the *Writing Culture* debate represent only a portion of those aspects of general anthropology that are necessarily part of doing research on conflicts. Just as the study of conflict is a part of anthropology (and related social sciences), so anthropology is a part of conflict studies. It can even be a part of the conflict.

Günther Schlee

References

Asad, T. (ed.) 1973. *Anthropology and the Colonial Encounter.* London: Ithaca Press.

Hymes, D. (ed.) 1969. *Reinventing Anthropology.* New York: Random House.

Acknowledgements

This volume grew out of a workshop entitled '*Beyond* Writing Culture' held at the Max Planck Institute for Social Anthropology in Halle/Saale, Germany, in September 2006, which took the twentieth anniversary of *Writing Culture's* publication as an occasion to think about current intersections of epistemologies and practices of representation. Being organized within the department 'Integration and Conflict' at the Max Planck Institute, we are very grateful to its director, Günther Schlee, both for his financial support and for his intellectual engagement. The workshop itself turned out to be a great and stimulating event, not least because of the excellent background coordination by Bettina Mann and Ralph Orlowski which was so effective to almost pass unnoticed – an adverse state we hereby wish to remedy. The subsequent revision of the manuscripts benefited greatly from the editorial work by the board members of the Berghahn series 'Integration and Conflict Studies' published in association with the Max Planck Institute, John Eidson, Peter Finke, Joachim Görlich, Jacqueline Knörr and Bettina Mann, as well as from helpful suggestions by two anonymous referees. Our endeavour to turn the different chapters into a consistent manuscript was also profoundly assisted at the Max Planck Institute by Cornelia Schnepel, to whom we are enormously indebted. Last, but not least, we wish to thank Richard Rottenburg and especially Steve Reyna for their ongoing intellectual and practical support throughout the whole project.

Olaf Zenker
Karsten Kumoll
Bern and Köln, August 2009

1

Prologue: Opening Doors Beyond *Writing Culture*

Olaf Zenker and Karsten Kumoll

❦

The publication of James Clifford and George E. Marcus's volume *Writing Culture: The Poetics and Politics of Ethnography* (Clifford and Marcus 1986b) has been represented in anthropology and beyond 'as something of a watershed in anthropological thought', as Allison James, Jenny Hockey and Andrew Dawson wrote a decade ago in their introduction to *After Writing Culture* (James, Hockey and Dawson 1997a: 1). In highlighting the epistemic and political predicaments adhering in ethnographic representation, *Writing Culture* indeed marked an important turn within anthropology, variously described as 'literary' (e.g., Scholte 1987), 'reflexive' (e.g., McCarthy 1992: 636), 'postmodern' (e.g., Wagner 1986: 99), 'deconstructive' (e.g., Sangren 1988: 405) or 'poststructural' (e.g., Nichols 1988: 57). The subsequent debate broadened to function as an important 'crystallization of uncertainties about anthropology's subject matter (traditionally, "the other"), its method (traditionally, participant observation), its medium (traditionally, the monograph) and its intention (traditionally that of informing rather than practice)' (James, Hockey and Dawson 1997a: 2). Given its impact on the discipline as a whole, few anthropologists today would deny that the volume has, in fact, come to be what Scholte (1987: 34) presaged in his review: *Writing Culture* has become a (post)modern 'classic' in anthropology.

Looking back with a historicizing gaze, the mid 1980s indeed appear as a *kairos* – a right and opportune moment – for an endeavour like *Writing Culture* and its companion volume *Anthropology as Cultural Critique* (Marcus and Fischer 1986), which itself evoked such a temporality in its subtitle, 'an experimental moment in the human sciences'. While it remains debatable whether *Writing Culture* and concomitant texts actually delivered a timely fulfilment (*kairosis*), this *kairos* nevertheless contributed to establishing the edition as 'both the culmination of earlier developments in the profession and the sign-post of a new era in the discipline' (Bunzl 1999: 260). *Writing Culture* thereby elaborated on earlier debates within the anthropological profession on objectivity, colonialism, reflexivity and literary sensibility, to mention but a few. At the same time, the edition also outlined alternative paths for anthropological scholarship that have also been absorbed and developed within various anthropological sub-fields and paradigms.

In the following, we briefly trace some of the dominant threads of debate that preceded and prepared the way for *Writing Culture*. Afterwards, we sketch the dominant positions in the subsequent debate on *Writing Culture* as well as some of the further impacts the volume turned out to have on various strands of anthropological thought. This discussion of some of the more important developments 'after' *Writing Culture* is subsequently followed by and to some extent contrasted with an overview of some of the general themes of *Writing Culture* itself. In reaching a final characterization of the volume only after pursuing a diachronic analysis of its intertextuality, we do not mean to imply any sort of telos. Rather, by first examining the context out of which *Writing Culture* emerged and into which it was grafted, and only later discussing the actual contents of the volume, we hope to provide a means of explaining the volume's success. Put differently, we hope this approach will show how it is that *Writing Culture* both met and made its *kairos*.

Against this backdrop, the second part of this chapter suggests the ways in which the present volume is meant to move 'beyond *Writing Culture*'. In our brief introduction to each of the chapters included in this volume, we elaborate on how these texts open different doors beyond *Writing Culture*, how they address the 'worldliness' of representations, and how they handle the 'recursivity' of the representational process, in that 'theorizing' about intersections between epistemology and representational practice inexorably entails already 'realizing' such intersections.

Writing Culture and Beyond

Before Writing Culture

One anthropological paradigm that highly influenced *Writing Culture* was Clifford Geertz's interpretive anthropology, which opened the discipline to the paradigmatic innovations taking place in literature departments at that time. Whereas Geertz's ethnographic studies in the early 1960s had been largely influenced by modernization theory, from the mid 1960s onward he began to write a series of essays in which he developed his well-known interpretive theory of culture (Geertz 1973, 1983), 'insisting that human social life is a matter of meaningful activity only very imperfectly studied through the objectifying methods of (certain kinds of) science' (Ortner 1997: 1). Geertz paved the way for blurring the lines between, on the one hand, a rising interest in poststructuralism, deconstructionism, and literary studies and, on the other, a growing epistemologically and politically motivated scepticism in anthropology concerning ways of 'doing' anthropological research.

While his own anthropological essays were not extended experiments in ethnographic writing, Geertz nevertheless contributed to a growing interest within anthropology about the ethnographic text itself. Of additional importance was Hayden White's *Metahistory* (1973) in which he examined the literary and tropological grounding of historical scholarship. In 'Ethnographies as Texts', George E. Marcus and Dick Cushman observed 'a growing trend of experimentation in ethnographic writing, largely as a philosophically informed reaction to the genre conventions of ethnographic realism' (Marcus and Cushman 1982: 25), by which they meant 'a mode of writing that seeks to represent the reality of a whole world or form of life' (ibid.: 29). At that time, they could already point to several ethnographies that explored new modes of ethnographic representation. Within the paradigm of dialogical anthropology, for instance, the person of the fieldworker and their interaction with other people in the field played an important role.[1] Dialogical forms of ethnographic writing also sought to transcend earlier forms of ethnographic reasoning in which personal experiences 'in the field' were textually separated from 'scientific' ethnographies (see also Clifford 1983).

New experimental forms of ethnographic writing were also informed by the growing importance of 'poststructuralism' and 'postmodernism'. While Claude Lévi-Strauss's structuralist theory had modernized anthropological theory in the 1960s (e.g., Lévi-Strauss 1966), by the 1980s it seemed as outdated as Radcliffe-Brownian structural-functionalism. Not that structuralism had lost its appeal completely. In American anthropology, for instance, Marshall Sahlins was still developing a structuralist theory of action (Sahlins 1981, 1985). In France, Pierre Bourdieu (1977) developed his highly influential 'theory of practice' as an attempt to synthesize the approaches of Lévi-Strauss, Durkheim, Weber and Marx. In general, however, structuralism seemed to be on the way out, giving rise to various modes of postmodern and poststructuralist reasoning.[2] According to Sahlins, 'Structural inversions were in the intellectual air' in the mid 1960s (Sahlins 2000: 24); by the 1980s, however, these inversions seemed to have been dissolved into a fundamental decomposition of Western logocentrism, promoted not only by Derrida and his followers in literary criticism and beyond, but also by other philosophical mavericks like Richard Rorty (1979).

---

1   See Rabinow (1977), Crapanzano (1980), Dwyer (1982), and Webster (1983).
2   This was exemplified in the works of Jacques Derrida (1976), Jacques Lacan (1977), Michel Foucault (1978) and Jean Baudrillard (1988), as well as in those of Gilles Deleuze and Felix Guattari (1987). These and other similar works, which can only artificially be labelled poststructuralist, were heavily influenced by Georges Bataille's (1985) deconstructive critique of Western rationality.

This growing interest in postmodernism and poststructuralism was complemented by various intellectual movements within anthropology and related disciplines that played an important role in reconfiguring the epistemological and political groundings of the discipline. Examples include the rise of the Birmingham school of Cultural Studies (e.g., Hall 1980), the growing importance of feminist scholarship (e.g., Rosaldo and Lamphere 1974; MacCormack and Strathern 1980), and the political critique of colonialism (e.g., Horowitz 1967; Asad 1973; Solovey 2001). During the 1960s and 1970s a reflexive awareness emerged that the process of doing anthropology could be embedded in various overarching power asymmetries between Western and non-Western life-worlds. Partly as a reaction to this situation, world systems analysis and political economy investigated the international division of labour and power asymmetries within the 'world system' with renewed verve (Wolf 1971, 1982; Wallerstein 1974). Marxists influenced by Althusser tried to apply Marx's ideas to non-capitalist societies in order to work out ideology, exploitation and power.[3] Within economic anthropology, Marxian approaches became important alternatives to the schools of formalism and substantivism.[4]

The emerging field of 'postcolonial studies' also contributed to a critique of international power asymmetries and colonialism. Edward Said (1978) argued that, far from being only a discipline with academic institutions, 'orientalism' should be understood as a complex discourse within Western societies and as a general style of thought and domination based upon epistemological and ontological distinctions made between 'orient' and 'occident'. Said's work – itself infused with Marxism, Foucault's discourse analysis, Gramsci's notion of hegemony, and Fanon's early critique of colonialism – served as a powerful epistemological critique of 'Western' representations of 'non-Western' life-worlds and contributed to the emerging 'crisis of representation' within anthropology, exemplified, for instance, in Johannes Fabian's timely study, *Time and the Other* (1983).

Reactions to 'That Damn Book'[5]

Published in 1986 in a climate constituted and shaped by such intellectual developments, *Writing Culture* engendered a debate that rapidly took up a broader discussion of the intricate relationship between epistemology, politics, practices and styles of ethnographic representation. Reactions, ranging from wholesale agreement to near complete rejection, exhibited a tone that oscillated between hyping 'the *Writing Culture* crowd' (Handelman 1994: 348) as

---

3   See, among others, Meillassoux (1972, 1981), Terray (1972), Friedman (1974) and Godelier (1977). On the philosophical grounding of structural Marxism, see Sebag (1964), and for an early account of the history of the relationship between anthropology and Marxism, see Bloch (1983).
4   For a Marxian critique of Sahlins's 'substantivist' work on the 'domestic mode of production', see Donham (1981).
5   This phrase is borrowed from Marcus (1998a).

anthropology's 'new avant-garde' (McCarthy 1992: 636) and polemically condemning the 'millennial ideology' of these self-styled 'high priest[s]', dismissing their intervention as a careerist 'sleight-of-hand' (Sangren 1988: 409, 411).

Early reviews already began to open up this spectrum. Roy Wagner, while showing a degree of scepticism towards 'the postmodern project' (Wagner 1986: 99), still saw *Writing Culture* as a chance to raise anthropology's self-awareness. In a similar but more emphatic vein, Bob Scholte praised 'Writing Culture's undeniable historical interest to our discipline' and expressed a 'genuine respect for the detailed, imaginative, and suggestive analyses found in the Clifford & Marcus volume' (Scholte 1987: 38). At the same time, Scholte's praise was tempered by misgivings regarding the 'literary turn' in anthropology; he feared that 'politics may become merely academic – literally so' (ibid.: 44). Howard S. Becker (1987) also praised *Writing Culture* as an example of the rising postpositivism in the philosophical spirit of Rorty (1979). Becker's critique therefore mainly related to what he saw as a neglect of comparable experiences and attempts to address these issues within sociology and, in particular, 'contemporary work in the sociology of science' (Becker 1987: 27). Bill Nichols (1988) found the epistemological debates on ethnography in *Writing Culture* equally useful because they were, he argued, similar to certain discussions in film studies.

In contrast to reviewers who received *Writing Culture* rather positively as an important contribution, P. Steven Sangren excoriated the postmodern rhetoric of reflexivity as 'ultimately misleading and surprisingly "unreflexive" in ways that diminish both the legitimacy and the logic of the arguments it produces' (Sangren 1988: 406). By criticizing 'traditional' ethnographic works for establishing textual authority, hegemony and power, and by proclaiming to transcend this strategy, postmodernists, Sangren claimed, committed the very sin they decried. Sangren suggested instead that an epistemological 'totalization' with a broadened focus on the reproduction of society and culture as a whole allowed for a better form of reflexivity than the mere literary analysis of ethnographic texts. *Writing Culture* and the companion volume *Anthropology as Cultural Critique* had thus failed as 'ethnography of ethnography', he argued, 'because they do not locate collective representations (texts) in the contexts within which they are produced and which they in turn are essential in reproducing' (ibid.: 422). Kevin K. Birth explicitly positioned his equally polemical critique as a continuation of Sangren's response. Arguing from the position of 'reader-response literary criticism,' Birth ultimately concluded that 'not only does *Writing Culture*'s version of anthropology as cultural critique fail logically and pragmatically, it also fails ethically' (Birth 1990: 555).

Paul A. Roth also discussed the then-recent wave of literary analyses of ethnographic authority, which confused 'literary, epistemological, and political issues' (Roth 1989: 555). He primarily criticized texts like *Writing Culture* for being 'epistemologically innocuous since the charge of partiality applies to all positions' and complained that 'this union of epistemology and literary criticism' had spawned no new epistemological insights (ibid.: 561, 555). As had been the case before with Sangren's (1988) article, Roth's article in *Current Anthropology* was followed by responses, some of which were written by contributors to *Writing Culture*. These exchanges began to exhibit the increasingly typical positions in this debate. Stephen A. Tyler (1989), for instance, reiterated that he was simply not playing the game of 'representations' anymore.

In another influential critique, Jonathan Spencer pointed out that 'despite its trappings of political and intellectual radicalism', *Writing Culture* was 'in some of its presuppositions a depressingly reactionary document' (Spencer 1989: 145). Spencer complained that within *Writing Culture* 'there is the abandonment of *any* consideration of problems of validation' (ibid.: 159). These, he argued, were subsumed under the term 'authority', which was characterized 'as a literary rather than a practical issue' (ibid.: 159). Furthermore, many contributors to *Writing Culture* assumed 'that texts can be wholly decontextualized and compared as formal objects, stripped of history and living in a social vacuum' (ibid.: 160). In addition, Spencer was afraid 'that the book will provoke a trend away from doing anthropology, and towards ever more barren criticism and meta-criticism' (ibid.: 161).

Likewise addressing the issue of decontextualization, Tony Free also focused on *Writing Culture*'s preoccupation with 'texts', which entailed a 'bracketing and ignoring' of 'the world' in three important facets: first, the world of 'the reader'; second, 'the world in which it [the text] is written'; and third, 'the world about or of which it is written' (Free 1990: 52). Arguing from a position primarily informed by phenomenology, Richard Sutcliffe aptly summarized his primary criticism by stating that 'it is not so much that members of the Writing Culture school are completely wrong – they do draw attention to problems, if not quite a "crisis", of representation – it is more that they are too late to be novel and, what is worse, they offer no genuine solutions to problems already recognized by others' (Sutcliffe 1993: 21). In questioning *Writing Culture*'s 'case against science', Stephen P. Reyna argued that 'literary anthropologists know little, not because they have shown that little is knowable, but because they have chosen, without reason, not to know' (Reyna 1994: 576).

The remedies suggested by *Writing Culture* were the main issue of contention in Don Handelman's discussion. Handelman argued that *Writing Culture*'s sceptical self-examination of anthropology and related experiments with innovative ethnographic writing styles had proven helpful to the discipline. However, important issues within this reflexivity debate were overlooked, most notably that 'fieldwork anthropology is unlike any of the humanities and other social sciences in that it is not a text-mediated discipline in the first place' (Handelman 1994: 341). Thus, rather than subjecting itself to a text-based literary deconstruction from outside the discipline, Handelman argued that anthropology should use its unique pre-textual potential for a self-critique that emerged from its struggling 'with the turning of subjects into objects rather than the turning of objects into subjects' (ibid.: 341).

Another fundamental line of criticism put forward against *Writing Culture* was advanced by various feminist writers. Frances Mascia-Lees, Patricia Sharpe and Colleen Ballerino Cohen, for example, argued rather dismissively that 'what appear to be new and exciting insights to these new postmodernist anthropologists ... are insights that have received repeated and rich exploration in feminist theory for the past forty years' (Mascia-Lees, Sharpe and Cohen 1989: 11). The same authors further criticized *Writing Culture* as well as *Anthropology as Cultural Critique* for dismissing feminist theory altogether, regardless of its insights for generating new forms of ethnographic writing and practice. In their reading, postmodern anthropologists thereby established and maintained unequal power relations within anthropology by downplaying feminism in favour of a male-dominated 'postmodern' ethnographic paradigm (ibid.: 16–17). In a somewhat similar vein, Ruth Behar (1993) summarized one of the prime feminist criticisms of *Writing Culture*, targeting Clifford's justification (Clifford 1986a: 21–22) of the absence of feminist perspectives in his introduction to the volume. Behar argued that according to Clifford's vision, 'to be a woman writing culture is a contradiction in terms: women who write experimentally can't seem to be feminist enough, while women who write as feminists write in ignorance of the textual theory that underpins their own texts' (Behar 1993: 309).

Despite these and other arguments addressing issues related to *Writing Culture*, the 'debate' as such nevertheless to some degree cooled down from the early 1990s onwards. This was evidenced by public statements like that of Maryon McDonald who wrote that she was 'already tired of Clifford and Marcus' collection *Writing Culture*' and the endless moaning about 'every novelty-claiming and enthusing espousal' of the edition (McDonald 1991: 19, 20). Nonetheless, 'modernist critiques' (Spiro 1996) and further attacks on *Writing Culture* continued to be launched a decade or more after the publication of the volume. For instance, Adam Kuper, echoing Spencer's critique, argued that 'the postmodernist movement has had a paralysing effect on the discipline of anthropology. It denies the possibility of a cross-cultural, comparative anthropology' (Kuper 1999: 223). Kuper further argued that the consequence of the Geertzian programme of the 'blurring' of different academic genres 'was to subordinate the theoretical concerns of cultural anthropology to those of the mainstream disciplines in the humanities' at that time – that is, literature and art (ibid.: 224).

The overall cooling down of the *Writing Culture* debate, however, may perhaps best be illustrated with reference to the edition *After Writing Culture* (James, Hockey and Dawson 1997b), which received much less attention than *Writing Culture*. This may have been the case because, as Matti Bunzl argued, '[f]ew today dispute the poetic and fictive qualities of ethnographic texts, while the invariable situatedness of ethnographic knowledge can hardly be called an issue of great contention' (Bunzl 1999: 261). Bunzl further pointed out that 'such an emphasis on the representational dimensions of anthropological knowledge production can hardly constitute a coherent body of analysis', because 'representation, in and of itself, can hardly serve as a viable unifying theme' (ibid.: 261). In contrast to this position, Clifford (1999) and Marcus (1999) each welcomed the publication in their respective reviews as part of a continuing debate on 'the poetics and politics of ethnography' that was, as Clifford characterized it, 'integral to contemporary work' (Clifford 1999: 644).

After Writing Culture

Beyond eliciting immediate reactions, *Writing Culture* also influenced, albeit in a more mediated manner, other important developments in anthropology. A brief and fragmentary elaboration of a few of these developments can contribute to an assessment of the overall reception of the volume. We should stress, however, that this exercise is difficult in methodological terms because common concerns and systematic equivalences cannot always be attributed to common intellectual genealogies. Keeping this in mind, we want to draw attention to elements of discussions about globalization, feminism, postcolonialism and the changing contours of ethnographic practice that, as we see it, profited from *Writing Culture*. First of all, however, a short look at Clifford Geertz's interpretive anthropology seems to be in order because this approach played such a central role in shaping the intellectual project that was to become *Writing Culture*.

Writing Culture could be characterized as a radicalization of Geertz's interpretative anthropology, 'but stripped of all reservations' (Kuper 1999: 206). This radicalization involved a serious critique of Geertz's interpretive programme. In particular, Geertz's writing style was criticized for a lack of the reflexive sensibility that was considered to be one of the central objectives of *Writing Culture* and various new forms of experimental ethnography (Crapanzano 1986; Gottowik 1997; Marcus 1997).[6] Thus it is interesting to recall that Geertz himself interpreted other anthropological works as literary enterprises in *Works and Lives* (Geertz 1988). Here, however, a certain ambivalence towards the literary and self-reflexive orientation of 'postmodern' ethnography was clearly visible. *Works and Lives* was concerned with a literary analysis of written ethnographic texts; at the same time, Geertz showed no interest in analysing his own work. Still, Geertz argued that *Writing Culture* and his own *Works and Lives* 'did induce a certain self-awareness, and a certain candor also, into a discipline not without need of them' (Geertz 2002: 11). Concerning experimental forms of ethnographic writing,

---

6 These critiques were complemented by attacks outside the 'writing culture crowd'. For instance, Mark A. Schneider criticized Geertz's approach to culture-as-text for suppressing cultural complexity (Schneider 1987). Advocates of approaches in the spirit of political economy and world systems theory were wary of the use of the culture concept by anthropologists such as Geertz and Sahlins because 'culture' often served as an ideological smokescreen for power asymmetries (Keesing 1987; Friedman 1994; Wolf 1999, 2001; on the relationship between Wolf's approach and postmodern anthropology, see Whitehead 2004 and Gledhill 2005).

however, Geertz remained sceptical. In *Works and Lives* he noted that the 'experimental' movement in ethnographic writing contributed to a sort of 'epistemological hypochondria' in the field (Geertz 1988: 71).[7]

The same ambivalence towards postmodernism in anthropology is visible in Geertz's essay 'The World in Pieces' (Geertz 2000: 218–63) in which he tried to find a middle ground between the dissolution of 'culture' and a model of cultural homogeneity. As this brief account suggests, Geertz's interpretive anthropology changed significantly over the years, partly in response to the postmodern critique in anthropology and partly in response to the anthropological critique of the culture concept, a move that was itself influenced by *Writing Culture* and subsequent discussions of the book.[8]

During the 1980s and 1990s, the critique of the culture concept in anthropology reached new heights. Much of this critique, also coming from political economy and practice theory, was not directly related to the attacks on 'culture' explicated in *Writing Culture*. However, *Writing Culture* marked an important step in the rising postmodern critique of 'culture' and thereby contributed to subsequent anthropological elaborations of the culture concept (e.g., Thornton 1988). Further developing his arguments from his introduction to *Writing Culture* in a series of related articles, Clifford (1992) pointed out that anthropologists invented boundaries around 'cultures' by 'localizing strategies' that were related to the exclusion of intercultural interaction from the writing of ethnographies. Clifford suggested that the anthropological concept of culture should perhaps be replaced by a Foucauldian 'vision of powerful discursive formations globally and strategically deployed. Such entities would at least no longer be closely tied to notions of organic unity, traditional continuity, and the enduring grounds of language and locale' (Clifford 1988a: 274).

Arjun Appadurai located the problem of the anthropological culture concept in 'its implication that culture is some kind of object, thing, or substance, whether physical or metaphysical' (Appadurai 1996: 12). Lila Abu-Lughod ingeniously modified the volume's title in her attempt to 'write against culture' by arguing that the culture concept was 'the essential tool for making other. As a professional discourse that elaborates on the meaning of culture in order to account for, explain, and understand cultural difference, anthropology also helps construct, produce, and maintain it' (Abu-Lughod 1991: 143). In 1995, Robert Brightman could thus observe that such 'terminological items as "habitus", "hegemony", and "discourse" are increasingly opposed to "culture" as new concept to old, as useful to defective' (Brightman 1995: 510).

The discussion about 'writing against culture'[9] was closely linked to debates on 'cultural hybridity'[10] as well as debates on cultural globalization wherein traditional

---

7   For a discussion of *Works and Lives*, see Hutnyk (1989).
8   On Geertz's intellectual development, see Inglis (2000).

notions of culture were seriously called into question.[11] In working out new models, anthropologists aimed to capture a sense of this changing, seemingly disjunctive new world in which the local and the global could no longer be properly separated from each other (see Marcus 1998b).[12] As Henrietta Moore argued, the changing configurations of cultural globalization thereby altered the building of theory and epistemology in anthropology, replacing older notions of part/whole relationships with radically new 'concept-metaphors' and 'pre-theoretical commitments' that 'may emerge from the bio, medical, and information sciences' (Moore 2004: 86). *Writing Culture* and the many debates surrounding the book to some degree directly influenced discussions of cultural globalization as some of the contributors to the volume extended the arguments they presented in the book in subsequent work on globalization and the changing contours of 'culture'. Furthermore, *Writing Culture* indirectly influenced debates about cultural globalization through its postmodern critique of 'traditional' anthropological concepts, which also came under fire in the anthropology of globalization. But whereas *Writing Culture* primarily focused on the written text, the growing anthropology of globalization was more concerned with the 'real world', which proved to be far too complex to be analysed with 'traditional' concepts of culture.

Anthropological discourses centred on cultural globalization and the epistemological fallacies of representation were also related to postcolonial scholarship in complex ways, calling into question the very idea of autonomous academic genres. For example, the 'writing against culture' critique was influenced by Said's *Orientalism* (1978; see Varisco 2004: 107–110). Furthermore, Said's postcolonial theory had itself been an important inspiration to the literary movement in anthropology (see Prakash 1995: 209). Said himself was rather sympathetic to reflexive, postmodern strands in anthropology (Said 1989: 208), while at the same time critical of 'revisionist anthropological currents' by anthropologists such as Sahlins (1985) and Wolf (1982) because they left 'the problematic of the observer' underanalysed (Said 1989: 212). Although it is often difficult to reconstruct intellectual linkages and genealogies between postmodernism in anthropology and postcolonial scholarship, at the least it can be observed that many postcolonial thinkers worked on themes that were complementary to the *Writing Culture* critique.[13] This is not altogether surprising as *Writing Culture* itself was already influenced by Said's critique of 'orientalism'. Postcolonial theory aimed to shift the prevailing ways in which the relation

---

9   See also Rosaldo (1989), Brumann (1999), Fox and King (2002) and Keane (2003).
10   Gupta and Ferguson (1997), Werbner and Modood (1997), Werbner (2001) and Scott (2005).
11   Clifford (1997), Wimmer (2001), Inda and Rosaldo (2002), Lewellen (2002) and Nederveen Pieterse (2004).
12   These models include notions such as 'creolization' (Hannerz 1996), global 'scapes' (Appadurai 1996), the changing relationship between 'roots' and 'routes' (Clifford 1997), 'alternative modernities' (Gaonkar 1999), 'millennial capitalism' (Comaroff and Comaroff 2000), 'the global as local practice' (Cunningham 1999), 'indigenizations of modernity' (Sahlins 2000) and the notion of global connections as 'friction' (Tsing 2005).

between Western and non-Western peoples were considered and investigated (Young 2003: 2). It sought to 'provincialize Europe' (Chakrabarty 2000) through varied deconstructions of Western metanarratives and epistemologies. Postcolonial scholars frequently focused on the deconstruction of established 'realist' epistemologies, showed a literary and deconstructive attitude towards theory-building, and furthered a political sensibility for changing world-historical 'colonial' and 'postcolonial' circumstances.

Postcolonialism was frequently criticized for its seemingly textualist orientation, its exportation of French 'high theory' into cultural analysis, and its concomitant exclusion of material realities 'on the ground'. Above all, postcolonialism was dismissed as an egoistic enterprise that primarily furthered the academic careers of postcolonial 'pop-stars' and, at the same time, reproduced unequal power relations in society and academia (see Ahmad 1992). Interestingly, as we have already shown, *Writing Culture* was criticized for similar reasons. In a way, this critique was echoed by the emerging field of cultural studies of Oceania which argued that anthropological representations of Oceanic cultures and life-worlds stabilize a neocolonial world order dominated by the West (see Wood 2003, 2006 for useful overviews). However, it has been precisely postcolonial scholarship that strengthened a reflexive sensibility to the production of scientific knowledge within overarching intercultural fields of power relations (Tsing 1993; Spivak 1999). Furthermore, 'Western' scholars actively engage in continuing dialogues with 'non-Western' intellectuals on the study of cultural change, history and the legacies of colonialism (see Borofsky 2000). Recent approaches suggesting such a move include research into 'indigenous articulations' (Clifford 2001), the anthropology of colonialism (Pels 1997), the rebuilding of anthropological theory on postmodern and postcolonial grounds (Mutman 2006), and the relationship between globalization and 'postcoloniality' (Gikandi 2001).[14]

As we already noted, *Writing Culture* has been heavily criticized for its extensive exclusion of feminism. After the publication of *Writing Culture*, however, anthropology benefited from various interventions ranging from a postmodern or deconstructionist ethnographic style to feminist anthropology on the Other. One such project that was influenced by *Writing Culture* and at the same time sought to overcome Clifford's and Marcus's exclusion of feminism was *Women Writing Culture*, edited by Ruth Behar and Deborah A. Gordon (1995). This project not only sought to cope with the exclusion of feminism in *Writing Culture* but also aimed to incorporate critiques by women of colour and lesbians of the white, middle-class presuppositions of mainstream feminism. The various contributors to *Women Writing Culture* tried to reappraise anthropological traditions on feminist grounds, to rework current anthropological theories from

---

13   See Spivak (1988, 1999), Said (1993), Bhabha (1994) and Chakrabarty (2000).
14   For the current state of postcolonial theory, see Loomba et al. (2005).

feminist perspectives, and to reflect on the complex and intersecting relationships between gender, power, marginalization and exclusion in academia and beyond. The rising interest in 'women writing culture' was also exemplified by a volume with the same title containing interviews with leading intellectuals on the relationships between and intersections of writing, feminism, power, rhetoric and cultural change (Olson and Hirsh 1995). Publications like Behar and Gordon's *Women Writing Culture* signalled a more mediated confrontation of feminism with *Writing Culture* and its limitations, thereby enabling more complex and original frames of research combining feminist, poststructural and critical research agendas.[15]

Writing Culture was enormously influential in changing writing styles and research practices and in the development of new experimental forms of ethnography (Poewe 1996). These experimental forms have included the further development of 'dialogical anthropology' (Tedlock 1987), 'narrative ethnography' (Tedlock 1991), and 'collaborative ethnography'. In a series of papers, Lassiter (2001, 2005) argued that collaborative ethnography sought to extend the ethnographic trope of 'dialogue' to its next step: the active collaboration of researchers and subjects in the production of anthropological texts, thus extending 'fieldwork collaboration more systematically into the writing of the actual ethnography' (Lassiter 2005: 84). From the perspective of Tyler's postmodern anthropology, these approaches may be criticized as hopeless attempts at recapturing a vanishing sense of ethnographic authenticity (Tyler 1987, 1989). However, Tyler's radical deconstruction of ethnographic style has not proven as influential as diverging modes of dialogical, polyphonic and autobiographical writing styles.

These diverging modes of ethnographic writing signal, as Marilyn Strathern (1987) has argued, new relationships between writer, audience and subject of research that deviate from a modernist writing style that creates a distance between the society that is studied, the society to which the anthropologist's audience belongs, and the anthropologist that mediates between the two contexts: 'If anthropologists write now about "other peoples", they are writing for subjects who have become an audience' (ibid.: 269). By doing this, anthropologists today have to solve the same technical problem as writers such as Frazer and Malinowski. Anthropologists apply 'specific literary strategies, the construction of a persuasive fiction: a monograph must be laid out in such a way that it can convey novel compositions of ideas' (ibid.: 257). What counts as persuasive may change dramatically over time; this, in turn, is linked to the identification and interpretation of the discipline's great epistemological shifts, for example the shift between Frazer and modernist anthropology, but also 'the alleged shift from

---

15 Recent work in feminist ethnography that goes in such a direction has included, for instance, Patti Lather's (2001) complex amalgamation of feminist theory, Derridean and Deleuzian poststructuralism, and postcolonialism.

modernism to postmodernism in the 1980s': 'we create historic shifts between past writers in terms persuasive to our own ears, thereby participating in a postmodern history, reading back into books the strategies of fictionalisation' (ibid.: 269).

Concerning the ethnographic practice of doing fieldwork, George E. Marcus has argued that:

> The *Writing Culture* critique was absorbed positively by anthropologists, but its implications were contained by the idea that it dealt only with writing, with strategies for composing ethnographic texts, thus leaving fieldwork – the true experiential core of the discipline – untouched. I always believed, however, that the most substantial implication of the critique was for the fieldwork process. (Marcus 2002: 192)

In Marcus's view, ethnography 'moves from its conventional single-site location, contextualized by macro-constructions of a larger social order, such as the capitalist world system, to multiple sites of observation and participation that cross-cut dichotomies such as the "local" and the "global"' (Marcus 1995: 95). In a similar vein, James Clifford saw the growing importance of 'postcolonial mobility' and 'diasporic routes' (Clifford 2001: 477). The changing relationships between 'roots' and 'routes' may alter ethnographic fieldwork, 'with short, repeated visits the norm and fully supported research years rare' (Clifford 1997: 90). Last but not least, recent developments in ethnographic practice have led to a growing interest in doing 'anthropology at home' (see Peirano 1998).

The Text Itself

Having traced some of the prior developments that set the scene for *Writing Culture* and provided a short synopsis of the diverse reactions to the book, as well as having finally tracked of some of the edition's more mediated impacts, we may now consider the text itself.

In its afterword, Marcus characterized *Writing Culture* as a kind of 'literary therapy' aimed at introducing 'a literary consciousness to ethnographic practice by showing various ways in which ethnographies can be read and written' (Marcus 1986b: 262). Clifford accordingly framed this overall project in his introduction to the volume, when he highlighted that the collected essays began 'not with participant-observation or with cultural texts (suitable for interpretation), but with writing, the making of texts' (Clifford 1986a: 2). Far from remaining a marginal or insignificant issue, the 'close analysis of one of the principle things ethnographers do – that is, write' (ibid.: 24) was henceforth to be central.

In rejecting the clear-cut Western distinction between fictional literature and factual science, Clifford insisted on the inseparable nature of the literary, poetic and rhetorical on the one hand and the factual on the other in ethnographic representations. The collected essays were thus unified in rejecting the older objectivist ideology 'claiming transparency of representation and immediacy of experience' (ibid.: 2). Instead, ethnographies were to be seen as 'true fictions', drawing on the word's Latin root (*fingere*) in the sense of 'something made or fashioned'. However, it was also crucial to 'preserve the meaning not merely of making, but also of making up, of inventing things not actually real' (ibid.: 6). Instead of being simply opposed to truth, the notion of ethnographic 'fiction' thus rather suggested 'the partiality of cultural and historical truths', in that 'all constructed truths were made possible by powerful "lies" of exclusion and rhetoric' (ibid.: 6, 7). It was in this sense, Clifford insisted, that the collected essays kept the oxymoron 'true fictions' sharp (ibid.: 6). (In a way, the question of whether this notion of 'true fictions' can be meaningfully maintained as a 'sharp oxymoron' or whether, when all is said and done, it necessarily dissolves epistemologically into a tautological truism epitomizes a crucial point of contention for the whole debate).

Clifford stressed that anthropology's ability to represent others had come under fire both through the powerful political critique of postcolonialism on the one hand and the epistemological undermining of scientific positivism and objectivity by a plethora of theoretical perspectives on the other. He further claimed that these critiques entailed a shift from a visual to a discursive conception of the ethnographic encounter. This shift, Clifford argued, had been accompanied by changes in ethnographic styles of representation that increasingly questioned the separation of authorial subjectivity from the objective referent of the text, turning instead towards dialogism and polyphony. While being generally in favour of such dialogic and polyphonic ways of writing, Clifford also cautioned the reader against the ideal of the scientific accumulation of facts by arguing that in addressing certain partialities, newly occupied positions necessarily produced their own partialities. That said, Clifford nevertheless insisted that the collected essays aimed at 'new, better modes of writing' and at an ethnographic poetics that could still be 'historical, precise, objective' and did not 'give up facts and accurate accounting' (ibid.: 25, 26).

Clifford wrote that most of the essays in *Writing Culture*, 'while focusing on textual practices, reach beyond texts to contexts of power, resistance, institutional constraint, and innovation' (ibid.: 2). While questions of politics and epistemology thus always lurked just below the surface, the primary focal point of the volume nevertheless remained the rhetorical dimensions of others' ethnographies as texts. This applied to Clifford's own chapter, 'On Ethnographic Allegory', in which he sought to work out the allegorical nature of ethnographic writing. Clifford argued that ethnography could be seen 'as a performance emplotted by powerful stories' which 'simultaneously describe real cultural events and make additional, moral, ideological, and even cosmological statements' (Clifford 1986b: 98). Recognition of the inescapably allegorical nature of ethnographic writing thereby highlighted its 'political and ethical dimensions' and complicated it 'in potentially fruitful ways' (ibid.: 120).

Vincent Crapanzano's contribution, 'Hermes' Dilemma: The Masking of Subversion in Ethnographic Description', likened the ethnographer to Hermes, the messenger of the gods: both were concerned with rendering the foreign familiar while preserving its foreignness, and both were confronted with the difficulty of making their message convincing while pretending that the truth of the message spoke for itself. Crapanzano then concentrated on this last aspect in analysing the use of rhetorical devices in three ethnographic texts as means for such persuasion. He suggested that in all three cases 'the very figures the authors use to convince their readers – and themselves – of their descriptions in fact render them suspect, and in all three cases this failure to convince is covered by an institutionally legitimated concern for meaning' (Crapanzano 1986: 53).

In her chapter, 'Fieldwork in Common Places', Marie Louise Pratt also explored the poetics of anthropology, concentrating on various tropes of ethnographic writing and how they were derived from earlier discursive traditions. She focused on the relationship within ethnography between impersonal description and personal narrative and 'the history of this discursive configuration, notably its history in travel writing' (Pratt 1986: 28). Pratt suggested that acknowledging one's tropes as 'neither natural nor, in many cases, native to the discipline' allowed for a self-liberation, 'not by doing away with tropes (which is not possible) but by appropriating and inventing new ones (which is)' (ibid.: 50). In 'From the Door of His Tent: The Fieldworker and the Inquisitor', Renato Rosaldo attempted to develop 'an anatomy of ethnographic rhetoric by exploring modes of authority and representation' (Rosaldo 1986: 77) in Evans-Pritchard's *The Nuer* and Emmanuel Le Roy Ladurie's *Montaillou*. Rosaldo contended that representations of the Nuer and late medieval French shepherds as idealized pastoralists within the genre of the 'pastoral' covered up issues of dominance and power underlying the courtly politeness of this literary form.

Various explorations in *Writing Culture* not only brought forward criticisms of pre-existing representational styles but also made pleas for new experimental forms. The most radical suggestion was presented by Stephen Tyler in his piece 'Post-Modern Ethnography: From Document of the Occult to the Occult Document'. In this 'generally unclassifiable' essay (Clifford and Marcus 1986a: viii), Tyler conjured 'post-modern ethnography' as 'a cooperatively evolved text consisting of fragments of discourse intended to evoke in the minds of both reader and writer an emergent fantasy of a possible world of commonsense reality, and thus to provoke an aesthetic integration that will have a therapeutic effect' (Tyler 1986: 125). Despite being somewhat at variance with Derrida (1973, 1976) in its celebration of orality, in its uncompromising gesture Tyler's chapter provided a clue as to what proper deconstructionist anthropology might look like.

In contrast, Talal Asad's discussion of 'The Concept of Cultural Translation in British Social Anthropology' provided a take on the issue of intercultural exchange that was more sceptical about the potential of experimental writing. Asad critically discussed Gellner's essay 'Concepts and Society' (Gellner 1970), dismissing the latter's critique as misconceiving the nature of cultural translation: 'the anthropologist's translation is not merely a matter of matching sentences in the abstract, but of *learning to live another form of life*' (Asad 1986: 149, original emphasis). In highlighting the historically situated nature of translations, power asymmetries between languages became an urgent issue. While urging anthropologists to study institutionalized inequalities in order to evaluate 'the possibilities and the limits of effective translation', in light of such asymmetries, Asad doubted that 'individual experiments in modes of ethnographic representation' could be effective in overcoming them (ibid.: 164, 158).

In his discussion of 'Contemporary Problems of Ethnography in the Modern World System', George E. Marcus was equally concerned with global power relations, yet he saw stylistic experimentation as the most promising means of accounting for power. For Marcus, the current challenge in anthropology consisted in the question of how to engage the interpretative analysis of cultural meaning with the explanatory investigation of social action as well as the micro with the macro without misrepresenting '[t]he world of larger systems and events' as 'externally impinging on and bounding little worlds, but not being integral to them' (Marcus 1986a: 166). This challenge posed a problem of 'textual representation' rather than a problem of 'grand theoretical synthesis' (ibid.: 169). Accordingly, Marcus concentrated on two such modes of textual construction: on the one hand, narratives based on multi-sited ethnography (in which each site is understood to be interrelated) and, on the other, narratives based on strategically selected single locales (understood against the backdrop of a broader global system).

Michael M.J. Fischer's essay, 'Ethnicity and the Post-Modern Arts of Memory', aimed to reveal parallels between contemporary ethnic autobiographies and recent 'textual theories of deferred, hidden, or occulted meaning' (Fischer 1986: 194). Ethnographic writing could therefore be informed by both genres, given that each textual form suggested 'powerful modes for cultural criticism' (ibid.: 230). Through an analysis of a wide array of ethnic autobiographies from five 'hyphen-American' communities, Fischer derived a number of textual strategies for a postmodern arsenal: 'bifocality or reciprocity of perspectives, juxtapositioning of multiple realities, intertextuality and inter-referentiality, and comparison through families of resemblance' (ibid.: 230). Fischer contended that these techniques had the potential to contribute to a necessary 'renewed beginning' in anthropology, given that the discipline had not yet fulfilled its 'promise of a fully bifocal cultural criticism' (ibid.: 233).

Finally, in 'Representations Are Social Facts: Modernity and Post-Modernity in Anthropology', Paul Rabinow demonstrated a number of implications following from his characterization of representations as social practices. In his critical reading of Clifford's own textual productions, Rabinow observed that Clifford's approach contained 'a refusal of self-reflection' in faulting others for textual omissions while making 'the same omission on another level' (1986: 251–52, 244). In addition, Clifford's position was shown to be ambiguous; on the one hand he stressed the superiority of dialogical and polyphonic modes of ethnographic representation, while also depicting all modes of representation as equal. Referring to Fredric Jameson's analysis of postmodern culture, Rabinow then 'socialized' Clifford's indecision as a symptom of (post)modernist textualism. Rabinow thereby drew attention to 'the politics of interpretation in the academy today' (ibid.: 253), in which experimental writing also had to be investigated in relation to academic careers. Rabinow observed that the new rhetoric of dialogue was advanced primarily by male experimentalists and was interpreted by feminists as yet another act of violence. This, argued Rabinow, underlined the need for analysing representations *sociologically.*

This cursory summary of the positions in the *Writing Culture* volume can now be used to highlight two points. First, 'the text itself' covered a quite broad and at times contradictory spectrum of positions, sequentially ordered in the book in a somewhat 'general progression from studies with a literary bent towards those that question this emphasis' (Clifford and Marcus 1986a: viii). Asad and Rabinow in particular were openly sceptical, critically elaborating on possible implications of the (post)modernist obsession with textualism. Given this 'rather wide range of positions and problems', the editors and some of the contributors to *Writing Culture* reacted quite negatively to critiques and reviews that 'conflated [the book] into a single "postmodern" anthropology' (Fischer, Marcus and Tyler 1988: 426; see also Clifford 1988b).

On the other hand, the degree to which the positions advocated in the volume can be seen as varied is also in the eye of the beholder. Despite their variation, the contributions were still primarily engaged with textual and literary analysis. Thus, while the 1984 seminar that led to *Writing Culture* may have indeed pursued 'a limited set of emphases self-critically in an attempt to come to terms with the politics and poetics of cultural representation' (Clifford and Marcus 1986a: viii), the poetics of ethnography thereby took centre stage with political analysis and epistemological reflection being sidelined.

The limitations of this specific focus, 'stressing textual form and ... privileging textual theory' (Clifford 1986a: 21) were acknowledged by the editors themselves. Clifford and Marcus repeatedly highlighted the partiality of their account of 'larger contexts of systematic power inequality, world-systems constraints, and institutional frameworks' (Clifford and Marcus 1986a: vii–viii) and characterized the overall approach as intrinsically 'partial' epistemologically as well as 'contestable' in its concrete textualist 'bias' that somewhat evaded 'concrete institutional forces' (Clifford 1986a: 18, 21). However, we feel that a degree of (self-)deception was nevertheless at work in this representation of the volume by its editors. Much of the subsequent ado about *Writing Culture* arose precisely because of its tone and proclamation of novelty, its overarching rhetoric of demystification, and its promising pathos of transcending hitherto unacknowledged barriers in order to reach greener pastures of 'true' encounter and 'just' representations (notwithstanding the somewhat incompatible hedging statements of modesty).

This leads back to the question posed at the beginning of this introduction: why is it that *Writing Culture* has become such a modern or postmodern classic in anthropology? To our minds, a number of reasons arise from the diachronic analysis of the volume's intertextuality. First, several contributions did indeed provide 'detailed, imaginative, and suggestive analyses' (Scholte 1987: 38), which at the time of their publication truly did open new doors. Second, several of the essays were effective primarily because of their emotive claims to relevance and the pathos produced through the simultaneous unmasking and transcending of the rhetorical misdeeds of the past. While it is true that some of these essays expressed a degree of caution about their own epistemological legitimacy, thereby explicitly rejecting the idea that the approaches deployed therein were superior to those critiqued, such caveats could be read as mere rhetorical gesture. Despite their explicit understatement, the implicit, affectively transmitted message was that the essays did in fact offer a superior epistemological perspective. Third, despite its primary focus on textual analysis, *Writing Culture* did link up with an impressive array of topics, concerns and contemporary currents of thought, the most important of which have been referred to above. The more or less explicit dismissal by several contributors of attempts to create cohesive metanarratives thereby effected the maintenance of a high connectivity for the volume: depending on interest and point of departure, many different things could be 'found', 'uncovered' and 'read into' the text, which equally contributed to its intensified reception. Fourth, the discussions in *Writing Culture* took place in an intellectual climate that was simply ripe for such an endeavour. As we have attempted to show, various theoretical developments prior to the volume's publication sensitized and thereby produced an audience for the publication. To put it differently, these trends ensured that *Writing Culture* was to meet its *kairos*.

To this last point should be added one final reason for *Writing Culture*'s success, namely, the ingenious capacity of several of the essays – and especially Clifford's introduction – to frame the various prior and coexisting debates in such a way as to actively forge contemporary time into its own *kairos*. In other words, *Writing Culture* came about in part as 'the culmination of earlier developments in the profession' (Bunzl 1999: 260) because its very take on these developments turned itself into their 'culmination'. Our own textual organization can thereby be seen as a conscious extension of this framing, aimed at showing both how *Writing Culture* became central through its situatedness at crucial junctures and how its own depiction of this 'situation' contributed to this very centrality. In sum, *Writing Culture* became a success story because it productively and creatively responded to important developments in its time in a way that refocused this very time as 'a right and opportune moment': the volume thus both met and made its *kairos*.

Beyond *Writing Culture*

Invoking a rhetoric of going 'beyond *Writing Culture*' raises questions and possibly apprehensions. The textbook realist may fear yet another cascade of occultist 'beyond-isms', while the postmodern critic might see this as a boomerang-like 'moving-beyond-as-a-return-to-square-one'. The business of this volume, however, is much more sedate. While the collected chapters in this edition do appropriate the notion of moving 'beyond *Writing Culture*' in idiosyncratic ways and take it in numerous directions, a common project can still be specified in five respects.

First of all, we take the move 'beyond' to stand for the unitary refusal of the various essays to exclusively discuss, as ends in themselves, either the book *Writing Culture* or its subsequent debate. This volume thus positions itself as clearly past and beyond the actual debate on *Writing Culture*. Second, against the backdrop of historicizing both book and debate, we hope to achieve an altogether more sober and modest tone, which goes well beyond the frequently encountered oscillation between emphatic celebration and polemical condemnation. The contributions to this volume refer to *Writing Culture* in quite divergent and nuanced ways, which cannot be easily classified as being either supportive or critical of the original book. Thus we do not conceive the arrangement of the chapters in terms of a simple differentiation between proponents and critics of *Writing Culture*, since such a one-dimensional organization of the volume would flatten the complexities and multitudinousness of the whole debate. Third, this volume moves beyond *Writing Culture's* preoccupation with textual analysis and focuses instead on the wider and arguably more 'foundational' question of how to conceptualize the mutual implications and intersections between epistemologies and practices of representations. Fourth, the volume thereby aims to transcend the largely uni-disciplinary background in anthropology that characterized the contributions to *Writing Culture*. Instead, this volume includes a diversity of perspectives by bringing together representatives from as many disciplines and approaches as possible. Such an endeavour was of course limited in numerous ways, not only in obvious ways like restrictions on publication length, but also by unforeseen occurrences that changed what was originally envisioned as the shape the volume would take.

This edition developed out of a workshop entitled 'Beyond *Writing Culture*' held at the Max Planck Institute in September 2006. The workshop took the twentieth anniversary of *Writing Culture's* publication as an occasion to think about current intersections of epistemologies and practices of representation. Our invitations to speakers were not only shaped by institutional and personal networks but also by our desire to achieve a maximum variety of perspectives. The conference participants included in this volume represent disciplines such as anthropology, sociology, cognitive science and history.[16] In addition, we tried to maximize diversity not only in terms of disciplinary, ethnographic and epistemological approaches, but also with regard to textual genres. We were fortunate enough to get Rozita Dimova contributing a substantial as well as personal account of how *Writing Culture* crucially shaped her development as both an ethnographer and writer, in making her realize the formative and powerful role of language in any research process and quest for knowledge. Today, however, facing the challenges of neoliberal capitalism, which seems to be stabilized rather than undermined by the multiplicity of critical voices, Dimova argues that anthropologists should strategically reclaim authorial authority by going back to the founding 'fathers' of social science who recognized the centrality of class and economy.

Being situated on the same meta-level as the prologue, Dimova's essay thus provides an important cross-cutting 'interlogue' to our own concerns in this introduction. The same applies to Günther Schlee's epilogue, which – equally drawing on personal experience – argues that for radical turning points to qualify as 'paradigm shifts', they need to be ultimately rooted in epistemological realism. However, if based on epistemological relativism (as was largely the case with *Writing Culture*), such shifts turn out to rather consist of playful and voluntaristic changes of fashion. In showing how anthropology in fact benefits, when self-declared relativists do not really keep their non-factual promises, Schlee pleads for (more) realism, which he sees as legitimated by both a rehabilitation of Popper and – usurping the logics of fashion – by a fatigue with playful relativism.

Besides maximizing diversity, a fifth and final way in which this volume aims to go 'beyond *Writing Culture*' actually consists of several *ways*, namely the concrete ways in which the authors of the eight chapters take up, rework and go about the challenge of configuring the intricate interrelation between epistemology and representational practice. All of the essays thereby suggest 'doors' that can be opened beyond *Writing Culture*, and it is to a brief discussion of these that we now turn.

Opening Doors

The chapter by Vincent Crapanzano sets out from a threshold – more so, in a way, than any other contribution. Written by a participant in the original 1984 workshop, the chapter's retrospective gaze elaborates on one failure of the original 'movement' and aims to move beyond this. Crapanzano insists that depictions of the *Writing Culture* group as a 'movement' were primarily externally ascribed dismissals of the project within a discipline that still resisted critical self-reflection on its products. The 1984 workshop participants themselves, however, did not

---

16 Five additional speakers (Marlies Heinz, Rozita Dimova, Richard Rottenburg, Purnima Mankekar and Akhil Gupta) were invited to attend the conference but had to cancel their presentations. Unfortunately, this produced an unwelcome reduction of perspectives, excluding approaches with a strong archaeological, feminist and postcolonial focus. We decided against artificially filling these gaps in the course of preparing this publication, especially since it remained unclear for a considerable time whether several of these invited speakers would still contribute a chapter.

really unite as a 'movement' and instead exhibited a contradictory range of perspectives. Nevertheless, most papers were united, he argues, in failing to appreciate how their own conception of language and text was consequential for their own approach. Crapanzano addresses this oversight by drawing on Silverstein's (1979) notion of 'linguistic ideologies', which – through the metapragmatic function – prioritize certain communicative functions like referentiality, the pragmatic-indexical or the poetic. This metapragmatic framing thereby tends towards mystification by erasing its own contingent privileging of certain functions. On the basis of different ethnographic examples, Crapanzano suggests an anthropology which is sensitive to diverse linguistic ideologies – not only because failing to acknowledge potentially divergent metapragmatic definitions can lead to seriously flawed interpretations of field encounters, but also, much more fundamentally, because the metapragmatic function literally empowers certain takes on reality while blinding us to others.

Steffen Strohmenger criticizes the assumption that judgements about non-moral matters are liable to empirical verification while judgements about moral matters are not. Strohmenger argues against the tenet that there is a non-value laden dimension of reality – the non-moral sphere – about which objective statements can be made, in contrast to a value laden dimension of reality – the moral sphere – about which empirically verifiable, objective statements are excluded. The author argues that such an assumption about the 'asymmetry' of knowledge cannot be maintained because both non-value and value questions share the same epistemological grounding. The epistemological assumption that only non-moral statements are objectively verifiable while value statements are not, according to the author, thereby entails a hidden moral dimension. As Strohmenger argues, James Clifford's essay 'On Ethnographic Allegory' (Clifford 1986b) can be read as an effort to make visible the asymmetry in anthropological discourse – an asymmetry that is still at the heart of our theoretical understanding and representational practices. However, while Clifford argues that ethnographic texts transport a hidden level of meaning concerning ethical and political significance, at some points in his text he nevertheless unwittingly re-inscribes the theoretical assumptions of epistemological asymmetry. Thus for Strohmenger, moving 'beyond' *Writing Culture* means striving for a 're-symmetrization' of scientific knowledge and ethnographic writing.

In his contribution, Karsten Kumoll begins with the assumption that the debate about the 'poetics and politics of ethnography' has led to a beneficial promotion of a reflexive sensibility in anthropological research and writing. However, the *Writing Culture* debate was predominantly a Western controversy within anthropology dealing with Western representations of non-Western life-worlds. Within various non-Western concepts of science, anthropology has been criticized for being an ethnocentric and neocolonial enterprise that stabilizes power asymmetries between Western and non-Western cultures. Kumoll points out that the political implications of representational practices seem to lie at the heart of the problem indexed by this critique. By examining the work of Marshall Sahlins, Kumoll explores some of the consequences 'indigenous' concepts of science may have for anthropology. The author suggests that anthropology could benefit from non-Western ways of knowing, from incorporating new narrative forms into ethnographic writing, and from a sensibility to the changing political status of ethnographic research in different socio-cultural contexts. However, these attempts themselves may ultimately be interpreted as politically motivated impositions of a universal epistemology on localized scientific strategies.

In his chapter, Thomas Kirsch argues that thus far anthropological reflexivity concerned with ethnographic writing has largely tended to be blind to its own epistemological treatment of informants' conceptions of speakership. He builds his argument by delving into an ethnographic case study of a charismatic Pentecostal Church in rural southern Zambia. Through an exemplary investigation of texts produced by Church secretaries, Kirsch shows how their representations come to be seen as expressing 'the total truth' from the Holy Spirit's point of view (although some variation exists among Church members as to what this 'total truth' exactly entails and how it comes about). The author argues that ethnographic cases like this one, in which the 'natives' reject the ethnographer's attempt to represent 'their' point of view and insist instead that 'the point of view of the Holy Spirit' is to be represented, unveil the possibility of conflicting 'appellations' of speakership. Kirsch points out that ethnographers have typically handled such problems by selectively representing some of the self-identified speakership positions of their interlocutors as real and others as less real. He suggests that this inconsistency can be read as both a symptom of and a strategy for anthropology's attempt to balance it's conflicting objectives of seeking propinquity while retaining distance.

In his chapter, Olaf Zenker briefly presents the ethnographic case of the recent Irish language revival in Catholic West Belfast, where practices and representations of the Irish language have come to be issues of contention for local actors. Amongst other issues, Zenker analyses how 'they' (language activists) have used representations and, in a second step, how he himself relies on representations to present 'their' case in his text. In generalizing the problem and drawing on the language philosophies of Wittgenstein and Austin, he suggests conceptualizing the ethnographic process as a cultural translation of 'truths' and 'facts' from 'their' into 'our' language-game of English-medium social science. The author thereby argues for an understanding of these two language-games as fundamentally symmetrical in that, apart from their mutual striving for truth and plausibility, in both language-games truth and meaning are mutually constitutive and facts reside at the intersection of their respective words and the world. Such an approach leads to two reflexive acknowledgements: first, the need to develop a sufficiently sensitive language competence in *both* language-games; and second, the need to go beyond the matter of language in persistently confronting 'their' as well as 'our' own factual statements with the world in order to produce approximate and more plausible truths.

Christophe Heintz characterizes *Writing Culture* as a project of naturalized epistemology, in which evaluative and normative positions are derived from a descriptive analysis of how anthropologists actually write their ethnographies. While arguing for such a position himself, Heintz suggests that *Writing Culture*'s strength – focusing on textuality – was also partly its weakness: such an approach neglected crucial contextual factors such as the specificities of the human mind that also determine the production of ethnographies. He therefore recommends improving anthropology's reflexivity through empirically studying ethnographic writing from the perspective of a cognitive anthropology of anthropology. As Heintz emphasizes, ethnographies are typically produced not by single individuals but are instead created through intense exchanges between colleagues. Ethnographic texts are hence authored by distributed cognitive processes of critical collaborative thinking rather than by the individual who functions as 'the author'. It is for this reason, Heintz argues, that acknowledgements can reveal the particularities of these distributed cognitive processes, while the general absence of 'the author' in ethnographic representations is more indicative of the multi-authored nature of such texts than any attempt at achieving a polyphonic style, whose 'voicing' of informants as co-authors remains largely pretentious.

Stephen P. Reyna suggests improving anthropological representations by establishing increasingly harder, 'approximate truths' according to the epistemological criteria of accuracy and reliability. He argues that *Writing Culture* was a relatively minor moment in the history of socio-cultural thought and a largely negative one that ultimately contributed to obscurantism. In fact, according to Reyna, there is an epistemological crisis in ethnography, and it was only heightened by *Writing Culture*. This crisis consists in the fact that ethnographers produce their texts in ways largely indifferent to questions of truth. Reyna criticizes the contributors of *Writing Culture* for having been indifferent to establishing a framework for 'true ethnography' – that is, ethnographic accounts that can be judged according to their veridicality. He then introduces the concept of 'approximate truths', a synthesis of pragmatic approaches to truth in the spirit of William James and C.S. Peirce. The primary concern here is not with the question of what truth actually is but rather with the task of formulating more accurate and reliable statements about reality. The business of producing approximate truths is, as Reyna points out, hard work. The alternative, however, may be much less desirable: if ethnographers are indifferent to the truth of their fictions, then their fictions are ultimately irrelevant.

John H. Zammito's analysis of the different usages of the culture concept in anthropology and sociology reveals that disciplinary conventions can create unacknowledged barriers that unnecessarily blind us to various epistemological issues and can lead to the premature abandonment of concepts in social analysis and representational practice. Zammito observes that while anthropologists seem to have grown disenchanted with the concept of culture, sociologists have taken it up in a decisive manner. As with anthropologists, the concern that drove sociologists to form the new field of cultural sociology was the desire to grasp concrete practices and to reject at one and the same time 'structural' and cultural determinism. But this endeavour also sought to grasp the specific contributions, both enabling and restraining, that cultural actors made to practices. That entailed, Zammito argues, a more differentiated notion of culture, breaking it out into more determinate structures of its own, and then finding out how these structures affected practices. Zammito claims that the new American cultural sociologists seek a balance between structure and agency, avoiding structuralist determinism and voluntarist freedom alike. In order to move beyond *Writing Culture*, the argument goes, this insight of the 'new' cultural sociology of structure and agency should be combined with a self-aware and critically attuned anthropological sensitization to the pitfalls of representation.

The Worldliness of Representations

Although the chapters in this volume proceed in rather divergent empirical, methodological and epistemological directions, all of the authors nevertheless touch on common problems related to a move 'beyond' *Writing Culture*. In this respect, one important epistemological problem that was somewhat marginalized in *Writing Culture* concerns the 'worldliness' of texts – that is, different aspects of the relationship between 'texts' and the 'world'. This relationship may concern the question of how to represent empirical realities in scientific texts; it may also refer to different 'worldly' contexts of textual production and reception; and it may point to the embeddedness of epistemological frameworks, theoretical paradigms and research practices in historical contexts, academic disciplines and cognitive processes. In what follows, we give a short overview of the main aspects of 'worldliness' that are addressed by the various contributions in this volume.

Crapanzano views representations as fundamentally implicated in the intertwined enactments of often unacknowledged linguistic ideologies, metapragmatically privileging certain communicative functions over others. As Crapanzano shows, this not only complicates communicative processes in the-world-to-be-represented, in that unacknowledged metapragmatic differences among informants can perpetuate mutual misunderstandings, distrust and negative stereotyping between and about them. In addition, divergent linguistic ideologies also affect the field encounter itself – that is, the-world-of-representing – which thereby turns into both the site and object of intense plays of power and desire when the metapragmatic definition of the situation itself is negotiated. It is here, Crapanzano reminds us, that the limits of mutual understanding are probed and shifted but also ultimately constituted.

The fact of such limited compatibilities emerging in fieldwork encounters also provides the focal point for Kirsch's discussion of the quandaries that result from the very question, in what sense representations actually are 'worldly'. In his exploration of a case of a Zambian Pentecostal Church, 'theoglossia' – speech that purports to be an unmediated transmission of the Divine – obviously affects the operation of the Church's bureaucracy. However, this 'self-appellation of speakership' also poses fundamental epistemological questions since it leaves the ethnographer in the awkward position of either treating the informant's speakership position as true (implying that they are not the true speaker) or else negating the informant's denial of speakership in order to restore their 'truly true native's point of view'. The ways in which ethnographies reflect informants' self-appellations of speakership thus provide certain takes on the 'worldliness' of representations and exclude others.

Zenker builds on approaches in the philosophy of language that see representations as intrinsically worldly in that representations are necessarily in, and only therefore possibly of, the world. The ordinary, situated and routinized usage of representations is thus taken as a precondition for their intelligible referencing of the world. As Zenker stresses, the 'worlds' of production, reception and referentiality of representations thereby interlock within common language-games. Rather than lamenting the inescapably historical, spatial and social situatedness of specific instances of language-games as precluding an objective vantage point, Zenker emphasizes that the specific worldliness of language-games and their representations not only allows for referentiality in the first place, but also simultaneously provides 'truth-conditions-in-progress' for checking and improving one's game-specific accounts of the world of facts.

Reyna wants to overcome *Writing Culture*'s indifference to empirical reality through recourse to 'approximate truths'. Within this framework, theories are always related to empirical reality through their confrontational stance towards the world, a stance that requires observations to produce 'validation histories' and 'evidential ladders'. Validation histories are records of confrontations between observational pictures and generalizations about reality; these generalizations are thereby liable to validation or falsification. As we try to acquire more positive evidence validating a generalization within validation histories, Reyna argues, we climb an 'evidential ladder' towards truer generalizations about reality.

Strohmenger presents a more philosophical account of the relationship between 'world' and 'text,' arguing that the 'world' is misrepresented within the 'text' if the realms of 'fact' and 'value' are separated from each other. This is so, Strohmenger points out, because both non-value and value statements share the same (im)possibility of being objectively answered. As a consequence, he argues that textual strategies should reflect what he calls the 'collapse of the fact/value dichotomy' – that is, the compatibility between these seemingly different epistemological domains.

By analysing the clash of apparently incompatible epistemological frameworks, Kumoll analyses the 'political' worldliness of theories and practices of research. He argues that Marshall Sahlins's cultural theory may serve as an example of the political location of epistemological and research practices in the world outside the text. Kumoll points out that Sahlins's cultural theory may be interpreted as a scientific rationalization of his political protest against the Vietnam War in the 1960s. However, Sahlins's universalist strategy of representation undermines his politically sensitive cultural relativism and collides with the emerging cultural studies of Oceania, a field that may be analysed as a radical political and epistemological alternative to Western anthropology. Kumoll concludes that both the development and the acquisition of theories, epistemologies and research practices are always embedded within changing historical and cultural contexts that shape their political dimensions and significance for different interpreters.

Focusing on the use of the culture concept in anthropology and sociology, Zammito also illustrates that scientific concepts are embedded in the world of different academic disciplines, paradigms, contexts and traditions that may shape their respective uses, connotations and meanings for different readerships. If anthropologists have been desperately seeking to extricate themselves from the culture construct, he argues, the situation in sociology has been just the opposite. The somewhat unexpected career of the culture concept in sociology may be at least partly explained by the attempt to overcome a *crise de conscience* in sociology in contrast to anthropology where the culture concept was alleged to have contributed to a crisis in representation. As Zammito's chapter shows, scientific concepts are also embedded in varying institutional structures that influence their respective uses in different academic fields.

A somewhat different account of the embeddedness of texts and research practices in the world is presented by Heintz, who seeks to investigate ethnographies with a more differentiated view of both the processes and diverse 'worlds' that, at different stages, influence the production of texts. Adopting a stance informed by cognitive anthropology, Heintz emphasizes that the production of ethnographies involves forms of cognition that take place in the field as well as back at the researcher's home university, though this second element remains undertheorized. During fieldwork, 'mind-reading' – the cognitive ability to attribute desires, beliefs, and intentions to others – is crucial and, as Heintz argues, autobiographical sections in ethnographies provide important information concerning the ethnographer's mind-reading acculturation in the 'world' of the field. Back in the 'world' of research institutions, however, colleagues become the relevant Other, thereby shaping the final text and turning it into a product of distributed cognition. This specific 'worldliness' of representations equally finds its way into the text through acknowledgments and a rightful absence of 'the author'. With this approach, Heintz addresses yet another facet of the worldliness of representations and thereby complements the other contributions in this volume, which open up various frameworks that, in locating the 'text' in the 'world', warrant further analysis.

Theorizing and Realizing Intersections of
Epistemology and Representational Practice

While it may initially sound trivial, it is worth noting that despite pointing towards various pitfalls and while airing certain reservations concerning the epistemological status of representations, all the contributors to this volume are united in continuing to represent. The mere act of representing sends a clear message that, notwithstanding evident costs, within this volume the gains are still seen as justifying a continual representational process. This observation draws attention to a more general issue, which we think was not sufficiently attended to in *Writing Culture*, namely the question of recursivity: to what extent is what is said by an author consistent with both that and how it is said in the text? Put differently, we must ask how an author handles the fact that in theorizing about intersections of epistemology and representational practice, they are always already realizing such an intersection. In a final consideration of the various chapters we thus provide our reading of how these texts actually deal with this issue.

In highlighting linguistic ideologies, which privilege the referential, indexical or poetical function within communication, Crapanzano cautions against approaches that unduly universalize their own metapragmatic position by misreading it in others' representations. This warning becomes necessary because such ideological frames have the power to obfuscate themselves. Crapanzano directs his admonition against scientisms that tend to assume that the referential is more important than the indexical, poetical or other metapragmatic functions of representations. However, Crapanzano himself does so within a scientific, 'denotational text' which also prioritizes referentiality. Reflexively taking up this issue, Crapanzano makes clear that although the project of a reflexive science can and should be maintained, it provides but one metapragmatic approach, which ultimately must remain blind to its own omissions.

The issue of referentiality and especially the problem of how to recursively handle it in a consistent manner also constitutes a central concern in Zenker's chapter. In his case study he attempts to theorize about 'their' language usages in terms of the same conditions that, as he retrospectively shows, he himself has realized in theorizing. In this process, a symmetry between 'their' and 'our' language-game is suggested in which notions of 'truth', 'meaning' and 'facts' rooted in situated representational usages are seen as underpinning rather than undermining the realist project of a referential social science. Zenker thereby suggests that what is needed is a realistic understanding of scientific realism rather than a change to non-realistic modes of writing.

Reyna argues that the indifference of postmodernism to empirically validated referentiality corresponds to the deplorable situation in which the chief intellectual products of anthropology – ethnographies – are often forgotten. Reyna's argument conceptually develops his notion of 'hard truths' and can thereby itself be seen as being based on such a 'hard truth', as Reyna reflexively suggests. Only if ethnographers care for and comprehensibly validate the truth of their accounts will their ethnographies less easily sink into oblivion. In addition, Reyna's plea for avoiding 'blurred concepts' is also mirrored by his own representational style, which seeks to follow his own rules of accuracy and reliability as much as possible.

Zammito suggests that the divide between sociology and anthropology concerning the different usages and understandings of culture concepts should be overcome by further advancing approaches that are both sensitive to the fallacies of representation and sympathetic to developing a systematic theorization of the relationship between structure and action. By providing various citations taken from texts that are central to anthropological and sociological debates on culture and by discussing a multitude of different paradigms and theories, Zammito's narrative may be read as being itself a textual reflection of this goal: he carefully constructs virtual dialogues between different paradigms and research traditions, thereby contributing to contemporary attempts to enrich both anthropological and sociological theories of culture.

Strohmenger discusses Clifford's move from an asymmetrical to a symmetrical understanding of non-value and value judgements. However, Strohmenger argues that Clifford is seduced by the vocabulary he uses and is led to a conclusion that ultimately fails to defend a symmetrical position. One example of this is what Strohmenger calls 'secret repetition compulsion'; that is, the confusion of non-factual with value statements. Strohmenger's analysis of Clifford's text can thereby be interpreted as an outcome of his attempt to overcome the fact/value dichotomy, as Strohmenger seeks to sensitively combine non-value and value judgments in Clifford's essay, thereby aiming at a 'symmetrical' position.

In his elaborations of ethnographic cognition and the process of writing (up) culture, Heintz suggests that we read the restricted information on 'the author' as well as the corresponding stylistic conventions within classic ethnography as reflecting crucial cognitive processes, which constitute the basis for such texts primarily aimed at representing cultural others. In accordance with these reflections, Heintz makes only a few, brief self-references in his text: in the introduction where Heintz introduces himself as a cognitive anthropologist of anthropology and in the concluding paragraph of his chapter, as well as several lines of his acknowledgements that provide information on his mind-reading acculturation during fieldwork. The remainder of his acknowledgements indicates critical academic exchanges, which ensure that his text is sufficiently saturated with distributed cognition.

Within quite a different ethnographic arena, Kirsch struggles with the question of how to maintain the anthropological ideal of dialogism and multivocality in giving voice to others when these others themselves adhere to monologism, monovocality, and the total truth from 'the spirit's point of view'. As Kirsch shows, there are no easy answers to this problem. In fact, Kirsch's own solution – such as his phrasing of 'self-appellation of speakership by interlocutors' rather than of 'God speaking through others' – already constitutes a position seeking allegiance with a secular, multivocal anthropology rather than with a sacred voicing of the Holy Spirit. Kirsch reflexively comments on this predicament, insisting that even if the tension cannot ultimately be resolved, we can at least make explicit the extent to which our representations reflect our interlocutors' self-appellation of speakership.

Also seeking to determine how far a dialogic integration of self and other can be taken, Kumoll looks at ways of overcoming the emerging epistemological and political divide between Western and Oceanic research practices. He argues that anthropology and related disciplines may benefit from incorporating specific elements of Oceanic ways of 'doing' science into their scholarly frameworks. At the same time, however, Kumoll's text is not an example of combining Western and Oceanic epistemologies and practices of representation, as the author emphasizes. Kumoll's narrative rather indicates that he wants to extend the limits of mutual compatibility without committing the error of giving up one's own otherness with regard to the other, as this would signify the end of any fruitful dialogue.

Creating a fruitful dialogue between different positions within and across academic disciplines on current intersections of epistemologies and representational practices has also been a primary driving force behind this volume. Though unified in general approach, the essays that comprise this volume nevertheless advocate different positions and are written in different tones, expressing varying degrees of scepticism towards social science's ability to deliver. Nevertheless, we believe that the essays in this volume are ultimately united in that they all suggest specific doors to be opened beyond *Writing Culture* in ways that exhibit their reflexivity less in terms of textual strategies of self-reference and more in terms of a heightened awareness of the individual condition and conditionalities of the author.

References

Abu-Lughod, Lila. 1991. 'Writing Against Culture', in Richard G. Fox (ed.), *Recapturing Anthropology: Working in the Present*. Santa Fe, NM: School of American Research Press, 137–62.

Ahmad, Aijaz. 1992. *In Theory: Classes, Nations, Literatures*. London: Verso.

Appadurai, Arjun. 1996. *Modernity at Large: Cultural Dimensions of Globalization*. Minneapolis: University of Minnesota Press.

Asad, Talal (ed.). 1973. *Anthropology and the Colonial Encounter*. London: Ithaca Press.

———. 1986. 'The Concept of Cultural Translation in British Social Anthropology', in James Clifford and George E. Marcus (eds), *Writing Culture: The Poetics and Politics of Ethnography*. Berkeley: University of California Press, 141–64.

Bataille, George. 1985. *Visions of Excess: Selected Writings 1927–1939*, ed. and trans. A. Stoekl. Minneapolis: University of Minnesota Press.

Baudrillard, Jean. 1988. *Selected Writings*, ed. M. Poster. Stanford, CA: Stanford University Press.

Becker, Howard S. 1987. 'The Writing of Science', *Contemporary Sociology* 16(1): 25–27.

Behar, Ruth. 1993. 'Women Writing Culture: Another Telling of the Story of American Anthropology', *Critique of Anthropology* 13(4): 307–25.

Behar, Ruth and Deborah A. Gordon (eds). 1995. *Women Writing Culture*. Berkeley: University of California Press.

Bhabha, Homi. 1994. *The Location of Culture*. London: Routledge.

Birth, Kevin K. 1990. 'Review: Reading and the Righting of Writing Ethnographies', *American Ethnologist* 17(3): 549–57.

Bloch, Maurice. 1983. *Marxism and Anthropology: The History of a Relationship*. Oxford: Oxford University Press.

Borofsky, Robert. 2000. 'An Invitation', in Robert Borofsky (ed.), *Remembrance of Pacific Pasts: An Invitation to Remake History*. Honolulu: University of Hawai'i Press, 1–30.

Bourdieu, Pierre. 1977. *Outline of a Theory of Practice*, trans. R. Nice. Cambridge: Cambridge University Press.

Brightman, Robert. 1995. 'Forget Culture: Replacement, Transcendence, Relexification', *Cultural Anthropology* 10(4): 509–46.

Brumann, Christoph. 1999. 'Writing for Culture: Why a Successful Concept Should Not Be Discarded' (with Comments and Reply), *Current Anthropology* 40(Supplement): S1–S27.

Bunzl, Matti. 1999. 'Review: *After Writing Culture: Epistemology and Praxis in Contemporary Anthropology*', *American Ethnologist* 26(1): 260–61.

Chakrabarty, Dipesh. 2000. *Provincializing Europe: Postcolonial Thought and Historical Difference*. Princeton, NJ: Princeton University Press.

Clifford, James. 1983. 'On Ethnographic Authority', *Representations* 1(2): 118–46.

———. 1986a. 'Introduction: Partial Truths', in James Clifford and George E. Marcus (eds), *Writing Culture: The Poetics and Politics of Ethnography*. Berkeley: University of California Press, 1–26.

———. 1986b. 'On Ethnographic Allegory', in James Clifford and George E. Marcus (eds), *Writing Culture: The Poetics and Politics of Ethnography*. Berkeley: University of California Press, 98–121.

———. 1988a. *The Predicament of Culture: Twentieth Century Ethnography, Literature, and Art*. Cambridge, MA: Harvard University Press.

———. 1988b. 'Comment', *Current Anthropology* 29(3): 425.

———. 1992. 'Travelling Cultures', in Lawrence Grossberg, Cary Nelson and Paula Treichler (eds), *Cultural Studies*. New York: Routledge, 96–117.

———. 1997. *Routes: Travel and Translation in the Late Twentieth Century*. Cambridge, MA: Harvard University Press.

———. 1999. 'After Writing Culture', *American Anthropologist* 101(3): 643–45.

———. 2001. 'Indigenous Articulations', *Contemporary Pacific* 13(2): 468–90.

Clifford, James and George E. Marcus. 1986a. 'Preface', in James Clifford and George E. Marcus (eds), *Writing Culture: The Poetics and Politics of Ethnography*. Berkeley: University of California Press, vi–ix.

——— (eds). 1986b. *Writing Culture: The Poetics and Politics of Ethnography*. Berkeley: University of California Press.

Comaroff, Jean and John L. Comaroff. 2000. 'Millennial Capitalism: First Thoughts on a Second Coming', *Public Culture* 12(2): 291–343.

Crapanzano, Vincent. 1980. *Tuhami: Portrait of a Moroccan*. Chicago: University of Chicago Press.

———. 1986. 'Hermes' Dilemma: The Masking of Subversion in Ethnographic Description', in James Clifford and George E. Marcus (eds), *Writing Culture: The Poetics and Politics of Ethnography*. Berkeley: University of California Press, 51–76.

Cunningham, Hilary. 1999. 'The Ethnography of Transnational Social Activism: Understanding the Global as Local Practice', *American Ethnologist* 26(3): 583–604.

Deleuze, Gilles and Félix Guattari. 1987. *A Thousand Plateaus: Capitalism and Schizophrenia*, trans. B. Massumi. Minneapolis: University of Minnesota Press.

Derrida, Jacques. 1973. *Speech and Phenomena and Other Essays on Husserl's Theory of Signs*, trans. D.B. Allison. Evanston, IL: Northwestern University Press.

———. 1976. *Of Grammatology*, trans. G.C. Spivak. Baltimore: Johns Hopkins University Press.

Donham, Donald L. 1981. 'Beyond the Domestic Mode of Production', *Man* 16(4): 515–41.

Dwyer, Kevin. 1982. *Moroccan Dialogues: Anthropology in Question.* Baltimore: Johns Hopkins University Press.

Fabian, Johannes. 1983. *Time and the Other: How Anthropology Makes Its Object.* New York: Columbia University Press.

Fischer, Michael M.J. 1986. 'Ethnicity and the Post-Modern Arts of Memory', in James Clifford and George E. Marcus (eds), *Writing Culture: The Poetics and Politics of Ethnography.* Berkeley: University of California Press, 194–233.

Fischer, Michael M.J., George E. Marcus and Stephen A. Tyler. 1988. 'Comment', *Current Anthropology* 29(3): 425–26.

Foucault, Michel. 1978. *Discipline and Punish: The Birth of the Prison*, trans. A. Sheridan. Harmondsworth: Penguin.

Fox, Richard G. and Barbara J. King (eds). 2002. *Anthropology Beyond Culture.* Oxford: Berg.

Free, Tony. 1990. 'Written or Living Culture?', *Journal of the Anthropological Society of Oxford* 21: 51–65.

Friedman, Jonathan. 1974. 'Marxism, Structuralism and Vulgar Materialism', *Man* 9(3): 444–69.

———. 1994. *Cultural Identity and Global Process.* London: Sage.

Gaonkar, Dilip P. 1999. 'On Alternative Modernities', *Public Culture* 11(1): 1–18.

Geertz, Clifford. 1973. *The Interpretation of Cultures: Selected Essays.* New York: Basic Books.

———. 1983. *Local Knowledge: Further Essays in Interpretive Anthropology.* New York: Basic Books.

———. 1988. *Works and Lives: The Anthropologist as Author.* Stanford, CA: Stanford University Press.

———. 2000. *Available Light: Anthropological Reflections on Philosophical Topics.* Princeton, NJ: Princeton University Press.

———. 2002. 'An Inconstant Profession: The Anthropological Life in Interesting Times', *Annual Review of Anthropology* 31: 1–19.

Gellner, Ernest. 1970. 'Concepts and Society', in Bryan Wilson (ed.), *Rationality.* New York: Harper and Row, 18–49.

Gikandi, Simon. 2001. 'Globalization and the Claims of Postcoloniality', *South Atlantic Quarterly* 100(3): 627–58.

Gledhill, John. 2005. 'Some Histories are More Possible than Others: Structural Power, Big Pictures and the Goal of Explanation in the Anthropology of Eric Wolf', *Critique of Anthropology* 25(1): 37–57.

Godelier, Maurice. 1977. *Perspectives in Marxist Anthropology.* Cambridge: Cambridge University Press.

Gottowik, Volker. 1997. *Konstruktionen des Anderen: Clifford Geertz und die Krise der ethnographischen Repräsentation.* Berlin: Reimer.

Gupta, Akhil and James Ferguson (eds). 1997. *Culture, Power, Place: Explorations in Critical Anthropology.* Durham, NC: Duke University Press.

Hall, Stuart. 1980. 'Cultural Studies: Two Paradigms', *Media, Culture and Society* 2: 57–72.

Handelman, Don. 1994. 'Critiques of Anthropology: Literary Turns, Slippery Bends', *Poetics Today* 15(3): 341–81.

Hannerz, Ulf. 1996. *Transnational Connections: Culture, People, Places.* London: Routledge.

Horowitz, Irving L. (ed.). 1967. *The Rise and Fall of Project Camelot: Studies in the Relationship between Social Science and Practical Politics.* Cambridge, MA: MIT Press.

Hutnyk, John. 1989. 'Clifford Geertz as a Cultural System: A Review Article', *Social Analysis* 26: 91–107.

Inda, Jonathan X. and Renato Rosaldo (eds). 2002. *The Anthropology of Globalization: A Reader.* Oxford: Blackwell.

Inglis, Fred. 2000. *Clifford Geertz: Culture, Custom and Ethics.* Cambridge: Polity Press.

James, Allison, Jenny Hockey and Andrew Dawson. 1997a. 'Introduction: The Road to Santa Fe', in Allison James, Jenny Hockey and Andrew Dawson (eds), *After Writing Culture: Epistemology and Praxis in Contemporary Anthropology.* New York: Routledge, 1–15.

——— (eds). 1997b. *After Writing Culture: Epistemology and Praxis in Contemporary Anthropology.* New York: Routledge.

Keane, Webb. 2003. 'Self-Interpretation, Agency, and the Objects of Anthropology: Reflections on a Genealogy', *Comparative Studies in Society and History* 45(2): 222–48.

Keesing, Roger M. 1987. 'Anthropology as Interpretive Quest' (with Comments and Reply), *Current Anthropology* 28(2): 161–76.

Kuper, Adam. 1999. *Culture: The Anthropologists' Account.* Cambridge, MA: Harvard University Press.

Lacan, Jacques. 1977. *Écrits: A Selection,* trans. A. Sheridan. New York: Norton.

Lassiter, Luke E. 2001. 'From "Reading over the Shoulders of Natives" to "Reading alongside Natives", Literally: Toward a Collaborative and Reciprocal Ethnography', *Journal of Anthropological Research* 57(2): 137–49.

———. 2005. 'Collaborative Ethnography and Public Anthropology' (with Comments and Reply), *Current Anthropology* 46(1): 83–106.

Lather, Patti. 2001. 'Postbook: Working the Ruins of Feminist Ethnography', *Signs* 27(1): 199–227.

Lévi-Strauss, Claude. 1966[1962]. *The Savage Mind.* Chicago: University of Chicago Press.

Lewellen, Ted C. 2002. *The Anthropology of Globalization: Cultural Anthropology Enters the 21st Century.* Westport, CT: Bergin and Garvey.

Loomba, Ania et al. (eds). 2005. *Postcolonial Studies and Beyond.* Durham, NC: Duke University Press.

McCarthy, Thomas. 1992. 'Review: Doing the Right Thing in Cross-Cultural Representation', *Ethics* 102(3): 635–49.

MacCormack, Carol and Marilyn Strathern (eds). 1980. *Nature, Culture and Gender.* Cambridge: Cambridge University Press.

McDonald, Maryon. 1991. 'Postmodernism, Socialism and Ethnography', *Anthropology Today* 7(5): 19–20.

Marcus, George E. 1986a. 'Contemporary Problems of Ethnography in the Modern World System', in James Clifford and George E. Marcus (eds), *Writing Culture: The Poetics and Politics of Ethnography.* Berkeley: University of California Press, 165–93.

———. 1986b. 'Afterword: Ethnographic Writing and Anthropological Careers', in James Clifford and George E. Marcus (eds), *Writing Culture: The Poetics and Politics of Ethnography.* Berkeley: University of California Press, 262–66.

———. 1995. 'Ethnography in/of the World System: The Emergence of Multi-Sited Ethnography', *Annual Review of Anthropology* 24: 95–117.

———. 1997. 'The Uses of Complicity in the Changing Mis-en-Scene of Anthropological Fieldwork', *Representations* 59: 85–108.

———. 1998a. '"That Damn Book": Ten Years after Writing Culture', *Etnográfica: Revista do Centro de Estudos de Antropologia Social* 2(1): 5–14.

———. 1998b. *Ethnography through Thick and Thin.* Princeton, NJ: Princeton University Press.

———. 1999. 'Review of Auto/Ethnography: *Rewriting the Self and the Social,* by D. Reed-Danahay, and *After Writing Culture: Epistemology and Praxis in Contemporary Anthropology,* by A. James, J. Hockey and A. Dawson', *American Journal of Sociology* 104(2): 582–85.

———. 2002. 'Beyond Malinowski and After Writing Culture: On the Future of Cultural Anthropology and the Predicament of Ethnography', *Australian Journal of Anthropology* 13(2): 191–99.

Marcus, George E. and Dick Cushman. 1982. 'Ethnographies as Texts', *Annual Review of Anthropology* 11: 25–69.

Marcus, George E. and Michael M.J. Fischer. 1986. *Anthropology as Cultural Critique: An Experimental Moment in the Human Sciences.* Chicago: University of Chicago Press.

Mascia-Lees, Frances, Patricia Sharpe, and Colleen Ballerino Cohen. 1989. 'The Postmodern Turn in Anthropology: Cautions from a Feminist Perspective', *Signs* 15(1): 7–33.

Meillassoux, Claude. 1972. 'From Reproduction to Production: A Marxist Approach to Economic Anthropology', *Economy and Society* 1(1): 93–105.

———. 1981. *Maidens, Meal, and Money.* Cambridge: Cambridge University Press.

Moore, Henrietta L. 2004. 'Global Anxieties: Concept-Metaphors and Pre-Theoretical Commitments in Anthropology', *Anthropological Theory* 4(1): 71–88.

Mutman, Mahmut. 2006. 'Writing Culture: Postmodernism and Ethnography', *Anthropological Theory* 6(2): 153–78.

Nederveen Pieterse, Jan. 2004. *Globalization and Culture: Global Mélange.* Lanham, MD: Rowman and Littlefield.

Nichols, Bill. 1988. 'Review of *Myth, Race and Power*, by K. Tomaselli et al. and *Writing Culture: The Poetics and Politics of Ethnography*, by J. Clifford and G.E. Marcus', *Film Quarterly* 41(3): 56–57.

Olson, Gary and Elizabeth Hirsh (eds). 1995. *Women Writing Culture.* Albany: State University of New York Press.

Ortner, Sherry B. 1997. 'Introduction', *Representations* 59(Special Issue): 1–13.

Peirano, Mariza G.S. 1998. 'When Anthropology is at Home: The Different Contexts of a Single Discipline', *Annual Review of Anthropology* 27: 105–128.

Pels, Peter. 1997. 'The Anthropology of Colonialism: Culture, History, and the Emergence of Western Governmentality', *Annual Review of Anthropology* 26: 163–83.

Poewe, Karla. 1996. 'Writing Culture and Writing Fieldwork: The Proliferation of Experimental and Experiential Ethnographies', *Ethnos* 61(3/4): 177–206.

Pratt, Mary L. 1986. 'Fieldwork in Common Places', in James Clifford and George E. Marcus (eds), *Writing Culture: The Poetics and Politics of Ethnography.* Berkeley: University of California Press, 27–50.

Prakash, Gyan. 1995. 'Orientalism Now', *History and Theory* 34(3): 199–212.

Rabinow, Paul. 1977. *Reflections on Fieldwork in Morocco.* Berkeley: University of California Press.

———. 1986. 'Representations are Social Facts: Modernity and Post-Modernity in Anthropology', in James Clifford and George E. Marcus (eds), *Writing Culture: The Poetics and Politics of Ethnography.* Berkeley: University of California Press, 234–61.

Reyna, Stephen P. 1994. 'Literary Anthropology and the Case against Science', *Man* 29(3): 555–81.

Rorty, Richard. 1979. *Philosophy and the Mirror of Nature.* Princeton, NJ: Princeton University Press.

Rosaldo, Michelle and Louise Lamphere (eds). 1974. *Woman, Culture, and Society.* Stanford, CA: Stanford University Press.

Rosaldo, Renato. 1986. 'From the Door of His Tent: The Fieldworker and the Inquisitor', in James Clifford and George E. Marcus (eds), *Writing Culture: The Poetics and Politics of Ethnography.* Berkeley: University of California Press, 77–97.

———. 1989. *Culture and Truth: The Remaking of Social Analysis.* Boston: Beacon.

Roth, Paul A. 1989. 'Ethnography Without Tears' (with Comments and Reply), *Current Anthropology* 30(5): 555–69.

Sahlins, Marshall. 1981. *Historical Metaphors and Mythical Realities: Structure in the Early History of the Sandwich Islands Kingdom.* Ann Arbor: University of Michigan Press.

———. 1985. *Islands of History*. Chicago: University of Chicago Press.

———. 2000. *Culture in Practice: Selected Essays*. New York: Zone Books.

Said, Edward. 1978. *Orientalism*. New York: Pantheon Books.

———. 1989. 'Representing the Colonized: Anthropology's Interlocutors', *Critical Inquiry* 15(2): 205–25.

———. 1993. *Culture and Imperialism*. New York: Knopf.

Sangren, P. Steven. 1988. 'Rhetoric and the Authority of Ethnography: "Postmodernism" and the Social Reproduction of Texts' (with Comments and Reply), *Current Anthropology* 29(3): 405–435.

Schneider, Mark A. 1987. 'Culture-as-Text in the Work of Clifford Geertz', *Theory and Society* 16(6): 809–839.

Scholte, Bob. 1987. 'The Literary Turn in Contemporary Anthropology', *Critique of Anthropology* 7(1): 33–47.

Scott, Michael W. 2005. 'Hybridity, Vacuity, and Blockage: Visions of Chaos from Anthropological Theory, Island Melanesia, and Central Africa', *Comparative Studies in Society and History* 47(1): 190–216.

Sebag, Lucien. 1964. *Marxisme et structuralisme*. Paris: Payot.

Silverstein, Michael. 1979. 'Language Structure and Linguistic Ideology', in Paul R. Cline, William Hanks and Carol Hofbauer (eds), *The Elements: A Parasession on Linguistic Units and Levels*. Chicago: Chicago Linguistic Circle, 193–247.

Solovey, Mark. 2001. 'Project Camelot and the 1960s Epistemological Revolution: Rethinking the Politics-Patronage-Social Science Nexus', *Social Studies of Science* 31(2): 171–206.

Spencer, Jonathan.1989. 'Anthropology as a Kind of Writing', *Man* 24(1): 145–64.

Spiro, Melford E. 1996. 'Postmodernist Anthropology, Subjectivity, and Science: A Modernist Critique', *Comparative Studies in Society and History* 38(4): 759–80.

Spivak, Gayatri C. 1988. 'Can the Subaltern Speak? Speculations on Widow Sacrifice', in Cary Nelson and Lawrence Grossberg (eds), *Marxism and the Interpretation of Culture*. Urbana: University of Illinois Press, 271–313.

———. 1999. *A Critique of Postcolonial Reason: Toward a History of the Vanishing Present*. Cambridge, MA: Harvard University Press.

Strathern, Marilyn. 1987. 'Out of Context: The Persuasive Fictions of Anthropology' (with Comments and Reply), *Current Anthropology* 28(3): 251–81.

Sutcliffe, Richard. 1993. 'Writing Culture: Towards "Postmodern" Ethnography or Much Ado about Nothing? An Exercise in Writing about Writing about Writing about the Other', *Canberra Anthropology* 16(2): 17–44.

Tedlock, Barbara. 1991. 'From Participant Observation to the Observation of Participation: The Emergence of Narrative Ethnography', *Journal of Anthropological Research* 47(1): 69–94.

Tedlock, Dennis. 1987. 'Questions Concerning Dialogical Anthropology', *Journal of Anthropological Research* 43(4): 325–37.

Terray, Emmanuel. 1972. *Marxism and 'Primitive' Societies*. New York: Monthly Review Press.

Thornton, Robert. 1988. 'The Rhetoric of Ethnographic Holism', *Cultural Anthropology* 3(3): 285–303.

Tsing, Anna L. 1993. *In the Realm of the Diamond Queen*. Princeton, NJ: Princeton University Press.

———. 2005. *Friction: An Ethnography of Global Connection*. Princeton, NJ: Princeton University Press.

Tyler, Stephen A. 1986. 'Post-modern Ethnography: From Document of the Occult to Occult Document', in James Clifford and George E. Marcus (eds), *Writing Culture: The Poetics and Politics of Ethnography*. Berkeley: University of California Press, 122–40.

———. 1987. *The Unspeakable: Discourse, Dialogue, and Rhetoric in the Postmodern World*. Madison: University of Wisconsin Press.

———. 1989. 'Comment', *Current Anthropology* 30(5): 566.

Varisco, Daniel M. 2004. 'Reading against Culture in Edward Said's *Culture and Imperialism*', *Culture, Theory and Critique* 45(2): 93–112.

Wagner, Roy 1986. 'Review: The Theatre of Fact and Its Critics', *Anthropological Quarterly* 59(2): 97–99.

Wallerstein, Immanuel. 1974. *The Modern World-System: Capitalist Agriculture and the Origins of the European World-Economy in the Sixteenth Century*. New York: Academic Press.

Webster, Steven. 1983. 'Ethnography as Storytelling', *Dialectical Anthropology* 8(3): 185–205.

Werbner, Pnina. 2001. 'The Limits of Cultural Hybridity: On Ritual Monsters, Poetic Licence and Contested Postcolonial Purifications', *Journal of the Royal Anthropological Institute* 7: 133–52.

Werbner, Pnina and Tariq Modood (eds). 1997. *Debating Cultural Hybridity: Multi-Cultural Identities and the Politics of Anti-Racism*. London: Zed Books.

White, Hayden. 1973. *Metahistory: The Historical Imagination in Nineteenth-Century Europe*. Baltimore, MD: Johns Hopkins University Press.

Whitehead, Neil L. 2004. 'Power, Culture, and History: The Legacies of Wolf, Sahlins, and Fabian', *Ethnohistory* 51(1): 181–85.

Wimmer, Andreas. 2001. 'Globalizations *Avant la Lettre*: A Comparative View of Isomorphization and Heteromorphization in an Inter-Connecting World', *Comparative Studies in Society and History* 43(3): 435–66.

Wolf, Eric. 1971. *Peasant Wars of the Twentieth Century*. London: Faber and Faber.

———. 1982. *Europe and the People without History*. Berkeley: University of California Press.

———. 1999. *Envisioning Power: Ideologies of Dominance and Crisis*. Berkeley: University of California Press.

———. 2001. *Pathways of Power: Building an Anthropology of the Modern World*. Berkeley: University of California Press.

Wood, Houston. 2003. 'Cultural Studies for Oceania', *Contemporary Pacific* 15(2): 340–374.

———. 2006. 'Three Competing Research Perspectives for Oceania', *Contemporary Pacific* 18(1): 33–55.

Young, Robert. 2003. *Postcolonialism: A Very Short Introduction.* Oxford: Oxford University Press.

2

Textualization, Mystification and the Power of the Frame

Vincent Crapanzano

In order to think beyond 'the writing culture movement', it is necessary, it would seem, to ask what that movement was. We might say that reference to the movement sets up, pragmatically, its sequel. It opens, as it closes, a direction of thought – possible futures.

The first question I want to ask is: Was all the fuss about writing culture, writing about culture, a movement? I do not, in fact, believe that it was ever a movement in the sociological sense, in which, as I take it, a group of people unite, however loosely, to achieve some goal or another. Though a group of us met in Santa Fe in 1984 to discuss 'the making of ethnographic texts', we never assumed that what we had to say would launch a movement.[1] We never even discussed the possibility. Yes, some of us hoped that what we had to say would call attention – anew – to the role of writing in the production of ethnographic texts. I stress 'anew' since, implicitly at least, most thoughtful anthropologists have had

---

1   In this paper I focus on the participants at the workshop that met at the American School of Research in 1984 and which resulted in the publication of *Writing Culture: The Poetics and Politics of Ethnography*, edited by James Clifford and George E. Marcus. I do not wish to exclude many other anthropologists and literary critics who anticipated or have participated in the 'movement'. Many were inspired by Clifford Geertz and Victor Turner's literary and theatrical concerns. Among the earliest of them, I would include James Boon (1972, 1983), Edward Bruner (1986), Richard Handler's (1983) essays on Edward Sapir, and Steven Webster (1982, 1983, 1986). See also edited volumes by Marc Manganaro (1990) and Doris Bachmann-Medick (1999). For a more extensive bibliography, see Marcus and Cushman (1982). I do not want to turn the Santa Fe meeting into an originary event. It has, however, been taken as such by many anthropologists, including, alas, some of the participants themselves. My focus is determined by my participation in the workshop and my contribution to the Clifford and Marcus volume. What I have to say may be of some historical interest.

to confront the task of describing in written form their findings in a manner that did justice to those facts and the experiences that lay behind their discovery. They were faced with problems of craft, though they did not necessarily articulate them in these terms. On occasion, their struggle to get it right, or more often the tentativeness of what they had written, was mentioned in prefaces and introductions. As such they integrated the struggle into the at times self-berating confession that has become a convention in ethnographic monographs in the United States. Rarely did they ask how the texts they had produced affected not just their ethnographic findings but, as a telos, the course of their field research. The fact that writing ethnography (with a stress on 'writing') was a significant goal was concealed behind other goals, usually scientifically formulated: the accumulation of knowledge, the testing of a hypothesis, contributing to one theoretical paradigm or another, the expansion (ever since Boas and particularly Margaret Mead) of the horizons of those who would became familiar with their findings, and finally, quite simply, social improvement.

Or, the role of writing in ethnography has been masked by one metaphor or another used to describe what ethnographers do. The most pertinent of these is translation: the translation of cultures.[2] I need not belabour the adequacy or inadequacy of this metaphor other than to point out that the understanding and evaluation of translation have varied enormously from culture to culture and throughout history.[3] It reflects a community's particular take on language. The translation metaphor (loosely, as translation is generally understood today) not only frames and organizes ethnographic data in a particular way – one conducive to the textualization of culture – but emphasizes the (re)presentational goal of the ethnography. It fosters the altogether problematic idea that presence – a presence – can be reproduced mimetically, that is to say in referentially adequate terms that escape (up to a point) contextual and co-textual adhesions.[4] What we might call the 'mimetic illusion' gives to the object of ethnographic representation a certain 'independence' – an essential quality that can be captured (*begreifen*) and carried across (*meta-phorein*) contexts and co-texts in another idiom with minimal distortion. It carries, of course, the risk of reification. Though often perceived as a passive activity, translation is, in fact, an active, at times aggressively prepossessing, activity in which the translation, as a palimpsest, overrides, as 'faithful' as it may be, its original. Never fully, to be sure, for as in any palimpsest, what is covered over, the fact that something is covered over, gives rhetorical, if not semantic, force to that which is covered over (Crapanzano 1997, 2001). The translator – the ethnographer – is, in other words, in a position of power, which

---

2   For recent examples, see collections edited by Maranhão and Streck (2003) and Rubel and Rosman (2003).
3   See, for example, Kelly (1979), Stierle (1996); more generally Budick and Iser (1996). See Crapanzano (2003) for a discussion of the translation metaphor in law.
4   By 'co-textual' I mean simply the textual environment in which the text of interest is embedded. In my understanding it extends to what is generally known as the intertextual.

is conventionally masked, epistemologically, in terms of the way translatability is accepted and, ethically, in terms of the translator's commitment to a 'true and faithful' rendition of the primary text or its equivalent. Though, accordingly, translation may be an inadequate metaphor for what ethnographers do, describe and interpret, its choice is itself, however unwittingly, revealing of dynamics that lie behind the ethnographer's task.

In 1972, John Szwed organized a session at the American Anthropological Association (AAA) meetings on the writing of anthropology. I believe it was the first time that a session was devoted to this topic. Clifford Geertz was one of the discussants, and I gave a paper on the status of ethnographies as a compromise between the demands of two sets of interlocutors, those of ones informants and those of ones colleagues.[5] I bring up this meeting since, though it wasn't all that well attended – there were maybe sixty people in the audience – it produced a quite negative reaction in the AAA at large. We were said, quite vulgarly, to be navel gazers, who would do better to get on with our research. Even Irving Goffman, who was in the audience, made the same plea. He was taken on by an Apache undergraduate, who had no idea who he was. She pointed out that there were many ways to express social and cultural reality, including poetry, as she believed her own people would prefer. She was treated with admiring condescension.[6]

I bring this meeting up to indicate the resistance with which the consideration of the writing of ethnography was greeted. None of us expected it. It seemed so obvious that writing would affect the articulation of findings and the conclusions we drew from them. This seemed especially true in an intellectual atmosphere which has been called 'the linguistic turn' and in which structuralist and poststructuralist thought focused on *parole*, *langue* and *discours* and how they articulated with and were influenced by prevailing notions of language (Lévi-Strauss's structuralism), literature (the *literaturnost* of the Russian formalists), ontology (Jacques Derrida's logocentrism), epistemology (Michel Foucault's linguistically endorsed epistemes), performance (John Austin and John Searle's performatives), conversation and dialogue (in ethnomethodology and in the works of Mikhail Bakhtin, Jan Mukarovsky and Hans-Georg Gadamer), narrative (in Vladimir Propp, Julien Greimas, Roland Barthes and Gérard Gennette), tropes (in Hayden White), power (in Foucault), desire (in Jacques Lacan), and orientalism (in Edward Said), and, of course, genre, convention and style. Though many of these approaches had not made their way into American anthropology, which has always looked askance at literary and philosophical fashions, some of them had inveigled their way into the interpretation and

---

5   See Crapanzano (1973). Today, I find that what I wrote is too simple.
6   I should point out that a few weeks before that meeting, Goffman's writing was compared favourably to Franz Kafka's by Marshall Berman in the book review section of *The Sunday New York Times*.

analysis of the texts collected by anthropologists. They were, after all, data. What was extraordinary was that anthropologists had resisted turning these modes of interpretation and analysis on the texts they themselves produced. We have to remember that it was in these same years that anthropology had become critically self-reflective. I suppose it was easier to condemn the discipline as a whole as an instrument of imperialism than to look in detail at our own products and how they bore the mark of putative power plays, including the imperial.

I should add two other factors that were making headway in the United States at the time: interdisciplinarity and feminism. Interdisciplinarity opened anthropology's purview. It was, however, treated with considerable ambivalence. Some hailed it as heralding new, if not revolutionary, intellectual paradigms; others saw it as a threat to scholarship, an encouragement of dilettantism. Feminism's influence on the conventions of ethnographic writing was indirect but equally significant. The feminists (as well as their avatars, proponents of gender and gay and lesbian studies) had, in my view, two important effects on the writing of anthropology. (I am not speaking here of the contributions of individual feminist anthropologists, many of whom wrote in conventional anthropological styles.) The first of these was calling attention to the relationship between social and political engagement and the putative objectivity of the social and psychological sciences. It raised the question of power in a way in which – in my reading – those critics of anthropology who maintained that anthropology was a handmaiden of imperialism did not (Hymes 1974). The feminists focused attention on how anthropology's exclusion of women – their perspective – from its purview framed and evaluated its subject matter, interpretive strategies and theorizing. They demanded an engaged, critical reflexivity. In consequence – my second point – their position required a change in the attitude toward, and practice of, the craft of anthropology, including writing. It is beyond the scope of this chapter to enter into the details of this transformation. Suffice it to say, that even the most superficial comparison of anthropological articles and books before and after the rise of feminism reveals important changes not only in subject matter and argument but also in rhetoric, style and authorial engagement. Obviously changes in attitudes toward science, positivism, objectivity, language and reflexivity also had their effect.

This all-too-brief description of the intellectual environment in which the writing culture movement developed, at least in the United States, offers us an inkling of why a group of heterogeneous approaches and concerns became a 'movement'.[7] It was, I believe, the critical, pejorative attitude of many anthropologists toward our focus on the writing of ethnography that defined our efforts as a movement rather than we ourselves.[8] This is not to say that James

---

7   Cf. Clifford (1986).

Clifford and George E. Marcus, in particular, did not attempt to orchestrate the reception of our work.

I have no intention of defending the writing culture school here. I do want to call attention, however, to the at times contradictory range of approaches encompassed by this stipulated movement. I will mention no names as I do not want to enter into specific characterizations and criticisms. Some of the researchers gave priority to the ethnographic texts themselves, paying little attention to their contexts of origin and reception. They treated these texts in a more or less conventional literary critical manner, examining how the texts constituted their subject matter generically, rhetorically and stylistically. They looked at the way perspective, voice, authorial authority, informants, what they said and did, were fashioned through narrative, figurative language, resonant images and most important the rhetorical use of ethnographic theory itself. Their calling attention to the way in which data and theory were manipulated in order to portray the society or culture under study was particularly troubling to their critics.

Other researchers did attempt to relate ethnographic writing to its contexts of origin and reception. Some, particularly those of a Marxist bent, focused on macro-political conditions; others on immediate contexts of textual production (i.e., fieldwork) or expected responses (usually by colleagues). Many invoked dialogical models, dialogue being understood in either Gadamer's (1960) or Bakhtin's (1981) sense. When contexts were invoked, they were usually phrased in broad sociological terms. With a few exceptions, little attention was paid to the historical or traditional foundations of the categories of ethnographic description and theorizing.

Some of the researchers confounded ethnographic fieldwork, indeed methodology, and ethnographic writing without studying their relationship. Many invoked text as a metaphor for culture, in the manner of Clifford Geertz (1973: 452–53), and fiction as a figure for textual artifice. They claimed to understand 'fiction' in its etymological sense, as something made or fashioned. But as James Clifford (1986: 7) remarked, it is important to recognize that *fingere*, hence fiction, implied a degree of falsehood, making up and inventing, which was ignored by those interpretivists who referred to ethnographies as 'true fictions'. Frequently they saw an overlap between the metaphorization of culture as a text and the textualization of culture. This double casting of culture as text produces, I believe, a textual illusion, a reduction and isolation of culture from its environmental and social surround. A few – the more daring – made reference to

---

8   The critics' dismissal of new, particularly intellectual, approaches in ethnography has, of course, a long history in American anthropology. One need only think of the initial reactions to symbolic, interpretive and postmodern anthropology. What, alas, characterizes these reactions is the frequent substitution of name-slinging for serious critical debate. At the time I am referring to, many 'scientific' anthropologists, as they called themselves, were quick to dismiss the interpretivists as 'intellectuals' in a manner reminiscent of the way Republicans in the U.S. castigate non-Republicans as 'liberals'.

Derrida and other deconstructionists, but they did not push deconstructive interpretation very far.

Most members of the school, as self-reflective as they claimed to be, failed to consider how their own understanding of language, discourse and literature affected their approach. I do not want to speculate as to why this failure was and is so widespread. I do want to suggest, however, that whatever its social, cultural and psychological origins, the way anthropology frames itself – its mission generally and its specific purview – facilitates its frequent failure to look critically at its own take on its subject matter. Facile ideological reflection often serves to cover up this shortcoming. Put another way, anthropology's announced commitment to critical reflexivity serves to mask the shortcomings of that critical attitude. There is, there can be, no ideal critical perspective or meta-perspective. There is no perspective from nowhere. We start from somewhere. This does not mean that we cannot – up to a point – step out of our conventional perspective to articulate our assumptions and look critically at them. We have, of course, to recognize that our meta-perspective is not without conventional constraint. A fully transgressive meta-perspective is as impossible as a view from nowhere, if only because every metalanguage is implicated in its target language.[9]

I want to focus attention on the writing-culture anthropologists' failure to consider how their formulations were affected by their attitudes towards language, discourse and textualization, because it suggests, I believe, one of the directions in which a refined anthropology should move. I should make it clear that my focus on language, discourse and textualization in no way precludes the recognition of the role of social, political, economic, cultural and psychological factors in the production of (ethnographic) texts, including those considered by the writing culture school, the occurrence, the fact, of the 'school' itself, and its reception. Nor am I denying their role in framing fieldwork, its findings, interpretation and analyses. I stress the importance of taking account of both our and our informants' understanding and evaluation of language, discourse and text since those understandings and evaluations mediate social, political, economic, cultural

---

9 I take a strong Wittgensteinian position, that is, until someone can demonstrate the possibility of a fully independent metalanguage. My stance here has been under critical assault for rendering the anthropological mission impossible by proclaiming an ultimately groundless or positionless hyper-reflexivity, an extreme relativism, a self-destructive iconoclasm, and an infinite regress that can lead nowhere. I find such criticism foolish. I am simply stating the obvious for any one living in as obsessively reflexive a world as ours, whatever its explanation: a world that is filled with longing, as attested by our fundamentalisms, for those simpler worlds where social and cultural assumptions were unquestioned or questioned in unthreatening ways. I would argue that we have to recognize the effects on the human sciences of the clash between ground and groundlessness, insistent perspectival conviction and equally insistent perspectival artifice, positional fixity and infinite regress, and ultimately, I suppose, justified objectivity and shiftless subjectivity. This clash is, I insist, a social fact whose effects cannot be dismissed through one slogan or another, the most common today being the promiscuous play of postmodernism, the irresponsible decontextualizations of cultural studies, or the stubborn clinging to one methodology or another. The failure to grasp the significance of this clash – or tension, if you prefer a more anemic characterization – by proclaiming one position at the expense of the other, is best exemplified by the failure of most postmodernists to have recognized the rise of fundamentalism.

and psychological determinants at both subjective and objective levels. Any serious ethnographic investigation has to be alert to both its own linguistic ideology and that of its informants. Michael Silverstein (1979, 1998; see also Crapanzano 1992: 12–14, 17–18), who first used 'linguistic ideology' in 1979, defined it as 'sets of beliefs about languages articulated by users as a rationalisation or justification of the perceived language structure and use'. Others, like Judith Irvine (1998), Susan Gal (1998) and Paul Kroskrity (1998, 2000), have stressed the moral and political weight of such linguistic ideologies. I myself have often suggested that we refer to both linguistic ideologies and axiologies.[10] Kroskrity (2000: 5) has argued that linguists' failure to consider linguistic ideologies until recently stems from their failure to consider (a) the linguistic awareness of speakers, and (b) the non-referential functions of language. He observes: 'In effect, the surgical removal of language from context produced an amputated "language" that was the preferred object of language sciences for most of the twentieth century' (ibid.). Put another way: the linguistic ideology of most twentieth-century linguists precluded consideration of their own linguistic ideology. Kroskrity relates this marginalization to institutional pressures, which were influenced by macro-political configurations of culture and society. I would also relate it to the way in which any language understanding precludes or at least limits awareness of the assumptions behind that understanding. In other words linguistic ideologies and axiologies so frame themselves as to insulate themselves from considering their own premises.

I would like to stress Kroskrity's second point: that the privileged position we give to the referential function of language blinds us to the significance of other linguistic functions. These other functions may be privileged in other language communities or in other genres in any one language community. Silverstein and his followers are indebted to Roman Jakobson's (1960) delineating of various language *Einstellungen* (poorly translated as 'functions' in English). Beside the referential or denotational function, the most important, for our purposes, are the pragmatic, or indexical, function, which calls up and fashions the context in which the utterance is made, and the poetic function which focuses on the language of the utterance. To Jakobson's *Einstellungen*, Silverstein has added a metapragmatic function which regiments and gives priority, among other things, to one or another of the functions or constellations of functions in accordance with the language being spoken or a particular genre. I am simplifying Silverstein's understanding of the metapragmatic, which is, in any case, not without different emphases in his various formulations over the years (Silverstein 1976, 1993). Among these, at least as I have argued, is its stipulation of appropriate hermeneutical strategies and reading practices. It should be clear that the

---

10 See Crapanzano (2000), especially (ibid.: 1–28), and (2002) for an illustration of the axiological dimension of language as expressed in American literalism.

metapragmatic is refracted in language ideologies and axiologies. Put another way, the metapragmatic function and its associated ideology and axiology serves a mystifying function insofar as it privileges one function at the expense of others. This has enormous political and moral consequences.

Let me first illustrate one role of linguistic ideological and axiological understanding in the writing culture movement. As heterogeneous as the putative members of the school were (and are), they are united by the claim that language is never fully transparent and as such has a formulating effect on that which it articulates. To German speakers this may appear to be a truism, hardly worth bothering about, for, unlike the English 'language', which is generally understood in Lockean terms as transparent and instrumental, *Sprache* is treated, I believe, in Herderian terms, as bearing all sorts of cultural, historical, philosophical, psychological, religious and nationalist orientations and values. What the writing culture anthropologists did not address was the way their take on language may differ from the Lockean position of mainstream American anthropology. Though I do not have the space to illustrate this point, I should note many of their studies confounded the two positions.

As the writing culture school was concerned primarily with texts, they did not, for the most part, delve into the way their particular understanding of language, discourse and literature affected their understanding of 'text' and its range of metaphorical possibilities. Their failure to grasp the implication of the metaphorization of culture as a text, as in Clifford Geertz's (1973: 452–53) characterization of culture as 'an ensemble of texts', which had a significant effect on the school, led to a concept of culture that was understood in referential rather than, dynamically, in interactional or dialogical terms. So understood, 'culture' serves as a reductive, detemporalizing gloss on the interactions, one that masks their complexity, fragility and transitoriness (*Vergänglichkeit*). This referential understanding was coordinate with anthropology's stress on classification, categorization and their organization, exemplified by componential analysis, then still in vogue. It fostered a tendency to reify culture and segregate it from its context of production and consequence much in the way 'texts' were taken to be separate from their contexts.[11] This isolation of culture as text was fortified by the literary critical referents that were frequently invoked. Geertz himself was, for example, influenced by the New Criticism that was in fashion during his student years. New Criticism argued ruthlessly that contextual features of literary

---

11 Put another way, much as the advocates of the translation metaphor for what ethnographers do, those advocates of the text metaphor for culture confounded what Silverstein (1993: 36ff.) calls denotational texts and interactional texts. To simplify and rephrase: Interactional texts are indexically saturated 'products' of discursive interaction which, under metapragmatic regimentation, give coherence to (speech-stipulated) events. Denotational texts are referentially saturated, grammatically structured 'products' of interactions that can – I would say – be 'extracted' from the discursive interaction in which they occur and may play pragmatic and metapragmatic functions. In metaphorizing culture as text, it is the denotational text that is so privileged that its contextual and co-textual embeddedness is likely to be lost or understood in facile ideological terms.

production, including the biographical, had to be bracketed off from literary interpretation and analysis. Just as the New Critics were opposed to sociological interpretations – read Marxism – so the textualists' isolation of culture has had enormous, though for the most part unacknowledged, political implication.[12]

I would like now to discuss briefly and all too generally how two different understandings of language affected the often tense relations between two intertwined populations: the English- and Afrikaans-speaking white South Africans during apartheid. *Taal*, 'language' in Afrikaans, a Germanic language derived from Dutch, bears the same semantic weight as *Sprache*. A 'new' language, developed in the last years of the nineteenth century, Afrikaans is a product of historical struggle and a source of great pride for Afrikaners. It carried and still carries particularly strong nationalist connotations. Afrikaners conflated it with their culture (*Kultuur*), religion, politics, tradition, land, history and community (*gemeenskap*). It gave them an intimate sense of social and cultural unity, which they called *gemeenlikheidsgevoel* (*Gemeinschafsgefühl*). They linked it with Africa, the African landscape (*land en landskap*) and claimed it bridged, as the Afrikaner poet N.P. van Wyk Louw (1959) put it, the 'enlightened West with magical Africa'.[13] There is in Paarl an Afrikaans language monument, memorializing that language's creation – a site of Afrikaner pilgrimage. On the walkway up to it are inscribed the words *Dit is ons erns* ('This is our ernest, our seriousness, our gravity'). For many Afrikaners, Afrikaans focused on the word (*woord, naam*), giving priority not only to a referential understanding of language but to literalist interpretation and a consequent mistrust of figurative language and irony, which are coordinate with the hermeneutics of the South African Dutch Reformed Church. The English-speakers understood language, as we might expect, in a transparent and instrumental fashion. Though they gave priority to reference, they were not given to literalist interpretation and mistrust of figurative and ironic expressions.[14]

These two contrastive takes on language affected, among other things, each speakers' characterization of the other as, respectively, boorish, thick, stubborn and dull, and as facile, superficial, hypocritical and amoral. They were, as such, symbolic vehicles for expressing and at times mediating the animosity between the two groups – an animosity that found (and no doubt still finds) its roots in economic competition, political struggle and the wounds of the past. The two different attitudes toward language also facilitated, or at least confirmed, mistrust in the daily encounters between members of the two groups. The Afrikaners felt the English propensity to treat their meetings, particularly the serious ones, with

---

12   I should note that Geertz was particularly beholden to Kenneth Burke, who recognized the importance of context.
13   See Crapanzano (1985: 27–34) for details.
14   I should note that they were not immune to the influence of the Afrikaner's linguistic ideology, as was apparent in their dealings with British businessmen who came to South Africa.

irony was condescending. No doubt on many occasions it was, but often enough the English speakers' ironic stance was an unreflected way to remove themselves (defensively, if you will) from the Afrikaners' power-laden 'serious' discourse – the way, for example, they read newspapers and propaganda tracts. They often made fun of Afrikaans, 'a bastard language', as they put it, which they and their children resented having to learn in school. They told jokes about a dolt, van der Merwe, who was always getting in trouble because of his insistent literalism. Afrikaners also told van der Merwe jokes but with a joviality I did not detect among English-speakers. There were many members of most groups who refused to speak the other's language.

Let me give a brief but hopefully illuminating example of this clash of linguistic understandings. I had been doing fieldwork for several months in a village near Cape Town, in which many English-speakers from Durban had recently bought family farms from the Afrikaners whose ancestors had settled there, when my wife and daughter arrived.[15] Everyone in the village was expecting them. We were immediately invited to dinner at the home of a wealthy English-speaking woman who had been raised in an Afrikaans-speaking area and was, therefore, able to bridge the two white communities. Conversation proceeded with requisite politeness and certain ironic turns of phrase, usually with reference to village gossip, by the English-speakers. The Afrikaner guests were mostly silent. Indeed they seemed irritated, for they assumed, I believe, that the ironic characterizations of villagers slighted them even when their ostensible subject was an English-speaker. We might say that they responded 'conventionally but unwittingly' to the indexical force of the ironic style, one that was deeply incrusted with historical memories. The English-speakers seemed oblivious to this 'slight', which intensified its effect on the Afrikaners.

The hostess changed the subject, introducing a topic of intense concern to everyone: a conspiracy theory that predicted the takeover of the world by communists, the UN, the Rothschild (red + shield – a cover for the 'Reds'), the Tri-Lateral Commission, the Council on Foreign Relations and Columbia University. Conversation livened. My wife Jane could not take it seriously. Responding perhaps to 'the critically ironic stance of the English-speakers', she started to ridicule the supposed conspiracy. It was nonsense. At this point I panicked, for I was afraid that she would reveal that she was a member of the Council on Foreign Relations and had attended Columbia (as I had). My carefully cultivated relations were about to collapse. As I was seated at the

---

15 Although the farmers regretted selling their farms, they could not resist the 'foolishly high' offers the English-speakers made. Many of them were convinced that the buyers would lose so much money that they would be forced eventually to sell the farms back to them at a price lower than they had paid. What they had not taken into account was the buyers' considerable capital which enabled them to carry out improvements that made the farms far more rentable than they had ever been. The Afrikaners felt duped and were filled with resentment.

opposite end of the long dining room table, I had no way to signal her. Fortunately, one of the Afrikaners interrupted her, insisting that he had read documents that proved the existence of the conspiracy, and went on to describe their contents. Realizing they were *all* serious – even the English-speakers – Jane fell silent. What was clear was not only the way the two different attitudes towards language and conversation clashed but that the English-speakers' ironic stance often masked an uncritical literalism that they themselves had probably not realized. Had the Afrikaners' take on language bled into their own? Had irony become a *façon de parler* that, like those exhausted metaphors Derrida (1982) obsessed over, had lost its ironic quality and become simply an identity marker? This coalescence of identities – identity styles – in white South Africa of the early 1980s was confirmed again and again in other domains in my research. Neither the Afrikaners nor the English-speakers, as inimical as they were, could admit either their similarities or any possible assimilation.

I want to stress the singular importance of the dynamics of fieldwork encounters in the production of ethnographic data, insight and interpretation. I think it important to recognize the advances made in ethnography over the last century. Today, it is near impossible to study a society that has not been carefully documented. This documentation permits a refinement of ethnography that was for the most part impossible earlier in the last century. (I will not comment on advances in anthropological theory, which, in my view, have not kept up with the increase in ethnographic knowledge.) Though there are many approaches to – and dramatically different sites for – anthropological research, it is the field experience that is central to them all. This has, of course, been acknowledged near-fetishistically, but curiously the dynamics of the encounters have been poorly analysed (Gupta and Ferguson 1997: 2 et passim). Often enough what transpires in the field is either glossed in detemporalizing simplification as 'participant observation' or reduced to narratives whose cultural and historical specificity is ignored.

In a number of papers (Crapanzano 1992: 70–112; 1998) I have argued that negotiations of interpersonal relations and their relevant context in fieldwork – indeed any negotiation – makes reference to what I have called the Third. It is a function whose functionality is stable but whose parameters are unstable, except in the most conventional of encounters, since they shift with the witting or usually unwitting appeals to them by all the parties to the encounter. I have suggested that this Third 'figures' the metapragmatic function by authorizing various pragmatic, or indexical, manoeuvres that define the encounter, its relevant context, its personnel, its modes of communication, how that communication is to be taken, the appropriate etiquette, and thereby fitting interpretive strategies and their transgressive possibility. I have argued further that this function may be conceptualized in terms of the law, grammar or convention and embodied in authoritative figures like gods, totems, fathers and even experts. I cannot do justice to my argument here, but I do want to make one important point. Sometimes, particularly in explicit or even implicit hierarchical situations, the Third may be embodied – for a time – in one of the parties to the encounter: say, the anthropologist as they question their informant or the informant who either assumes control of the encounter or is allowed to do so by the anthropologist – in the open-ended interview, for example. In complex encounters that have not yet become fully conventionalized through habit, like the idealized ethnographic, the Third appealed to may at times be 'outside' the encounter – a colleague back home or an omniscient deity. Under such circumstances, as the authority appealed to by either party to the encounter is unknown or alien to the other, there is a significant danger that their respective definitions of the situation will clash, producing misunderstandings, confusion and, in the extreme, the collapse of communication. Of course, rarely are the participants aware of the appeals they make.

Though I did not phrase it this way when I wrote *Tuhami* (Crapanzano 1980), I could have described early changes in the relationship between Tuhami and myself as the result of two different attitudes towards language. I was, of course, interested in data (about Moroccan religious brotherhoods), referentially understood; Tuhami was, I believe, interested in developing, pragmatically, a particular relationship with me. (In this case, you might want to substitute rhetorical.) I was oblivious at first to his pragmatic-rhetorical strategies and read what he said in referential terms, noting thereby dramatically contradictory changes in what he told me in even one interview. Tuhami *en revanche* appears to have been blinded to my semantico-referential request for data by his pragmatic-rhetorical stance. When once he understood through my insistent questioning what I wanted, he began to give me the data I wanted in a referentially consistent manner, but to see this as a conversion to my way of looking at language would, I believe, be a mistake, for now he was using the referential pragmatically, rhetorically, as a way to develop his desired relationship. My position also changed, for I became fascinated by his pragmatic-rhetorical strategies, which I now took referentially as data.[16] Our positions reversed themselves several times before we finally arrived at a shared communicative convention which eventually led to my adopting, as I believe Tuhami desired, a hierarchically superior or empowered therapeutic role. (Had I come to embody the Third?) I might add that submission to my putative authority was in some respects a repetition of his experiences with Europeans and their authority during the French Protectorate.

At least in such micro-encounters, desire cannot be separated from power, as Hegel – the Hegel of Alexandre Kojève – understood (Hegel 1949: 229–40; Kojève 1969). Through power, desire (may) be fulfilled; through desire, power

---

16 I used a semantical-referential metapragmatic language – most notably psychoanalytic theories of transference and counter-transference – to describe his pragmatic and, indeed, metapragmatic, strategies without fully realizing the implications of my, I suppose, unavoidable stance. I converted his strategies into referentially understood data. The social significance of this seemingly inevitable conversion or translation has yet to be explored. See Crapanzano (1992: 115–35) for a discussion of this sort of translation in Freud's theory of transference and counter-transference.

(may) become effective. Both desire and power and their objects are mediated in complex ways by language.[17] Certainly, linguistically mediated desire and power are central to the ethnographic encounter as they are to any encounter. The difference is that the idealized ethnographic encounter, at least in its initial stages, is not bound by conventional and habitual discursive and interpersonal relations. In consequence, its definition, including that of its interlocutors, can become an object of intense desire and of a struggle for power to determine it. (I do not want to reduce the ethnographic encounter to an arena for plays of power and desire, but I do believe this struggle, however attenuated, has to be acknowledged if we are to evaluate as accurately as possible the data that emerge from such encounters.) One obvious example of this is that in the anthropologist's manifest desire to foster an egalitarian relationship with each informant, they often fail to recognize that the informants frequently see the egalitarian relationship as a sham, understand it as a product of a hierarchical position in which the researcher is on top, and would prefer to preserve the hierarchy for many reasons, both psychological and material. This was clearly the case in my encounters with Tuhami.

A second example is the way in which the people we work with, even if they understand our research goals and the 'objectivity' it demands, will attempt to use our meetings politically. They may attempt to convert the field researcher into a sympathetic witness who will publicize the wrongs they have suffered. This puts considerable strain on the anthropologist as they try to resist the role in which they are being cast and on their informants as they try one strategy after another to convict the anthropologist. It certainly affects the data we collect and influences the way we interpret it. But it is also a datum. In my encounters with white South Africans, our shared privileging of referentiality masked the rhetorical undersong, which rendered the referentially-describable rhetorical. Their seemingly objective characterizations of each other or of the coloureds and blacks, for example, concealed, often poorly, the ways these characterizations, this objectivity, was used rhetorically to persuade me of the justice of apartheid or their victimization by the other white group or by the peoples of colour.

More recently, in my work with the Harkis – those Algerians who sided with the French during the Algerian war of independence and were either massacred by the Algerians upon independence or placed in camps in France if they managed to escape, some for as long as sixteen years – I was immediately cast as a witness and messenger.[18] The style of their appeal, at least that of the Harki children who had been educated in France, was, in my view, mixed, reflecting perhaps – I have to be very cautious here – the mixture of two different linguistic ideologies and

---

17 For Lacan (1966: 628) – in one of his inconsistent formulations – 'desire is an effect in the subject, which is imposed on him by the existence of the discourse, to make his need pass through the defiles of the signifier' (*le désir est en effet dans le sujet de cette condition qui lui est imposée par l'existence du discours de faire passer son besoin par les défilés du signifiant*). Can we give power a similar formulation? We might have to distinguish between two different levels of meaning of 'power' – analogous perhaps to need and desire. See also Butler (1997).

axiologies: those of the French and those of the Algerian Berbers and Arabs. Their appeal was, in other words, expressed at once in a strongly referential language, which, like that of the South Africans, exploited the rhetorical force of the referentially expressed, and in immediate rhetorical fashion – characterized, at times by exaggeration, poignant silences, stoicism and tears – a sentimentality focused on the wounds they suffered, their moral distress and political outrage. The cleverest of them played on the contradictions between the two approaches to language, producing in a manner reminiscent of the trickster a paradoxical effect in me – a confusion they attempted forcefully to clarify in the terms they desired. They sometimes used this same technique, with mixed reception, in their political protests.

I should note the significance of these observations for those ethnographies that claim an experiential or phenomenological perspective. I have argued elsewhere (Crapanzano 2004: 106–112) that our phenomenological descriptions are linguistically bound by the language in which they are cast. The *epoché* cannot free our phenomenological accounts (if not our actual experiences) of linguistic determination. Unless we are conscious of how our informants understand and evaluate language and its elaborations, we risk being conned or, if you prefer, mystified by our own take on language usage. We may assume, as I did with Tuhami, that descriptions of experience, including those of 'inner' life, which are expressed in referential language, are mimetic; that is, they attempt to be as faithful to experience as possible. But this is not necessarily the case. Stress may be placed on the rhetorical – to create a desired effect in one's interlocutor, as in many baroque descriptions of mystical states (de Certeau 1992: 113, 11–16); on the poetic, where pleasure is taken in the beauty of the language without regard to its accuracy; or simply on the phatic, that is the establishment of contact and communion. Experiential and phenomenological ethnographies based on such descriptions may not in fact meet realistic or mimetic standards, for the referential in such cases may be used rhetorically, poetically or phatically and in consequence be subject to different standards and modes of evaluation and interpretation.

In this chapter I have argued that many of the contributions to the writing culture movement as well as many of its critiques were caught in what I would call the textual illusion. By 'textual illusion' I mean so framing a text that it overrides conceptually its contexts of production and its aftermath and becomes an independent artefact, which in the extreme (as in Geertz's notion of 'culture as an ensemble of texts') becomes the model for what it depicts. So framed, the text permits a series of (critical) self-reflective manoeuvres, including seemingly transgressive ones, that, as illuminating as they may be, can and inevitably do mask some of the presuppositions that constitute the text's textuality and the range of responses to it. These responses include both 'appropriate' interpretive

---

18   For details and bibliography, see Crapanzano (2006).

strategies and an appreciation of the text's rhetorical and figurative capacity for modelling cultures as isolated sites for epistemological investigation and sources of continuity over time.

By advocating an anthropology sensitive to the ways in which diverse attitudes towards language, and by extension discourse, texts and literature, formulate its findings, I do not want to focus simply on the production of ethnographies. That would, in the end, be of little significance. Rather I want to stress the way in which attitudes towards language empower certain takes on reality and blind us to others. Inherent in the play of linguistic *Einstellungen* is mystification; for the predominance of one linguistic function masks the functioning of others. Insofar as the pre-eminence of functions, as well as the nomination of appropriate interpretive strategies, is determined metapragmatically, I suggest that the metapragmatic is one of the principal mechanisms by which power (and desire), understood either in institutional terms, as in Marxism, or diffusely, as Foucault conceives of it, orders our apprehension of reality. Supported by one linguistic ideology or another, one axiology or another, the metapragmatic function determines the way we frame, interpret and evaluate that reality. I believe that such a focus will promote a more rigorous approach to the formulating role of power and desire in our construction of reality than the rather more facile generalizations about the effectiveness of power in that construction, those constructions. I have stressed that fieldwork, more accurately encounters in the field, and their textualization may be seen as interacting arenas in which particular definitions of reality are empowered and others disempowered. Taken as such, fieldwork becomes a complex site which mirrors, if not the way the play of power and desire functions in the society under study then the way that society responds to divergent depictions and interpretations of reality, in its response to divergent depictions and interpretations of reality and their empowerment and desirability. Say, those of the anthropologist. The scrutiny of fieldwork and its textualization should not be an end in itself but an entry point for uncovering how power and desire inflect the world in various societies including our own, and, of singular importance today, the encounters between and among societies and their members.

References

Bachmann-Medick, Doris (ed.). 1999. *Kultur als Text: Die anthropologische Wende in der Literaturwissenschaft.* Frankfurt am Main: Fischer.

Bakhtin, Mikhail. 1981. *The Dialogical Imagination.* Austin: University of Texas Press.

Boon, James. 1972. *From Symbolism to Structuralism: Lévi-Strauss in a Literary Tradition.* Oxford. Blackwell.

———. 1983. 'Functionalists Write, Too: Frazer/Malinowski and the Semiotics of the Monograph', *Semiotica* 46: 131–49.

Bruner, Edward. 1986. 'Ethnography as Narrative', in Victor Turner and Edward Bruner (eds), *The Anthropology of Experience.* Urbana: University of Illinois Press, 139–58.

Budick, Sanford and Wolfgang Iser (eds). 1996. *The Translatability of Cultures: Figuration and the Space Between.* Stanford, CA: Stanford University Press.

Butler, Judith. 1997. *The Psychic Life of Power: Theories in Subjection.* Stanford, CA: Stanford University Press.

Clifford, James. 1986. 'Introduction', in James Clifford and George E. Marcus (eds), *Writing Culture: The Poetics and Politics of Ethnography.* Berkeley: University of California Press, 1–26.

Clifford, James and George E. Marcus (eds). 1986. *Writing Culture: The Poetics and Politics of Ethnography.* Berkeley: University of California Press.

Crapanzano, Vincent. 1973. 'The Writing of Ethnography', *Dialectical Anthropology* 2: 69–73.

———. 1980. *Tuhami: Portrait of a Moroccan.* Chicago: University of Chicago Press.

———. 1985. *Waiting: The Whites of South Africa.* New York: Random House.

———. 1992. *Hermes' Dilemma and Hamlet's Desire; On the Epistemology of Interpretation.* Cambridge, MA: Harvard University Press.

———. 1997. 'Translation: Truth or Metaphor', *Res* 32: 45–51.

———. 1998. '"Lacking Now Is Only the Leading Idea, That Is – We, the Rays, Have No Thoughts": Interlocutory Collapse in Daniel Paul Schreber's *Memoirs of My Nervous Illness*', *Critical Inquiry* 24: 737–67.

———. 2000. *Serving the Word: Literalism in America from the Pulpit to the Bench.* New York: New Press.

———. 2001. 'Transfiguring Translation', *Semiotica* 128(1/2): 113–36.

———. 2002. 'Estilos de interpretação e a retórica de categorias sociais', in Yvonne Maggie and Claudia Barcellos Rezende (eds), *Raça çomo Retórica a Construção da Diferença.* Rio de Janeiro: Civilização Brasileira, 443–58.

———. 2003. 'The Metaphoricity of Translation: Text, Context, and Fidelity in American Jurisprudence', in Tullio Maranhão and Bernhard Streck (eds), *Translation and Ethnography: The Anthropological Challenge of Intercultural Understanding.* Tucson: University of Arizona Press, 44–63.

————. 2004. *Imaginative Horizons: An Essay in Literary-Philosophical Anthropology*. Chicago: University of Chicago Press.

————. 2006. 'Eine Wunde, die nie verheilt', in Erika Fischer-Lichte, Robert Sollich, Sandra Umathum and Matthias Warstat (eds), *Auf der Schwelle: Kunst, Risiken und Nebenwirkungen*. München: Wilhelm Fink Verlag, 206–26.

de Certeau, Michel. 1992. *The Mystic Fable: The Sixteenth and Seventeenth Centuries*. Chicago: University of Chicago Press.

Derrida, Jacques. 1982. 'White Mythology: Metaphor in the Text of Philosophy', in Jacques Derrida, *Margins of Philosophy*. Chicago: University of Chicago Press, 207–72.

Gadamer, Hans-Georg. 1960. *Truth and Method*. New York: Seabury.

Gal, Susan. 1998. 'Multiplicity and Contention among Language Ideologies: A Commentary', in Bambi Schiefflin, Kathryn Woolard and Paul Kroskrity (eds), *Language Ideologies: Practice and Theory*. Oxford: Oxford University Press, 317–32.

Geertz, Clifford. 1973. *The Interpretation of Cultures*. New York: Basic Books.

Gupta, Akhil and James Ferguson (eds). 1997. *Anthropological Locations*. Berkeley: University of California Press.

Handler, Richard. 1983. 'The Dainty and the Hungry Man: Literature and Anthropology in the Work of Edward Sapir', *History of Anthropology* 1: 208–31.

Hegel, Georg Wilhelm Friedrich. 1949. *The Phenomenology of the Mind*. London: George Allen and Unwin.

Hymes, Dell. 1974. *Reinventing Anthropology*. New York: Vintage.

Irvine, Judith. 1998. 'Ideologies of Honorific Language', in Bambi Schiefflin, Kathryn Woolard and Paul Kroskrity (eds), *Language Ideologies: Practice and Theory*. Oxford: Oxford University Press, 51–67.

Irvine, Judith and Susan Gal (eds). 2000. 'Language Ideology and Linguistic Differentiation', in Paul Kroskrity (ed.), *Regimes of Language: Ideologies, Polities, and Identities*. Santa Fe, NM: School of American Research Press, 35–84.

Jakobson, Roman. 1960. 'Closing Statement: Linguistics and Poetics', in Thomas Sebeok (ed.), *Style in Language*. Cambridge, MA: MIT Press, 350–77.

Kelly, Louis G. 1979. *The True Interpreter: A History of Translation Theory and Practice in the West*. Oxford: Blackwell.

Kojève, Alexandre. 1969. *Introduction to the Reading of Hegel: Lectures on the Phenomenology of the Spirit*. Ithaca, NY: Cornell University Press.

Kroskrity, Paul. 1998. 'Arizona Twa Kiva Speech as a Manifestation of a Dominant Language Ideology', in Bambi Schiefflin, Kathryn Woolard and Paul Kroskrity (eds), *Language Ideologies: Practice and Theory*. Oxford: Oxford University Press, 103–22.

———— (ed.). 2000. *Regimes of Language: Ideologies, Polities, and Identities*. Santa Fe, NM: School of American Research Press.

Lacan, Jacques. 1966. *Ecrits.* Paris: Editions de Seuil.

Manganaro, Marc (ed.). 1990. *Modernist Anthropology: From Fieldwork to Text.* Princeton, NJ: Princeton University Press.

Maranhão, Tullio and Bernhard Streck (eds). 2003. *Translation and Ethnography: The Anthropological Challenge to Intercultural Understanding.* Tucson: University of Arizona Press.

Marcus, George E. and Dick Cushman. 1982. 'Ethnographies as Texts', *Annual Review of Anthropology* 2: 25–69.

Rubel, Paula G. and Abraham Rosman (eds). 2003. *Translating Cultures: Perspectives on Translation and Anthropology.* Oxford: Berg.

Said, Edward. 1978. *Orientalism.* New York: Pantheon.

Silverstein, Michael. 1976. 'Shifters, Linguistic Categories, and Cultural Description', in Keith Basso and Henry Selby (eds), *Meaning in Anthropology.* Albuquerque: University of New Mexico Press, 11–55.

———. 1979. 'Language Structure and Linguistic Ideology', in Paul R. Cline, William Hanks and Carol Hofbauer (eds), *The Elements: A Parasession on Linguistic Units and Levels.* Chicago: Chicago Linguistic Circle, 193–247.

———. 1993. 'Metapragmatic Discourse and Metapragmatic Function', in John Lucy (ed.), *Reflexive Language: Reported Speech and Metapragmatics.* Cambridge: Cambridge University Press, 9–32.

———. 1998. 'The Uses and Utility of Ideology: A Commentary', in Bambi Schiefflin, Kathryn Woolard and Paul Kroskrity (eds), *Language Ideologies: Practice and Theory.* Oxford: Oxford University Press, 123–48.

Stierle, Karlheinz. 1996. 'Translatio Studii and Renaissance: Vertical to Horizontal Translation', in Sanford Budick and Wolfgang Iser (eds), *The Translatability of Cultures: Figuration and the Space.* Stanford, CA: Stanford University Press, 55–67.

Van Wyk Louw, N.P. 1959. *Berigte te Velde.* Cape Town: Nasionale Pers.

Webster, Steven. 1982. 'Dialogue and Fiction in Ethnography', *Dialectical Anthropology* 7: 91–114.

———. 1983. 'Ethnography as Storytelling', *Dialectical Anthropology* 8: 125–65.

———. 1986. 'Realism and Reification in the Ethnographic Genre', *Critique of Anthropology* 6(1): 39–63.

3

Reading James Clifford: On Ethnographic Allegory

Steffen Strohmenger

In this contribution I shall provide a close reading of James Clifford's essay 'On Ethnographic Allegory' (Clifford 1986), first published in *Writing Culture: The Poetics and Politics of Ethnography*. While most of the postmodern debates, in one way or another, touch upon the problem of objective knowledge in general, I want to shift the attention towards the question of the objectivity of value statements in particular. In this regard, I will first briefly introduce a line of argument which provides the background against which the text of Clifford will be subsequently discussed. It will then be shown that the author tries to come to grips – but ultimately fails to do so – with a theoretical problem that I will call 'the asymmetry'.[1] I will thereby speak about 'non-moral' as opposed to 'moral statements', or (and these are to be seen as synonyms) 'non-value' and 'value judgements'.

A Symmetrical Perspective on the Objectivity of Non-Value and Value Statements

To begin with, there are four preliminary points I want to make. Firstly, as a point of departure I want to focus on an epistemological theorem which, particularly in the second half of the eighteenth century, has entered Occidental philosophical thought. It is the assumption that judgements about *non-moral* matters are liable to empirical verification, while judgements about *moral* matters are not. In other words, the tenet is that there is a non-value dimension of reality about which objective

---

1   For a more extensive development of the argument put forward here, see Strohmenger (2006).

statements can be made, in contrast to a value dimension of reality where the statements are forever excluded from the possibility of achieving the status of an empirically valid or objective answer. It is this doctrine – non-value judgements are objectifiable, value judgements are not – which I refer to in terms of 'the asymmetry'.

I shall give a brief example of where the asymmetry can be traced in the common language we use. Take the pair of terms: *facts and values*. In this formula we find the term facts being opposed to the term values. However, instead of using the term facts to denote the opposite of values we may also use the term *non-values*, as well as the opposite of facts being called *non-facts*. If we do so we can see that the pair of terms facts and values carries the meaning that non-value statements correspond to facts, and value-statements correspond to non-facts.

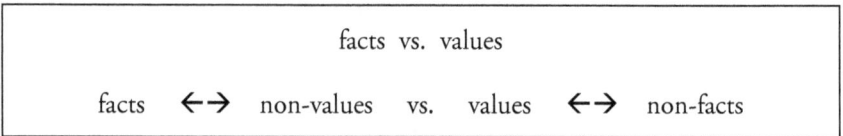

---

facts vs. values

facts ←→ non-values vs. values ←→ non-facts

Figure 3.1 Facts and values

We therefore automatically read that non-value judgements belong to the realm of the factual (the objective, empirically verifiable) while value statements belong to the realm of the non-factual (the [inter]subjective, empirically non-verifiable). Later, when discussing Clifford's text, we will encounter some more examples of this asymmetry being inscribed into the language employed.

Secondly, if we proceed from the notion of general epistemological scepticism – the impossibility of absolute truth – it becomes clear that the tenet of an asymmetrical relation cannot be maintained. Instead, we will have to assume a symmetrical relation. Both non-value *and* value questions share the same epistemological grounding of what I call an 'inescapable transcendentality' of knowledge. Both of them in principle share the same (im)possibility of being objectively answered, and thus the same right to participate in empirical scientific discourse. Regarding this theoretical move towards a symmetrical understanding, Hilary Putnam for instance has spoken of 'The Collapse of the Fact/Value Dichotomy' in a book with this title (Putnam 2002).[2]

The assumption of an inescapable transcendentality or relativity as the epistemological grounding of all kinds of knowledge – which thus applies to

---

2   Putnam here argues: 'The fact/value dichotomy is, at bottom, not a *distinction* but a *thesis*, namely the thesis that "ethics" is not about "matters of fact"' (2002: 19). In order not to misunderstand what Putnam wants to express by the formulation 'the collapse of the fact/value dichotomy' we have to unfold it. It is not the 'distinction' between non-value and value statements that he rejects, but the tenet of the asymmetry, the 'thesis' that non-ethical judgements are objectifiable and ethical judgements are not. Once we know that both kinds of judgements share the same (im)possibility of being matters of fact, we will also no longer use the term 'facts' to denote the opposite of 'values'. Instead, we will symmetrize our vocabulary and just talk about non-value and value statements (or the like) which then may be tested as to whether they can belong to the side of facts or to the side of non-facts.

value and non-value statements alike – will need no explicit illustration. The voices in support of it are countless and can be traced through cultural times and spaces. Max Weber, to name one, has talked about the 'transcendental presupposition of any culture science' (Weber 2006: 503), since 'all cognitive knowledge of infinite reality by the finite human mind rests upon the implicit presupposition that at any one time only a finite part of this reality can be subjected to scientific scrutiny' (ibid.: 499). To the same effect one can speak of the rhetoricity (de Man), performativity (Austin), constructivity (Derrida), 'culturalicity' (Geertz), or narrativity (Marquard) of knowledge. These concepts in one way or another all point to the impossibility of absolute truth. And the secret behind this story is that we do not have to worry about it. There is simply no way we could stop to distinguish between, if not true and false, then between more or less true, valid, plausible statements about what is the case and what is not. In this sense, Hans Vaihinger (1952) has introduced the term 'idealistic positivism'. We cannot help but continue operating under the assumption 'As if' that distinction is valid (ibid.). Again, the specific point to be made here is that this applies to moral and non-moral judgements alike.

Thirdly, the historical appearance of asymmetry in Occidental philosophical thought particularly in the second half of the eighteenth century – the reasons for which cannot be discussed here – initiated a process by which modern science found itself compelled to abstain and free itself from value statements. In order to grant objectivity it was held that science has to retreat completely to the production of knowledge about a non-value dimension of reality, thus holding on to the idea that at least in this field of knowledge true objectivity can be found. Regarding this, Wolf Lepenies has spoken of an agenda by which modern science sees the 'most important precondition of its acting in an explicit renunciation of orientation in political-social questions … The history of modern science thus represents a history of decreasing moral commitment' (Lepenies 1997: 27, 47; my translation).

The fourth point to be made is well known. Whenever science tried to refrain and to purify itself from value statements, it never succeeded. Put simply, there is no such thing as value-free science. One argument for this is that on a theoretical level moral and non-moral knowledge cannot ultimately be separated. Another argument holds that without referring to a value dimension of reality we would not be able to make sense of any narrative. In this respect, Putnam has spoken of the 'entanglement of fact and value' (Putnam 2002: 28).[3]

There is a remark I feel I should make. When using the term 'value-free' we have to be careful of what precisely is meant. In the sense being used here it just means that there is no science which is free from value statements. We must not confuse it with another statement that there is no science which is free from

---

3 In order not to misunderstand what Putnam means by the 'entanglement of fact and value' we should call it here the entanglement of non-value and value judgements.

transcendentality. Though we certainly agree with both of these statements, we have to be aware that we are dealing with two completely different meanings: there is no pure objective knowledge *and* there is no pure value-free knowledge. This is important to note, because soon we will see what happens if we mistake one for the other.

Next to these theoretical arguments there is also an empirical observation to be made. It is often quite obvious that scientific texts are far from being reduced to the production of non-moral knowledge alone. In many instances we can easily see that they are quite openly engaged in also making moral statements. Even where this seems not to be the case, we can, at a second look, often find that scientific texts carry what I shall call a *hidden* moral dimension. In this regard, Albert Hirschman (1983) talks about an unconscious smuggling in of moral considerations.[4] This frequently hidden moral dimension of scientific texts, I shall argue, can be understood as the *symptom* of the asymmetry. The epistemological verdict that only non-value judgements are objectively verifiable while value judgements are not pushes the latter into the discursive subtext. The pretension of modern science to be free from moral statements has always been a theoretical façade behind which, to use the phrase of Bruno Latour, 'we have never been modern' (Latour 1993).

In this regard, it is also important to note that the move towards a resymmetrization – in the sense that non-value and value statements share the same epistemological grounding, and thus the same right to participate in scientific empirical discourse – is merely a *theoretical* one. It cannot mean to move from a scientific practice which is free from moral judgements to one which is, let us say, enriched by moral judgements. We do not have to reintroduce value statements into our scientific *practice* because they have never been absent.

I will now turn to James Clifford's text and demonstrate how we can read this as an effort to make visible the asymmetry in anthropological discourse, which remains still at the heart of our theoretical understanding and representational practice. I will also show that Clifford can be understood as actually attempting to make the theoretical move from an asymmetrical towards a symmetrical understanding. However, seduced by the vocabulary he employs he is led to a conclusion which makes him ultimately fail to defend a symmetrical position. The effect – although we know that the asymmetry cannot be sustained – is that we would yet be condemned to submit to its theoretical regime as the eternal order of anthropological discourse.

---

4   In his text Hirschman is calling for 'a moral-social science … where moral considerations need no longer be smuggled in surreptitiously nor expressed unconsciously but are displayed openly and disarmingly' (Hirschman 1983: 31).

Reading James Clifford

In his essay, Clifford wants to direct attention to the fact that ethnographic reports of the other prove to have a 'twofold structure' by which they maintain 'a double attention to the descriptive surface and to more abstract, comparative, and explanatory levels of meaning … What one *sees* in a coherent ethnographic account, the imaged construct of the other, is connected in a continuous double structure with what one *understands*' (Clifford 1986: 101). Clifford refers to this hidden dimension of meaning as its allegorical content. 'Most descriptions of others continue to assume and refer to elemental or transcendent levels of truth' (ibid.: 102). 'Embodied in written reports', ethnographies 'simultaneously describe real cultural events and make additional, moral, ideological, and even cosmological statements' (ibid.: 98). 'To focus on ethnographic allegory', the author continues, 'draws attention to aspects of cultural description that have until recently been minimized. A recognition of allegory emphasizes the fact that realistic portraits, to the extent that they are "convincing" or "rich", are extended metaphors, patterns of associations that point to coherent (theoretical, aesthetic, moral) additional meanings' (ibid.: 100).

What Clifford states in these passages is that next to its manifest surface, ethnographic texts carry an additional and hidden level of meaning which he refers to as, for example, moral, ideological, theoretical, aesthetic, cosmological statements and meanings. Elsewhere in his text he also speaks of messages of ethical and political significance (ibid.: 102) and moral, practical lessons (ibid.: 103). It is difficult to say what Clifford exactly means by each of these terms. Yet, it certainly allows us to say that he is pointing at what I have called a 'hidden moral dimension' of scientific, here anthropological, texts. This phenomenon, as I have argued, can be interpreted as the symptom of the theoretical assumption of the asymmetry. Since the verdict decrees that only non-value judgements can epistemologically qualify for objectivization and to participate in scientific empirical discourse, value statements are pushed to hide under the discursive surface or to come along in the guise of non-value statements.

In order to illustrate these moral, ethical and political dimensions of ethnographic writing, Clifford then focuses on two examples: Marjorie Shostak's *Nisa* (Shostak 1981), as well as the 'Samoa controversy' involving Margaret Mead and Derek Freeman. In addition to this, Clifford discusses specific forms of the allegorical structuring of ethnographies; that is, as 'culturalist and humanist allegories' (ibid.: 101); 'socialist-humanist allegory' (ibid.: 120); 'pastoral allegories' (ibid.: 115); 'salvage or redemptive ethnography' (ibid.: 113).

Aside from this, Clifford then also argues that not only some – the usual suspects – but in fact all ethnographic reports entail an allegorical level of meaning. He argues 'that these kinds of transcendent meanings are not abstractions or interpretations "added" to the original "simple" account. Rather, they are the conditions of its meaningfulness. Ethnographic texts are inescapably allegorical' (ibid.: 99). This 'claim that nonallegorical description was possible', he continues, 'was closely allied to the romantic search for unmediated meaning in the event. Positivism, realism, and romanticism … all rejected the "false" artifice of rhetoric'. However, 'the recent "revival" of rhetoric by a diverse group of literary and cultural theorists', by authors like Roland Barthes, Kenneth Burke, Michel de Certeau, Hayden White, Paul de Man, and others, 'has thrown serious doubt on the positivist-romantic-realist consensus' (ibid.: 100). At the end of his essay Clifford concludes by a similar statement: 'There is no way definitely, surgically, to separate the factual from the allegorical in cultural accounts. The data of ethnography make sense only within patterned arrangements and narratives, and these are conventional, political, and meaningful in a more than referential sense. Cultural facts are not true and cultural allegories false … Abandoning allegory – an impossible aim' (ibid.: 119). Therefore, 'a recognition of allegory inescapably poses the political and ethical dimensions of ethnographic writing. It suggests that these be manifested, not hidden. In this light, the open allegorizing of a Mead or a Benedict enacts a certain probity' (ibid.: 120).

Let me highlight two main theoretical arguments Clifford makes in the passages quoted above: First, he states that ethnographic texts are inescapably allegorical. There are none which are free from meanings that are moral, political, ethical and so forth. The reason he gives for this is that there is no way to 'surgically' separate between the allegorical and the non-allegorical, as the allegorical content is the condition for the meaningfulness of any ethnographic account. Abandoning allegory – an impossible aim! This, I would argue, we can easily identify with what Putnam called the 'entanglement of fact and value',[5] and with our insight into the impossibility of value-free science. There is simply no science which proves to be free from value judgements and which could be reduced exclusively to judgements about a non-value dimension of reality.

A second argument Clifford makes in these passages is that 'cultural facts are not true and cultural allegories false'. Here he quite explicitly points at a symmetrical relation. Both non-value and value statements – that what Clifford calls 'cultural facts' and 'cultural allegories' – share the same status of being neither true nor false. Both are subjected to the same epistemological marker of what would be here the 'culturalicity' of knowledge, and what in a general sense I have referred to as the grounding of an inescapable transcendentality of knowledge. The same conclusion can also be deduced – although Clifford does not make it explicit – when he refers to those literary and cultural theorists who by 'the recent "revival" of rhetoric' have 'thrown serious doubt on the positivist-romantic-realist consensus'. Again, one sees the argument for a symmetrical position here. Rejecting the notion of positivism and realism is also rejecting the theoretical assumption of the asymmetry. Not only value statements but non-value

---

5   Regarding this phrase see footnote 3.

statements as well are submitted to the same marker of an inescapable rhetoricity of knowledge. They are both in the same epistemological boat.

We can thus see that to a certain extent Clifford is supporting the theoretical move from an asymmetrical towards a symmetrical understanding of value and non-value statements. By sharing the same epistemological status, both have the same right to participate in empirical scientific discourse. I want to elaborate on this point a little further: when adopting a symmetrical perspective nothing is said about which value statements – if any – would pass our tests to qualify as a scientifically valid answer. What is said is that moral judgements cannot in advance and for all times be excluded from their right to be subjected to empirical verification.

We of course know that on a theoretical level no such thing as a pure non-value judgement as opposed to a pure value judgement would eventually exist. For, if there is no way to ultimately – 'surgically', as Clifford puts it – separate the two, how could we ever say: This is a value statement and this is not?[6] But then why do we talk about non-moral and moral statements at all? First, we have done so in order to make the asymmetry in scientific discourse visible and to reject those who would be defending its supposition. And secondly, once we know that due to their epistemological qualification we can treat all statements alike there is simply no harm anymore in whether we keep on talking about non-value, value or whatsoever statements. As Putnam has put it:

> There is a distinction to be drawn (one that is useful in some contexts) between ethical judgements and other sorts of judgements. This is undoubtedly the case, just as it is undoubtedly the case that there is a distinction to be drawn (and one that is useful in some contexts) between *chemical* judgements and judgements that do not belong to the field of chemistry. *But nothing metaphysical follows from the existence of a fact/value distinction in this (modest) sense.* (Putnam 2002: 19)[7]

To re-emphasize: we do not have to abandon the use of the distinction between non-moral and moral judgements, but we have to abandon the notion of the asymmetry that the former are objectifiable and the latter are not.

Let us now come back once more to Clifford's text. By adopting a symmetrical perspective we have thus removed the reason for value statements to be hidden. And we have paved the way for what Clifford called the probity of 'open allegorizing'. However, though we can certainly consider Clifford to hold to the tenets of symmetry, there are some instances in his text, inscribed in the language

---

6 This also leads to the argument that we cannot hold that statements about a non-value dimension of reality are objectifiable and statements about a value dimension of reality are not. For, on a theoretical level, these two dimensions cannot ultimately be apart.

7 Regarding the pair of terms 'fact/value', Putnam here keeps on to employ, see footnote 2.

employed, where the author still carries the theoretical tenet of the asymmetry, therefore invoking the notion that only non-value statements can qualify as factual whereas value statements cannot. There are three examples from the above quoted passages I want to point out.

This proves to be the case when Clifford points out that 'cultural facts are not true and cultural allegories false', and when he says that there is no way to 'separate the factual from the allegorical in cultural accounts'. We here find that Clifford is using the terms allegory (allegorical), and facts (factual), in order to denote the distinction between the value content and the non-value content in cultural accounts. Similar to what I have illustrated regarding the juxtaposition of the terms values and facts, by opposing the terms allegory (allegorical), and facts (factual), the assumption of the asymmetry that the former is something that does not qualify as fact or as being factual is evoked again.

A second example, again quoted above, is when Clifford talks on the one hand about moral, political and ethical meanings, but then on the other hand refers to this value dimension of ethnographic writing as 'transcendent levels of truth', or 'kinds of transcendent meanings'. Here we find that the criterion of the moral is substituted by the epistemological criterion of the transcendental. This shift seduces us, making us assume that value statements adhere to a transcendental level in contrary to their counterparts, the non-value statements, which adhere to a non-transcendental level of meaning.

A third and maybe more subtle example is that Clifford declares that ethnographies 'simultaneously describe real cultural events and make additional, moral, ideological, and even cosmological statements'. Here the author talks about 'real' events on the one side as opposed to 'moral' and other statements on the other side. This again implies the assumption that these moral statements do not describe *real* cultural events and therefore do not belong to what can be validated by empirical science as being real. Apart from that we find that Clifford mentions the term 'moral' along with the term 'ideological'. However, insofar as the term 'ideological' is used in most cases to distinguish between the ideological and the non-ideological, between prejudice and non-prejudice, it generates the effect that the moral becomes infected by the epistemological marker of the ideological. Moral statements are then assumed to be always ideological, while non-moral statements may prove to be non-ideological.

As these examples clearly show, when being on the way towards a symmetrical understanding of value and non-value statements we have to be attentive to the language conceptions being employed. To avoid becoming unconsciously seduced once more by its theoretical doctrine, we must free our vocabulary from the traces which the asymmetry has left in the ways that we speak.

In the final section of my chapter, I want to turn to another theoretical problem we have to resolve on our way towards a symmetrical science. This is what I will call the 'secret repetition compulsion' of the asymmetry. I will show how we can find that rhetorical mechanism at work in Clifford's text.

Let me start by coming back once again to the pair of terms fact and allegory (the factual and the allegorical) which the author applies. As I have argued, when opposing fact to allegory it evokes the idea that the latter belongs to the side of non-facts. By doing this, the term allegory is thus simultaneously loaded with two distinct meanings: it denotes the class of value statements *and* the class of non-factual statements. Considering this we can then look at another rhetorical effect that is created in the text. Take the sentence: 'Abandoning allegory – an impossible aim'. Insomuch as the term allegory in the course of the text has become charged with that double meaning, we are brought to understand the sentence in a double sense as well. We read: 'abandoning allegory – an impossible aim'. And we understand: firstly, abandoning value statements is an impossible aim; and secondly, abandoning the non-factual (the transcendental) is an impossible aim. Though we agree with both of these statements, it generates an effect which rhetoricians would call metalepsis. By having one and the same lexical sentence loaded with two different semantic meanings it makes them enter into a causal relation. Although we are dealing with two completely distinct statements, a causal nexus between their meanings builds up. We then come to read that the transcendental cannot be abandoned because value judgements cannot be abandoned. We understand there is no objective science because there is no science free of value judgements.

In order to give an example that shows that Clifford assumes such a causal nexus, let us turn once again to the following passage: 'The claim that nonallegorical description was possible ... was closely allied to the romantic search for unmediated meaning in the event ... The recent "revival" of rhetoric by a diverse group of literary and cultural theorists ... has thrown serious doubt on the positivist-romantic-realist consensus'. What seems to be said in this passage is that putting into doubt the notion of positivism – that is, by demonstrating the inevitable rhetoricity of knowledge – has proved nonallegorical description, description free of value judgements, to be impossible. Or, said the other way round: rejecting the possibility of value-free science is to reject the possibility of science free from transcendentality.

We thus find that its value content is seen to be responsible for the transcendentality of knowledge. Since science entails value judgements it cannot be objective in an absolute, positivistic or realistic sense. However, if value judgements are seen to be the reason for the non-objectivity of non-value statements, what would be the reason for value judgements being non-objective in the first place? Is it because value judgements entail value judgements? If, therefore, we would hold on to the idea that non-value statements are non-objective because they contain value-statements, we would lack any proof why the latter cannot be objective. We would have just presupposed it without knowing why. This is to say that the factor proving the transcendentality of knowledge cannot be found in its value content. It has to be a factor that is responsible for the transcendence of non-value and value judgements alike. We can find this factor by simply saying that all knowledge – both non-value and value knowledge – rests on drawing a distinction between what shall be the case, and what shall be not; or, as Weber put it, that 'all cognitive knowledge of infinite reality by the finite human mind rests upon the implicit presupposition that at any one time only a finite part of this reality can be subjected to scientific scrutiny' (Weber 2006: 499). All kinds of knowledge are subjected to their inescapable rhetoricity, performativity, constructivity, culturality, narrativity and the like. And what is important to note is that when thus giving up our ideal of value-free science, we are not giving up our ideal of objective science. Although we cannot dismiss epistemological scepticism, we cannot help but 'doing as if' and deciding what we think is true and what is not. However, what we can help is that value statements can now be perceived to be a legitimate part of scientific discourse.

If, therefore, we have to dismiss the idea that value judgements would be liable for the transcendentality of non-value statements, there is still another point I want to make. Before doing so let me give one last example from the above quoted passages where we may find that Clifford wrongly assumes such a causal nexus: 'A recognition of allegory emphasizes the fact that realistic portraits, to the extent that they are "convincing" or "rich", are extended metaphors, patterns of associations that point to coherent (theoretical, aesthetic, moral) additional meanings'. Again, what seems to be said in this passage is that realistic portraits have to be perceived as metaphors or as metaphorical – which can be understood as an epistemological marker to denote the 'metaphoricity' of knowledge – to the extent that they are enriched by additional theoretical, aesthetic and moral meanings. What makes ethnographic accounts transcend their referentiality is their inevitable content of moral, political, ethical and similar messages. And what seems to be said here as well is that the more messages of this kind are included, the more metaphorical the whole story becomes.

This leads me to my last point. If we assume value judgements to be responsible for the transcendentality of non-value statements, we are taken to what I shall call a 'contamination theory'. It brings about the idea that non-value knowledge could actually be objective if it did not contain value knowledge. Unfortunately, as we know, this is not the case. There is no science free from value statements. Nonetheless, it makes us believe that by decreasing the share of moral knowledge in our ethnographic writing we are increasing its share of objectivity. The less value knowledge it contains, the more objective, the more empirical, the more factual our reports become. And it is exactly this idea that will put into force the asymmetry once again. We would be forever condemned to follow its programme on a practical level, though we have long seen that on a theoretical level its verdict – non-value statements are objectifiable, value statements are not – cannot be maintained. We would be bound to keep on trying to purify our reports from their moral content and, since this never proves to be successful, to reproduce the symptom of what Hirschman called the 'unconscious smuggling in of moral considerations' (Hirschman 1983: 31). And this would prevent us once again from having the 'political and ethical dimensions of ethnographic writing', as Clifford suggested, become 'manifested, not hidden'.

References

Clifford, James. 1986. 'On Ethnographic Allegory', in James Clifford and George E. Marcus (eds), *Writing Culture: The Poetics and Politics of Ethnography*. Berkeley: University of California Press, 98–121.

Hirschman, Albert O. 1983[1981]. 'Morality and the Social Sciences: A Durable Tension', in Norma Haan, Robert N. Bellah, Paul Rabinow and William M. Sullivan (eds), *Social Science as Moral Inquiry*. New York: Columbia University Press, 21–32.

Latour, Bruno. 1993[1991]. *We Have Never Been Modern*, trans. C. Porter. Cambridge, MA: Harvard University Press.

Lepenies, Wolf. 1997. *Benimm und Erkenntnis*. Frankfurt am Main: Suhrkamp.

Putnam, Hilary. 2002. *The Collapse of the Fact/Value Dichotomy, and Other Essays*. Cambridge, MA: Harvard University Press.

Shostak, Marjorie. 1981. *Nisa: The Life and Words of a !Kung Woman*. Cambridge, MA: Harvard University Press.

Strohmenger, Steffen. 2006. *Sachfragen und Glücksfragen: Von der Asymmetrie zur Re-Symmetrisierung ihrer Wahrheitsfähigkeit*. Munich: Wilhelm Fink Verlag.

Vaihinger, Hans. 1952[1911]. *The Philosophy of 'As If': A System of the Theoretical, Practical and Religious Fictions of Mankind*. London: Routledge.

Weber, Max. 2006[1904]. 'The "Objectivity" of Knowledge in Social Science and Social Policy', in Henrietta L. Moore and Todd Sanders (eds), *Anthropology in Theory: Issues in Epistemology*. Malden, MA: Blackwell, 494–505.

4

Indigenous Research and the Politics of Representation: Notes on the Cultural Theory of Marshall Sahlins

Karsten Kumoll

❧

Within some branches of sociological theory, the 'social' seems to have been redefined as the 'cultural' in recent decades (see Reckwitz 2002). Furthermore, since the 1980s, concepts like the 'new cultural history' (Hunt 1987) and 'historical anthropology' (Biersack 1991) have become increasingly influential in historical studies. One important source of this 'cultural turn' within sociology and history, though by no means the only one, is American cultural anthropology. However, within anthropology itself, cultural theories have been seriously questioned from various perspectives, including those held by proponents of the *Writing Culture* debate, which turned anthropology's attention towards both the literary status of ethnographic texts and the political implications of ethnographic representation.

Though the literary movement in anthropology and related disciplines has been criticized for neglecting the importance of empirical realities, the debate over the literary and political dimensions of ethnography has helped to broaden the reflexive sensibility of anthropological research and writing. However, discussions about the 'poetics and politics of ethnography' were predominantly Western ones within anthropology on Western representations of non-Western societies. In the last twenty years, however, there have emerged distinctive 'indigenous' ways of doing science that may be understood as explicitly anti-Western research practices. From the perspective of these studies, anthropology and related disciplines, including the *Writing Culture* debate itself, may be seen as neocolonial enterprises. In the Pacific, for example, Oceanic researchers and intellectuals incorporate indigenous epistemologies into their paradigms; furthermore, they use non-Western narrative forms and question the Western legitimacy of representing Oceanic ways of living. Thus, these 'cultural studies for Oceania' seem to undermine anthropology's cosmopolitical and comparative project.

Focusing on the work of Marshall Sahlins, I wish to explore some of the consequences that this intercultural politics of representation may have for the practice of 'doing' anthropology. Sahlins's work may be particularly suited for this investigation, because Sahlins is frequently criticized for 'Orientalizing' Oceanic cultures, although Sahlins's cultural theory may be understood as at least partly based on a politically motivated concept that stresses cultural difference and that is deeply rooted in his experience of the movement against the Vietnam War. Why is it that Sahlins's politically motivated critique of Western universalism is interpreted by some representatives of postcolonial theory and 'indigenous' Oceanic studies as just another form of Western universalism? This question may turn out not only to be of central importance with respect to the usefulness of Sahlins's work; it may also point us to some general observations about the pitfalls of the politics of representation.[1]

My starting point is the debate between Sahlins and Gananath Obeyesekere on the death of Captain James Cook in Hawaii. What is often ignored in the numerous analyses of the debate is the importance of Hawaiian responses that are highly critical of both Sahlins and Obeyesekere. In the second section of this chapter, I provide a sketch of the emerging 'cultural studies for Oceania', which may be understood as a critique of Western research on non-Western cultures. Subsequently, I investigate Sahlins's political protest against the Vietnam War in the 1960s, which has been largely overlooked by scholars analysing his work. Finally, I discuss the postcolonial and indigenous critique against the background of Sahlins's intellectual development and provide some indication of how to overcome the emerging divide between the different research practices.

The Sahlins–Obeyesekere Debate

In the 1970s, Marshall Sahlins, one of the leading American anthropologists of the twentieth century, developed a powerful theory of culture that combines Franz Boas's relativism with Claude Lévi-Strauss's structuralism (Sahlins 1976), thereby partly abandoning his earlier work on cultural evolution and economic anthropology (e.g., Sahlins 1958, 1972). Sahlins later reshaped this theory of culture within a historical framework and applied it to the history of the Pacific (Sahlins 1981, 1985). His influence on cultural history has been widespread and substantial. Though they also drew criticism (e.g., Friedman 1988), Sahlins's

---

1 For a more extensive discussion of Sahlins's cultural theory, see Kumoll 2007.

interpretations of the death of Captain James Cook in Hawaii and of contact histories in New Zealand and Fiji nevertheless stimulated important research at the intersection of anthropology and history with respect to colonialism, ethnohistory and cultural change (see Biersack 1991). In 1992, however, Sahlins's study on Cook's death was sharply criticized by the Sri Lankan anthropologist Gananath Obeyesekere (see Obeyesekere 1997). Obeyesekere refuted Sahlins's claim that Cook was perceived by the Hawaiians as the manifestation of their god Lono and argued instead that this 'apotheosis' of Cook was a Western invention. Obeyesekere's critique and Sahlins's angry response (Sahlins 1995) provoked a heated debate that generated widespread interest in several disciplines, including sociology, history and philosophy (see Borofsky 1997).

Reading Sahlins and Obeyesekere, one gets the impression that the empirical question of Captain James Cook's death, seemingly the focal point of the entire debate, is in fact a rather minor issue. Instead, Sahlins and Obeyesekere quarrel about the right way to do anthropology – methodologically, ontologically and epistemologically. Apart from the serious problems of interpreting the relevant sources (see, for example, Merry 2003), the debate between Sahlins and Obeyesekere is structured around their theories of social action. Marshall Sahlins's theory of culture is an example of a 'cultural turn' within social theories of action, though it obviously would be going too far to argue that 'social theory' in general has been transformed into some sort of 'theory of culture'. In contrast to other theories of action, such as rational choice theory and the 'homo sociologicus' of the norm-following actor, theories of culture may be defined as paradigms that conceive or explain human action and social order by establishing their basis in symbolic codes and schemes that order and regulate meaning (see Reckwitz 2002). This approach may be the common framework of the otherwise quite different theories advanced by Lévi-Strauss, Pierre Bourdieu, Alfred Schütz, Clifford Geertz and Michel Foucault. In Sahlins's view, people perceive reality and act according to cultural schemes, but culture does not determine action. Rather, culture should be seen as an enabling framework within which cognition and action take place. Thus, Sahlins's approach is somewhat similar to Bourdieu's concept of habitus (Bourdieu 1977). Action proceeds within structures of significance, thereby reproducing and modifying these structures. Sahlins argues that the Hawaiians were able to flexibly surmount empirical contradictions in their own cultural terms, thereby eventually altering their cultural traditions. Obeyesekere, on the other hand, argues that Sahlins's 'flexibility' is immovably embedded within a fundamentally static cultural cosmology. He develops an alternative, Weberian notion of 'practical rationality', or 'the process whereby human beings reflectively access the implications of a problem in terms of practical criteria' (Obeyesekere 1997: 19). In doing so, Obeyesekere aims to avoid an 'othering' of the Hawaiians by stressing a human feature common around the world.

The relationship between 'practical rationality', 'flexibility' and the symbolic organization of reality is, at first, an ontological problem, and I would argue that

Sahlins's and Obeyesekere's accounts should be combined in order to avoid the one-sidedness of their concepts, which also becomes evident in their methods of interpreting sources. Furthermore, Sahlins's concept of cultural homogeneity must be abandoned, even though Sahlins in no way develops a theory of cultural determinism. In the debate between Sahlins and Obeyesekere, neither Sahlins nor one of those commenting on his work refers to Sahlins's concept of 'humiliation', which is an important element of his overall theory of cultural change (see Robbins and Wardlow 2005). It may be that Sahlins has invited critical interpretations of his work by reducing the considerable complexity of his cultural theory in his polemical comments on Obeyesekere's critique. However, the problem of the relationship between culture and action is also linked to the epistemological one about representation. According to Obeyesekere, Sahlins does not properly represent the Hawaiians because he interprets them within his cultural relativism, that is Sahlins's argument that different cultures give rise to different rationalities. Therefore, the Sahlins–Obeyesekere debate has a specific political component, and the political charge of Obeyesekere against Sahlins is similar to Adam Kuper's critique of anthropological theories of culture (Kuper 1999). The culture concept developed by Sahlins and others seems to support essentialist representations of other cultures, to be a specific realization of 'Orientalism', and to support nationalist movements or even fascist politics.

After a reply by Obeyesekere in the second edition of his book (Obeyesekere 1997), both Sahlins and Obeyesekere apparently lost interest in the controversy. In general, interest in the Sahlins–Obeyesekere debate seems to have declined significantly in anthropology; one may even argue, as George E. Marcus does, that within anthropology there was never much interest in the debate to begin with (Marcus 1998: 248–49). In contrast to Marcus, Bruce Kapferer argues that many anthropologists were indeed very interested in the debate because it made apparent a deep-seated crisis within anthropology 'which involves a sense of loss among anthropologists of the relatively distinct project of anthropology' (Kapferer 2000: 175). In fact, the battle between Sahlins and Obeyesekere raised important epistemological questions. One of the most important aspects of the debate concerns critiques by Hawaiian scholars and intellectuals, which have been marginalized within the debate itself.

Hawaiian scholar Lilikala Kame'eleihiwa argues that 'I have been hard put to understand why haole scholars (like Marshall Sahlins) persist in writing about Cook, and since such scholars ... invariably misinterpret Hawaiian cultural acts, we generally laugh at such works' (Kame'eleihiwa 1994a: 111–12). These words indeed touch on an important aspect of both Sahlins's and Obeyesekere's work. In her review of Obeyesekere's book, Anne Salmond states that 'in the heat of the debate Hawaiians (and Maori), and what they (rather than Sahlins or Obeyesekere) thought about Cook are marginalised, while on occasion their accounts are contemptuously dismissed. I would not be surprised if for Hawaiians, as for many Maori, post-colonial humanism in such contexts seems about as pertinent to their interests as its colonial precursor' (Salmond 1993: 54). Kame'eleihiwa not only criticizes Sahlins's work, but also questions Obeyesekere's approach. Obeyesekere 'is not a Hawaiian and does not know our culture, nor does he speak our language; thus he makes mistakes common to a foreign scholar. I applaud his critical analysis of his field of anthropology, of colonialist myths, and of Sahlins's work, but before he ventures further into the writing of Hawaiian history, he should at least become fluent in my language' (Kame'eleihiwa 1994a: 117).

In a review of Sahlins's monumental study of Hawaiian history, *Anahulu*, Kame'eleihiwa attacks Sahlins's thesis that Hawaiian chiefs 'maintained a purely extractive relation to the resources of the Islands, preferring to enjoy their power over the land and people than to expend their wealth on them' (Sahlins 1992: 135). Kame'eleihiwa points out that 'Sahlins misunderstands Hawaiian culture. The *ali'i* were like our parents, and while we may dislike the tasks they have given us, we love and cherish them nonetheless' (Kame'eleihiwa 1994b: 216). She argues that Sahlins's version 'will be used by the colonial powers, and their academic supporters, to attack the Hawaiian sovereignty movement' (ibid.: 214).

As early as the 1980s, Haunani-Kay Trask attacked Sahlins's approach for similar reasons. In *Islands of History*, Sahlins argues that the Hawaiian category *kama' āina* 'refers to someone "native" to a place. Yet one may equally be a *kama' āina* by action or by prescription: by long-term residence or by birthright' (Sahlins 1985: 28). Thus, even Europeans and Americans could reach an 'indigenous' status in nineteenth-century Hawaii. Trask argues that Sahlins seriously misrepresents Hawaiian culture: 'What Sahlins believes to be cultural evidence continuing through time and across vastly different historical periods is rather the increasing appropriation by foreigners of a source of legitimacy' (Trask 1985: 786). Both Trask and Kame'eleihiwa argue that Sahlins's work is politically dangerous because it undermines the Hawaiian sovereignty movement. They suggest that not only Sahlins's work in particular, but large parts of anthropology in general, serve neocolonial powers and threaten indigenous sovereignty movements. This critique is one of the main legacies of the controversy between Sahlins and Obeyesekere.

Epistemological Elements of the 'Cultural Studies for Oceania'

Kame'eleihiwa is critical not only of anthropology in particular, but also of what she sees as the continuing influence of neocolonialist powers in Hawaii. In 2002, for example, she criticized plans to produce a Hollywood movie about the Hawaiian king Kamehameha. In a letter to screenwriter Greg Poirier, she wrote, 'For Hawaiians it is not acceptable that Hollywood should be allowed to misrepresent the history of our ancestors in any way. Nor do we want Hollywood's warped sense of "Hawaiiana" portrayed to the world. The story of Kamehameha should wait for a culturally knowledgeable Hawaiian to write the screen play, for a Hawaiian movie company to make the film, and for a Hawaiian descendant of Kamehameha to play the role' (see Burlingame 2002). Perhaps one is inclined to think that Kame'eleihiwa's views represent an exceptional case of indigenous nationalism that should not be taken too seriously, at least in academic terms. Furthermore, Trask's statement that anthropologists are part of the 'colonizing horde' (Trask 1991: 162) is more than fifteen years old, and anthropology has changed significantly since the early 1990s. Perhaps not every Hawaiian or Oceanic scholar is automatically a critic of Western anthropology. However, the Hawaiians' critiques of Sahlins's and Obeyesekere's views in particular and anthropology in general exemplify a general problem of the politics of representation. In the Pacific, there have emerged multiple 'indigenous' ways of doing science that 'emphasize Pacific Islander ways of knowing', as Houston Wood states (Wood 2003: 341). In what follows, I provide a sketch of the epistemological foundations of the emerging 'cultural studies for Oceania' (ibid.). I rely primarily upon discussions in the journal *Contemporary Pacific*, a major English-language platform for 'indigenous' scholarship and research.[2]

First of all, many Oceanic scholars demand that indigenous epistemologies – that is, 'a cultural group's ways of theorizing knowledge' (Gegeo 2001b: 491) – should be one of the bases of research on indigenous peoples (Smith 1999: 187–88; Wood 2003: 355).[3] Vilsoni Hereniko points out that the Western preoccupation with writing obscures the multiplicity and ambiguity of indigenous pasts in favour of one apparently true account (Hereniko 2000: 84–85; see also Wood 2003: 360). In his view, Western anthropologists and historians neglect the emotional truth, 'which is the essence of literature, oral or written ... novelists are concerned with the unseen as well as the seen and, if they are good at their craft, give better insights into history in its totality than social scientific accounts in textbooks' (Hereniko 2000: 85). Hereniko attacks the application of Western epistemologies to non-Western cultures; these applications, he argues, are intellectual bits and pieces that are not useful to the respective indigenous communities. As David Welchman Gegeo argues, 'we need once and for all to eliminate the Anglo-European categories that still tend to imprison us in outdated, meaningless terminologies that divide rather than unite us' (Gegeo 2001a: 179). Moreover, Konai Helu Thaman maintains that decolonizing Pacific studies involves reclaiming indigenous Pacific perspectives that have been suppressed because they were not considered important or worth further development (Thaman 2003: 2; see also Smith 1999: 38). Many indigenous scholars argue that epistemologies can be applied only locally (see Meyer 2001); furthermore, many Pacific scholars plead for multiple ways of expressing scientific knowledge. Wood

---

2 See Trask (1991), Kame'eleihiwa (1992), Hau'ofa (1993), Smith (1999), Hereniko (2000), Diaz and Kauanui (2001), Gegeo (2001a, 2001b), Gegeo and Watson-Gegeo (2001), Meyer (2001), White and Tengan (2001), Firth (2003), Hanlon (2003), Hviding (2003), Thaman (2003), Wood (2003, 2006) and Huffer and Qalo (2004).

3 See also Gegeo (2001b), Gegeo and Watson-Gegeo (2001), Meyer (2001) and Huffer and Qalo (2004: 88).

argues that poems may be as scientific as ethnographic works. He rejects the Aristotelian distinction between rhetorical and poetic texts as well as the distinctions between fact and fiction and between persuasion and entertainment (Wood 2003: 362; see also White and Tengan 2001: 402). In fact, many respected Oceanic scholars, including Haunani-Kay Trask and Epeli Hau'ofa, have also published poetic works on Oceanic ways of life and histories. The historian David Hanlon argues that these forms of expressing knowledge contribute to a decentering of Pacific history. 'History, it seems to me, can be sung, danced, chanted, spoken, carved, woven, painted, sculpted, rapped as well as written ... A decentering of history in Oceania also requires an awareness of the local knowledges and epistemologies that inform the many varied and particular practices of history in the region' (Hanlon 2003: 30). These practices may be understood as critiques of Western colonialism, because, as Kame'eleihiwa argues, 'We have evolved from a complex oral society and mistrust the power that the written words seems to wield' (Kame'eleihiwa 1992: 380, n.25).

Secondly, many Oceanic scholars demand that the historical process of colonialism be explicitly taken into account, because Western social science is considered to be an epistemological continuation of political colonialism. 'What good', Gegeo asks, 'is political independence if we remain colonized epistemologically?' (Gegeo 2001a: 182). Hereniko argues that colonialism has played an important role in the ongoing destruction of indigenous cultures. 'As native people were taught to read and write, they paid less and less attention to oratory. This process ... radically altered islanders' perceptions of themselves' (Hereniko 2000: 83). Western epistemologies are thus said to undermine cultural renaissance and to support epistemological colonialism in the Pacific by Western culture (see also Thaman 2003: 2). 'Pacific Islands research based on Euro-American answers ... generally helps perpetuate Euro-American dominance in the region, even when the goals of this work are supposed to be anti-hegemonic' (Wood 2003: 354). Hereniko argues that many islander students fail because the education systems work against indigenous ways of learning (Hereniko 2000: 84). As a consequence, many Oceanic scholars argue that indigenous epistemologies should be moved into the very centre of Pacific education systems. 'Institutions of high education must recognize ownership and control of indigenous knowledge by indigenous peoples rather than by the academy. Pacific studies centers and programs need indigenous cultural knowledge in order to validate and legitimize their work, particularly in the eyes of indigenous peoples' (Thaman 2003: 11).

Thirdly, many indigenous scholars in Oceania epistemologically and politically distinguish between 'islanders' and 'outlanders'. This distinction raises doubts about whether outlanders can legitimately make statements about Oceanic societies and histories. 'Do outsiders have the right to speak for and about Pacific Islanders? I was brought up to believe that the right to speak in public is not God-given' (Hereniko 2000: 86). Hereniko complains about Western scientists who make authoritative and objectified statements about

Oceanic cultures without expressing any doubt about whether they have the legitimacy to do so. 'I have been in numerous situations where natives sit and listen while white academics discuss and analyze their cultures and people in an objectified fashion' (ibid.: 86). He argues that indigenous voices were largely ignored in the Sahlins–Obeyesekere controversy. 'Both Sahlins and Obeyesekere say their ultimate desire is that native voices be heard, but how can we hear those voices when they are screaming at each other so loudly?' (ibid.: 87). Hereniko also suggests that Western scientists should invite indigenous scholars 'to share the space with them, either as copresenters or as discussants or respondents. Not to do so is to perpetuate unequal power relations between colonizer and colonized' (ibid.: 86). More generally, sometimes it is even argued that Western scientists should no longer be permitted access to indigenous ways of knowing. 'Non-Natives ... should no longer be allowed to claim for their disciplines, organizations, or corporations whatever resources they wish to take from the immense sea of Native knowledges scattered across Oceania. Such restrictions in access are necessitated by the contemporary asymmetries of power present throughout the region' (Wood 2003: 342).

However, precisely these distinctions between islanders and outlanders or between indigenous and foreign are contested by some because they are seen as part of the neocolonial order (Gegeo 2001b: 502).[4] Geoffrey M. White and Ty Kawika Tengan blame anthropology for having introduced the distinction between insider and outsider into the very investigation of Pacific cultures. Discussing the invention-of-tradition approach and Trask's radical critique thereof, they argue 'that this kind of separation has been fostered by anthropology's mythos of otherness and related practices that intensify native wariness of research practices associated with the colonial past' (White and Tengan 2001: 400). The distinction between islanders and outlanders may be understood as a process of identity-building. However, this distinction itself is sometimes criticized because, it is argued, it downplays asymmetries of power within indigenous communities and life-worlds (see Balawanilotu et al. 2003: 201).

Finally, many Oceanic scholars are convinced that 'doing' research is a deeply political activity.[5] This assertion is interwoven with the other elements of Oceanic

---

4   The concepts used in these controversies may have different meanings in different changing historical and cultural contexts. For example, the distinctions between the concepts 'Pacific' and 'Oceanic' and between 'indigenous' and 'native' may not be understood as arbitrary. '*Indigenous* now has two meanings among Pacific Island scholars and activists. First, it refers to fourth-world people such as Maori, Hawaiians, and Aborigines – people who were colonized and are still colonized in their own society; this is a political definition. Second, someone who is not of mixed blood. *Native* now means people who are of mixed ancestry living in the place of one or other parent. For example, persons of part-Hawaiian ancestry who were born and live in California can call themselves "native Hawaiian" but not "indigenous"' (Gegeo 2001a: 183 n. 1). Diaz and Kauanui use the terms 'native' and 'indigenous' synonymously, but they acknowledge that these terms may have different meanings in different contexts (Diaz and Kauanui 2001: 333 n. 1).

5   This claim should not be confused with the assertion that 'culture' is always 'political'. Within indigenous concepts of social science, this claim, which gained prominence in the invention-of-tradition literature, is explicitly criticized (Diaz and Kauanui 2001: 323).

concepts of science discussed so far in this chapter, because both the call for using indigenous epistemologies and the distinction between islanders and outlanders may be understood as politically motivated. Furthermore, the political basis of indigenous science in Oceania implies a practice of decolonization. As Diaz and Kauanui argue, 'Scholarship for us involves at least two interconnected fronts: the identification and dismantling of colonial structures and discourses variously conceptualized and theorized, and cultural reclamation and stewardship' (Diaz and Kauanui 2001: 318). Wood points out that the emerging 'cultural studies for Oceania' serves processes of identity-building in the Pacific rather than global scientific progress. 'Cultural studies in Oceania … exists first for Oceania and only secondarily, if at all, to further the theoretical or institutional goals of the international cultural studies movement. Helping to build a regional identity for the region, then, can be a first priority for a cultural studies for Oceania' (Wood 2003: 347). An individual who studies Oceanic cultures without taking an interest in the well-being of the people stabilizes the neocolonial status quo, according to Hereniko (2000: 88). As a consequence, many Oceanic scholars demand a code of ethics for Pacific ways of doing science: 'A body of Pacific thought should contribute to the establishment or affirmation of a Pacific philosophy and ethic – a set of applicable concepts and values to guide interaction within countries, within the region, and with the rest of the world. The ethic must be acknowledged, understood, and respected by all who interact with Pacific Island communities' (Huffer and Qalo 2004: 89). This suggestion is linked to a critique of knowledge transfers between Oceanic and Western societies. As Hereniko points out, 'The scholarly practice that says that the first to publish certain facts or information about a culture has "ownership" over that material ensures that knowledge that belonged to indigenous people, like their land in many cases, is slowly appropriated by the colonizers' (Hereniko 2000: 88; see also Smith 1999: 190).

Sahlins's Intellectual Development

From the perspective of the emerging 'cultural studies for Oceania', Sahlins's work on Hawaii seems to be an ethnocentric, neocolonial enterprise. It is thus ironic that Sahlins's cultural theory may be at least partly understood in the context of his political protest against the Vietnam War in the 1960s. In what follows, I give a brief outline of Sahlins's intellectual development until the publication of *Culture and Practical Reason* (Sahlins 1976).

In the late 1950s, Sahlins developed a universalist model of the evolution of culture, and he argued that different forms of society are adaptations to changing ecological circumstances (see Sahlins 1958). At that time Sahlins was deeply influenced by the neo-evolutionists Leslie A. White and Julian H. Steward. He also became increasingly interested in the work of Karl Polanyi. From the early 1960s onwards, he focused his attention on economic processes in so-called 'primitive' societies; his aim was to give an economic foundation to his evolutionary model. Sahlins thus used Polanyi's model of exchange systems in order to explain the evolutionary performances of different societies. Through the use of Polanyi's work, he slowly shifted his approach towards a more 'culturalist' position.

This shift may have been accelerated by the formalism–substantivism debate within economic anthropology in the 1960s. As early as the 1930s, anthropologists such as Raymond Firth had attempted to apply neoclassical economics to what they called 'primitive' societies. Polanyi and his followers, however, criticized this application of universal models of neoclassical economics and argued that these models could be applied only to a capitalist market system. In the 1960s, journals such as *American Anthropologist* and *Current Anthropology* were sometimes dominated by angry statements defending either the formalist or the substantivist position. In the late 1960s, Sahlins was viewed as a leading substantivist. In his seminal article 'The Original Affluent Society' (Sahlins 1972: 1–39), he argued that hunters and gatherers are more affluent than people in capitalist societies because they, unlike ourselves, do not have unlimited wants. Sahlins thus moved away from his earlier evolutionism and towards a position that acknowledged cultural distinctiveness.[6] At the time of publication, this article was very well received and had a substantial impact; indeed, it still seems to be one of the most well-known papers within anthropology in general. However, 'The Original Affluent Society' was not quite as 'culturalist' as it initially seemed. Sahlins only partly abandoned his earlier ecological perspective, for he explained the lack of wants among hunters and gatherers in terms of the ecological strains that forced them to move around; in such a situation, he argued, goods would be rather obstructive. Furthermore, Sahlins did not criticize 'the common understanding of "economy" as a relation between means and ends'; he only denied that hunters find any great disparity between the two (Sahlins 1972: xii). Sahlins tried to develop a culturally sensitive approach to consumption, but he did not completely abandon his earlier ecological position, nor did he construct a satisfying alternative to neoclassical economics. Thus, at this point in his intellectual development, Sahlins needed a new way to frame his evolving interest in cultural distinctiveness (see also Bird-David 1992).

One may question why this theoretical move to cultural distinctiveness happened at all. Presumably there were many reasons for Sahlins's 'cultural turn', and I have already argued that Sahlins moved towards a culturalist position through his use of Polanyi's work and his involvement in the formalism –substantivism debate. However, there may be factors behind his 'cultural turn' that lie beyond his anthropological work. I want to suggest that Sahlins's political protest against the

---

6   I focus on 'The Original Affluent Society' here as only one example of several articles published in the late 1960s in which Sahlins's turn to culture became apparent. For a detailed analysis of *Stone Age Economics*, see Kumoll (2007: 71–136).

Vietnam War in the 1960s may be one important political foundation of his turn to culture and which is already partly apparent in *Stone Age Economics*.

In 1965, Sahlins worked at the University of Michigan and became involved in the early anti-war protests. The main reason for these was the American bombing of North Vietnam under President Lyndon Johnson in 1965. This military action was particularly significant because Johnson had promised an end to the Vietnam War during his election campaign in 1964. Many intellectuals critical of the war had supported Johnson, yet in early 1965 Johnson escalated the war when he ordered the bombing of communist North Vietnam. As a consequence, many academics were upset, and they decided to protest against US policy in Vietnam by cancelling classes. These concerns were the intellectual foundation of the so-called 'teach-ins' at Michigan and other universities. In fact, the term 'teach-in' seems to have originated from Sahlins himself, who interrupted a discussion on the night of 17 March 1965 with the statement, 'Let's show them how responsible we feel. Instead of teaching out, we'll teach in – all night' (Harder 1968: 60). In the night of 24–25 March, the first teach-in was held at the University of Michigan, with more than 3,000 students attending the event. Within one week, there were teach-ins at more than thirty American universities, and in May 1965 the so-called National Teach-In was organized in Washington, DC. There, professors discussed American policy towards Vietnam with members of the administration (see Menashe and Radosh 1967).

In August 1965, Sahlins went to Vietnam on a fact-finding mission. While there, he spoke with American soldiers who supported what they called 'mental torture'; he saw the effects of the war on the Vietnamese countryside; and he was able to gain new insights into the administration in South Vietnam. In Sahlins's view, the Vietnam War was not a war against the Vietnamese, at least not in the first place. 'After all, we are fighting Chinese there. There are no Chinese there. So *Vietnamese* die by way of demonstration' (Sahlins 2000: 233). Sahlins argued that the Vietnam War was a proxy war within the context of the cold war, a war against communism. In Sahlins's view, Americans did not understand the complex cultural reality in Vietnam; people who were opposed to the Americans or the South Vietnamese government were routinely labelled communists. However, as Sahlins pointed out, the Americans misunderstood the nationalist movement in Vietnam, considering it to be a communist movement. Furthermore, Sahlins argued that the South Vietnamese government was corrupt and had no democratic legitimacy. He observed a 'destruction of consciousness in Vietnam' (ibid.: 229–60), an attitude towards the war that ignored the deplorable state of affairs.

There was much discussion of the war at the time among anthropologists and within the American Anthropological Association. These debates became even more heated when it was revealed in 1965 that the US Department of Defense had planned a multimillion-dollar study of the so-called revolutionary process in Latin America and other parts of the world. 'Project Camelot' was the latest example of the US army's support of various projects dealing with research into and the practice of 'insurgency' and 'counter-insurgency'. Many scholars protested against this project, which they said violated the ethical standards of the anthropological profession (see Horowitz 1967; Solovey 2001). Among the academics critical of Project Camelot was Sahlins, who criticized it as just another realization of American cold war policy (Sahlins 2000: 261–68).

These critiques by Sahlins and other respected anthropologists such as Eric Wolf and Marvin Harris were directed not only against the Vietnam War, but also against what came to be known as the 'military-industrial-academic complex', the ever-expanding connection between policymakers, the military and social scientists who were financed by the US army, the Central Intelligence Agency (CIA) or other government agencies. Within the cultural context of the cold war, there emerged a new paradigm of modernization theory that was highly influential on American policy. In the 1950s, social scientists who researched modernization and development in the areas that came to be known as the 'Third World' often also worked as advisors to the US administration and received substantial funding from the government. Some modernization theorists, especially those from the CIA-financed Center for International Studies at the Massachusetts Institute of Technology (MIT), even argued for the support of military dictatorships in postcolonial nations as a means against the expansion of communism (see Gilman 2003).

Some of the most important theoretical developments within American anthropology at that time may be at least partly understood as a reaction to the Vietnam War, the paradigm of modernization theory and the military-industrial-academic complex. One example is, of course, Eric Wolf's Marxian theory of history, which was influenced by world systems analysis and dependency theory (Wolf 1969, 1982 and 2001). Another example is the cultural relativism of Sahlins, as exemplified in *Culture and Practical Reason* and his later work on history. Both Wolf and Sahlins were active in the anti-war movement, and in the 1960s both even worked together at the same department in Michigan. However, in terms of their theoretical approach, Wolf and Sahlins were very different, though both took a position against American universalism. Whereas Wolf developed a Marxian theory that focuses on unequal power relations within the capitalist world system, Sahlins focused on 'islands of history' and cultural distinctiveness.

Between 1967 and 1969, Sahlins worked at the Collège de France in Paris in Claude Lévi-Strauss's department. In 1972 he published *Stone Age Economics*, thereby elaborating his 'anthropological economics'. In 1976, however, Sahlins published *Culture and Practical Reason*, which was based on lectures he gave at the City University of New York in 1973. In this book, he relied much more on Lévi-Strauss's structuralism than he had in *Stone Age Economics*. At the most basic level, *Culture and Practical Reason* is a radical critique of ecological, material and utilitarian anthropological theories. Sahlins argues that ecological and material forces are significant only if they are mediated by culture, that is, by meaningful perception. At the same time, the work can be read as a comment on the debate between Marxism and structuralism in France. Yet the book also can be read as a critique of his own earlier work on cultural evolution and anthropological economics. Sahlins implicitly criticizes his earlier work and thereby overcomes the problems he faced within the context of his anthropological economics by replacing his mixture of ecological anthropology and substantivism with a rather radical cultural relativism.

Furthermore, with *Culture and Practical Reason*, Sahlins arrives at a concept of cultural relativism that could be analysed as a scientific realization of his political protest against the Vietnam War and against the universalization of American-dominated modernity. To be sure, the proposition that Sahlins's 'cultural turn' was accelerated or even initiated by his protest against the Vietnam War is speculative. Sahlins himself stated that 'sympathy and even admiration for the Vietnamese struggle, coupled to moral and political disaffection with the American war, might undermine an anthropology of economic determinism and evolutionary development' (Sahlins 2000: 22–23). This remark, almost in passing, and other comments in his introduction to *Culture in Practice* provide only a hint of a causal relationship between Sahlins's protest against the war and his cultural turn; there are not enough historical documents available to demonstrate a strong link between theoretical text and historical context. At the very least, however, a content-related correspondence – and, at the same time, a difference – between his protest against the Vietnam War and his cultural theory becomes apparent: instead of criticizing the political universalism of the United States in Southeast Asia, through his cultural theory Sahlins criticizes the Western epistemological universalism inherent in utilitarian concepts.

The Politics of Representation

Within contemporary anthropology, Sahlins is rather routinely accused of being a cultural essentialist and a cultural determinist. Postcolonial and postmodern researchers criticize Sahlins's work as ethnocentric because it does not focus on cultural hybridity and because it reinforces a concept of cultural homogeneity (see Li 2001). As I have argued, it is difficult to prove a causal link between Sahlins's protest against the war and his cultural turn in the late 1960s, though it seems plausible that the war accelerated his critique of Western epistemologies which was already apparent in his early work on economic anthropology. Thus, against the backdrop of his political protest in the anti-war movement and his critique of the universalism of Western epistemologies within his cultural theory, it may at first seem a mystery why certain Oceanic intellectuals and Obeyesekere criticize Sahlins as just another Western anthropologist who applies Western theories to non-Western cultures. Although Sahlins protested against the violence of the United States in Vietnam, and although he has tried to develop an anthropological theory that does epistemological justice to non-Western cultures, some representatives of some cultures criticize Sahlins for committing an act of symbolic violence against the Hawaiians.

One reason for this is Sahlins's concept of representation. Whereas Sahlins attacks the seemingly universalist tradition of utilitarianism, his own work, one could argue, is based on a universalist concept of representation. Sahlins argues throughout his body of work that it is a legitimate goal of anthropologists to represent non-Western cultures in ethnographic texts. In his writings on the Vietnam War, Sahlins criticizes the US policy in Vietnam; however, his very process of representing Vietnamese culture and the Vietnam War does not seem to him to be problematic. In his paper on Project Camelot, Sahlins argues that 'the least we can do is protect the anthropologist's relation to the Third World, which is a scholarly relation. Fieldwork under contract to the U.S. Army is no way to protect that relation' (Sahlins 2000: 263). From the perspective of several Oceanic scholars, however, this 'scholarly relation' may itself be political and may stabilize unequal power relations between different cultures. The Western representation of non-Western cultures seems to have lost its 'legitimate' epistemological centre.

Anthropology and related disciplines may benefit from incorporating into their scholarly frameworks certain elements of Oceanic social science practice. At the same time, this incorporation raises serious epistemological problems. For example, the emerging 'cultural studies for Oceania' points to the importance of multiple forms of expressing anthropological knowledge. 'We see literature and the creative imagination as legitimate vehicles to explore, review and refine *niu* approaches to Pacific history. In a region where oral history carried knowledge across hundreds of years of history, Albert Wendt's bold decision to choose poetry rather than academic prose to write history is commendable and adds an exciting dimension to the representations of ourselves and our past' (Balawanilotu et al. 2003: 199–200). These ideas are not alien to so-called Western epistemologies, for within the *Writing Culture* debate the blurring boundaries between rhetoric and poetic expressions of scientific knowledge have been discussed extensively. Thus, controversies in anthropology and history on the relationship between empirical reality and narrative form should be revisited by acknowledging the claims made by Oceanic scholars that poetic language can function as a legitimate representation of Oceanic life-worlds. This claim, of course, is quite controversial, and many historians and anthropologists would deny that their disciplines depend on poetic narrative forms to represent empirical realities. A further complication arises from the assertion that the choice of specific epistemologies is a political action that may stabilize or undermine neocolonial political and epistemological orders. The very decision to choose a specific narrative form in order to express cultural and historical realities may be understood as a political activity.

One possible solution to this problem is a dialogue between different scholars from different disciplines as well as different cultural contexts. To be sure, sometimes such a dialogue does not seem to be very promising: one is reminded of the apparently failed dialogue between Jocelyn Linnekin and Haunani-Kay Trask on invented traditions in the early 1990s (see Linnekin 1991; Trask 1991;

see also Tobin 1994). However, the incommensurability of Western and Oceanic ways of doing research should not be overemphasized. Different academic traditions should not be understood as monolithic blocs. As Robert Borofsky argues, 'Islanders and Outlanders share overlapping standards for assessing credibility in the Pacific as well as more than three centuries of overlapping pasts. Together these offer a foundation for meaningful conversations across differences of representation, differences of silence, differences of perspective' (Borofsky 2000a: 20). For example, Sahlins integrated important indigenous concepts into his anthropological approach, in particular from Epeli Hauʻofaʻs essay 'Our Sea of Islands' (Hauʻofa 1993). Furthermore, Trask's critique that anthropologists are 'part of the colonizing horde' (Trask 1991: 162) does not seem to represent the attitude of most Hawaiians towards Western anthropology. 'What is left unsaid in Trask's statement is that diverse voices exist within the Hawaiian community, and many take strong exception to her views' (Borofsky 2000a: 17). The sharp distinction between Western and Oceanic ways of knowing and of doing social science seems to be as essentialist as the assertion by cultural relativists that there are monolithic cultural blocs 'out there' that are homogenous and unchanging. In fact, the representation of each other's intellectual tradition seems to be part of the problem. For instance, Kameʻeleihiwaʻs and Trask's critiques of Western anthropology shift into an unacceptable cultural nationalism that undermines the possibility of any fruitful dialogue. Furthermore, Trask and Kameʻeleihiwa seriously misrepresent Sahlins's anthropology by not acknowledging the relationship between his anthropological work and his protest against the Vietnam War.

One question open to debate is precisely whether such a dialogue between different cultural research traditions is possible at all. Sahlins views such a dialogue as a necessary basis of anthropological knowledge. 'True, in any intersubjective dialogue – including now ethnography and history – there is always a kind of Nietzschean moment, or a built-in will to power, insofar as the world is egocentrically constituted by the "I" of the speaker. But this hubris is necessarily reversible if there is to be communication … If the assertion of an "I" is a claim to *power*, the reversibility of "I" and "you" is alternatively *competition* or *reciprocity*, even as the mutual recognition of personhood is the germ of *sociability*' (Sahlins 1997: 276). Such a dialogue, however, may be understood as stabilizing the asymmetries between Western and Oceanic scholars by marginalizing non-Western epistemologies. The journal *Contemporary Pacific* and Robert Borofsky's *Remembrance of Pacific Pasts* (2000b) may be understood as exceptionally rich platforms for debating Oceanic epistemologies and thereby destabilizing Western intellectual traditions. At the same time, however, these publications may reinforce Western ways of doing research because most of the texts published in them are written in English; furthermore, these publications do not undermine the Western preoccupation with written texts. Therefore, within these works one finds many discussions about Oceanic ways of practising social science, but not many examples of these activities themselves. As Gegeo observes, the most successful and well-known indigenous scholars seem to be those who 'play' Western scientific and narrative games – that is, who publish written texts predominantly in English. 'It is rather hypocritical of us to argue for a Pacific Islander voice while we uncritically employ the standards and evaluations of Anglo-Europeans' (Gegeo 2001a: 179). It is not surprising, therefore, that Oceanic scholars discuss extensively whether they should publish in English or even publish at all, and whether such activity would undermine the neocolonial order or in fact support it. As a consequence, a dialogue on Oceanic versions of science does not automatically lead to a more 'balanced' approach to Pacific life-worlds and histories. Part of the problem are the spaces for argumentation themselves, as they are at least partly based on the Western 'scientific field', to borrow a phrase from Pierre Bourdieu, epistemologically as well as institutionally. Oceanic scientists are obliged to play the 'scientific game' in order to be heard, and in order to gain influence within the scientific community. This legitimate goal, however, does not necessarily correspond with the emancipatory ideals of indigenous scholarship.

This chapter faces similar problems. I have argued that anthropology and related disciplines may benefit from incorporating elements of indigenous epistemologies, such as poetic narrative forms, into their research frameworks. My chapter, however, exemplifies no radical challenge of Western social science discourse and may be criticized for stabilizing the neocolonial order through its attempted assimilation of Oceanic epistemologies into an overarching Western epistemological framework. I do not have a solution to this problem, but part of dealing with it may be the development of a reflexive framework that systematizes the 'politics of representation' discussed in this chapter. In my view, there are at least three levels of the politics of representation: First of all, a theory or analysis may have an immanent political component, what Hayden White calls 'ideological implication' (see White 1973). Examples include Marshall Sahlins's cosmopolitical goal of anthropological scholarship as well as the emancipatory aims of Oceanic forms of scientific activity. The second level of the politics of representation concerns the various debates within scientific fields about the authority and legitimacy of making scientific statements. As the Sahlins–Obeyesekere controversy shows, these spaces of argumentation are increasingly multicultural and interdisciplinary. Furthermore, what counts as a 'scientific' debate at all is increasingly contested, because the controversy may touch on various political problems, such as the Hawaiian sovereignty movement. Finally, a scientific analysis may have specific political consequences that lie beyond scientific fields and epistemologies. For example, in the eyes of Hawaiian scholars the invention-of-tradition literature seriously eroded the Hawaiian sovereignty movements. To be sure, such a reflexive stance towards the politics of representation does not solve the problems concerning the emerging 'cultural studies for Oceania'. However, any social scientific analysis may benefit from incorporating a self-reflexive component that includes a consideration of these three deeply interrelated levels of the politics of representation, even if this effort may be interpreted as a further application of a universal epistemological framework to the research on non-Western life-worlds and histories.

References

Balawanilotu, Gina, Anurag Subramani and Robert Nicole. 2003. 'Review of R. Borofsky (ed.) *Remembrance of Pacific Pasts*', *Contemporary Pacific* 15(1): 198–203.

Biersack, Aletta (ed.). 1991. *Clio in Oceania: Toward a Historical Anthropology.* Washington, DC: Smithsonian Institution Press.

Bird-David, Nurit. 1992. 'Beyond "The Original Affluent Society": A Culturalist Reformulation' (with comments and reply), *Current Anthropology* 33(1): 25–47.

Borofsky, Robert. 1997. 'Cook, Lono, Obeyesekere, and Sahlins', *Current Anthropology* 38(2): 255–82.

———. 2000a. 'An Invitation', in Robert Borofsky (ed.), *Remembrance of Pacific Pasts: An Invitation to Remake History.* Honolulu: University of Hawai'i Press, 1–30.

———. (ed.). 2000b. *Remembrance of Pacific Pasts: An Invitation to Remake History.* Honolulu: University of Hawai'i Press.

Bourdieu, Pierre. 1977. *Outline of a Theory of Practice.* Cambridge: Cambridge University Press.

Burlingame, Burl. 2002. 'Hawaiian Studies Head Fears Hollywood Movies', *Honolulu Star-Bulletin.* Retrieved from http://starbulletin.com/2002/07/04/features/story4.html.

Diaz, Vicente M. and J. Kehaulani Kauanui. 2001. 'Native Pacific Cultural Studies on the Edge', *Contemporary Pacific* 13(2): 315–41.

Firth, Stuart. 2003. 'Future Directions for Pacific Studies', *Contemporary Pacific* 15(1): 139–48.

Friedman, Jonathan. 1988. 'No History Is an Island', *Critique of Anthropology* 8(3): 7–39.

Gegeo, David W. 2001a. '(Re)visioning Knowledge Transformation in the Pacific: A Response to Subramani's "The Oceanic Imaginary"', *Contemporary Pacific* 13(1): 178–83.

———. 2001b. 'Cultural Rupture and Indigeneity: The Challenge of (Re)visioning "Place" in the Pacific', *The Contemporary Pacific* 13(2): 491–507.

Gegeo, David W. and Karen A. Watson-Gegeo. 2001. '"How We Know": Kwara'ae Rural Villagers Doing Indigenous Epistemology', *Contemporary Pacific* 13(1): 55–88.

Gilman, Nils. 2003. *Mandarins of the Future: Modernization Theory in Cold War America*. Baltimore, MD: Johns Hopkins University Press.

Hanlon, David. 2003. 'Beyond "the English Method of Tattooing": Decentering the Practice of History in Oceania', *Contemporary Pacific* 15(1): 19–40.

Harder, Kelsie B. 1968. 'Coinages of the Type of "Sit-In"', *American Speech* 43(1): 58–64.

Hau'ofa, Epeli. 1993. 'Our Sea of Islands', in Eric Waddell, Vijay Naidu and Epeli Hau'ofa (eds), *A New Oceania: Rediscovering Our Sea of Islands*. Suva: University of the South Pacific, 2–16.

Hereniko, Vilsoni. 2000. 'Indigenous Knowledge and Academic Imperialism', in Robert Borofsky (ed.), *Remembrance of Pacific Pasts: An Invitation to Remake History*. Honolulu: University of Hawai'i Press, 78–91.

Horowitz, Irving L. (ed.). 1967. *The Rise and Fall of Project Camelot: Studies in the Relationship between Social Science and Practical Politics*. Cambridge, MA: MIT Press.

Huffer, Elise and Ropate Qalo. 2004. 'Have We Been Thinking Upside-Down? The Contemporary Emergence of Pacific Theoretical Thought', *Contemporary Pacific* 16(1): 87–116.

Hunt, Lynn (ed.). 1987. *The New Cultural History*. Berkeley: University of California Press.

Hviding, Edvard. 2003. 'Between Knowledges: Pacific Studies and Academic Disciplines', *Contemporary Pacific* 15(1): 43–73.

Kame'eleihiwa, Lilikala. 1992. *Native Land and Foreign Desires: Pehea Lā E Pono Ai? How Shall We Live in Harmony?* Honolulu: Bishop Museum Press.

———. 1994a. 'Review of G. Obeyesekere, *The Apotheosis of Captain Cook*', *Pacific Studies* 17(2): 111–18.

———. 1994b. 'Review of M. Sahlins, *Anahulu*', *Contemporary Pacific* 6: 214–18.

Kapferer, Bruce. 2000. 'Star Wars: About Anthropology, Culture and Globalisation', *Australian Journal of Anthropology* 11(2): 174–98.

Kumoll, Karsten. 2007. *Kultur, Geschichte und die Indigenisierung der Moderne: Eine Analyse des Gesamtwerks von Marshall Sahlins*. Bielefeld:Transcript.

Kuper, Adam. 1999. *Culture: The Anthropologists' Account*. Cambridge, MA: Harvard University Press.

Li, Victor. 2001. 'Marshall Sahlins and the Apotheosis of Culture', *New Centennial Review* 1(3): 201–87.

Linnekin, Jocelyn. 1991. 'Defining Tradition: Variations on the Hawaiian Identity', *American Ethnologist* 10: 241–52.

Marcus, George E. 1998. *Ethnography through Thick and Thin*. Princeton, NJ: Princeton University Press.

Menashe, Louis and Ronald Radosh (eds). 1967. *Teach-Ins: U.S.A.: Reports, Opinions, Documents*. New York: Praeger.

Merry, Sally E. 2003. 'Kapi'olani at the Brink: Dilemmas of Historical Ethnography in 19th Century Hawai'i', *American Ethnologist* 30(1): 44–60.

Meyer, Manu Aluli. 2001. 'Our Own Liberation: Reflections on Hawaiian Epistemology', *Contemporary Pacific* 13(1): 124–48.

Obeyesekere, Gananath. 1997. *The Apotheosis of Captain Cook: European Mythmaking in the Pacific*, 2nd edn. Princeton, NJ: Princeton University Press.

Reckwitz, Andreas. 2002. 'Toward a Theory of Social Practices: A Development in Culturalist Theorizing', *European Journal of Social Theory* 5(2): 243–63.

Robbins, Joel and Holly Wardlow (eds). 2005. *The Making of Global and Local Modernities in Melanesia: Humiliation, Transformation and the Nature of Cultural Change*. Burlington: Ashgate.

Sahlins, Marshall. 1958. *Social Stratification in Polynesia*. Seattle: University of Washington Press.

———. 1972. *Stone Age Economics*. New York: Aldine.

———. 1976. *Culture and Practical Reason*. Chicago: University of Chicago Press.

———. 1981. *Historical Metaphors and Mythical Realities: Structure in the Early History of the Sandwich Islands Kingdom*. Ann Arbor: University of Michigan Press.

———. 1985. *Islands of History*. Chicago: University of Chicago Press.

———. 1992. *Anahulu: The Anthropology of History in the Kingdom of Hawaii, Volume 1: Historical Ethnography*. Chicago: University of Chicago Press.

———. 1995. *How 'Natives' Think: About Captain Cook, For Example*. Chicago: University of Chicago Press.

———. 1997. 'Comment', *Current Anthropology* 38(2): 272–76.

———. 2000. *Culture in Practice: Selected Essays*. New York: Zone Books.

Salmond, Anne. 1993. 'Whose God, or Not?' *Social Analysis* 34: 50–55.

Smith, Linda T. 1999. *Decolonizing Methodologies: Research and Indigenous Peoples*. New York: Zed Books.

Solovey, Mark. 2001. 'Project Camelot and the 1960s Epistemological Revolution: Rethinking the Politics-Patronage-Social Science Nexus', *Social Studies of Science* 31(2): 171–206.

Thaman, Konai Helu. 2003. 'Decolonizing Pacific Studies: Indigenous Perspectives, Knowledge, and Wisdom in Higher Education', *Contemporary Pacific* 15(1): 1–17.

Tobin, Jeffrey. 1994. 'Cultural Construction and Native Nationalism: Report from the Hawaiian Front', *Boundary 2* 21(1): 111–33.

Trask, Haunani-Kay. 1985. 'Review of M. Sahlins, *Islands of History*' *American Ethnologist* 12(4): 784–87.

———. 1991. 'Natives and Anthropologists: The Colonial Struggle', *Contemporary Pacific* 3: 159–67.

White, Geoffrey M. and Ty Kawika Tengan. 2001. 'Disappearing Worlds: Anthropology and Cultural Studies in Hawai'i and the Pacific', *Contemporary Pacific* 13(2): 381–416.

White, Hayden. 1973. *Metahistory: The Historical Imagination in Nineteenth-Century Europe.* Baltimore, MD: Johns Hopkins University Press.

Wolf, Eric. 1969. *Peasant Wars of the Twentieth Century.* New York: Harper and Row.

———. 1982. *Europe and the People without History.* Berkeley: University of California Press.

———. 2001. *Pathways of Power: Building an Anthropology of the Modern World.* Berkeley: University of California Press.

Wood, Houston. 2003. 'Cultural Studies for Oceania', *Contemporary Pacific* 15(2): 340–74.

———. 2006. 'Three Competing Research Perspectives for Oceania', *Contemporary Pacific* 18(1): 33–55.

5

From the Spirit's Point of View: Ethnography, Total Truth and Speakership

Thomas G. Kirsch

In 1985, the president of the African Spiritual Churches Association (ASCA), Archbishop Nbumiso Ngada, published a booklet entitled *Speaking for Ourselves* in which he notes, with regard to African-initiated churches: 'Anthropologists, sociologists and theologians from foreign churches have been studying us for many years and they have published a whole library of books and articles about us ... The view from outside ... tends to distort the picture and to prevent the outsider from seeing the real point about what we believe and what we are doing' (Ngada 1985: 5). Calling into question the authority of Western representations of African churches, the Archbishop's text is illustrative of common reactions when 'they read what we write' (Brettell 1996). Moreover, it is an example of the idea that there exists a non-subjective truth behind empirical phenomena and that the latter should be represented accordingly; Archbishop Ngada states that 'the variety of sometimes contradicting opinions is itself an indication of how much we are being misunderstood' (Ngada 1985: 6).

But most important for this article, the Archbishop gives his argument a special twist in also pointing out that:

> there is one enormous omission throughout the whole history that has been written by outsiders. The work of the Holy Spirit throughout our history has simply been left out. The events of our history have been recorded as if everything could be accounted for simply by sociology and anthropology... We would like to write our own history *from the point of view of the Holy Spirit.* (ibid.: 16, emphasis added)

The Archbishop's choice of words is remarkable. In this passage, he does not write that the Holy Spirit should be 'taken account of' in African Christian historiography. Rather, the phrasing 'the point of view of the Holy Spirit' bears resemblance to Bronislaw Malinowski's famous expression 'the native's point of view' (Malinowski 1922: 25). The Holy Spirit here is not only a nonhuman actor whose presence in the history of African-initiated churches should be documented; instead, it is said to be a spiritual entity whose epistemological outlook should be deliberately adopted by the historian in the act of representation.

In the following, I look at the linkages between epistemology, representation and what I call the 'appellation of speakership' – that is, the self- and other-referential denotation of the identity of interlocutors.[1] In the first part of this article, I do this by picking up certain themes of Archbishop Ngada's reasoning and by examining how – in a contemporary Pentecostal-charismatic church in southern Africa – spiritual epistemologies and the idea of a speakership of the Holy Spirit shape the church secretaries' representational practices and, in doing so, give rise to written reports considered to be authored by the Holy Spirit. This discussion will then – in the second part of the article – provide us with the momentum to develop some preliminary reflections on what I take to be a meaningful inconsistency in linkages between anthropological epistemology and ethnographic representation.

As concerns the latter, the major dimensions of these linkages appear to be straight forward and can – in part following the debates on *Writing Culture* (Clifford and Marcus 1986) – be outlined as follows: First, anthropological epistemology is about 'the way we image others as human beings' (Moore and Sanders 2006: 19). Secondly, in ethnographic representations these imageries are translated into acts of signification which, thirdly, endow ethnographers with a speakership that – despite claims and attempts to the contrary – more or less inevitably rules out the speakership of those studied ethnographically.

Although I would assent to this (self-critical) description, I suggest that there is an important dimension which is not captured in it and which touches on the anthropological politics of difference: while it has become common in recent decades to reflect on the ethnographer's positionality, what to my understanding has not yet received sufficient attention outside specific thematic fields in anthropology – like linguistic anthropology and the anthropology of the person and the self (Carrithers, Collins and Lukes 1985; Morris 1994) – is how anthropologists deal with their interlocutors' self-identification as speakers.[2] This question is of particular interest in cases in which the anthropologist's

---

1   In this article, I follow the convention of using the term 'speaker' for 'anyone who speaks, signs, writes, or uses some other medium for language' (Johnstone 2000: 405). My use of the term 'speakership', in turn, is informed by its use in conversational analysis (e.g., Sacks, Schegloff and Jefferson 1974).

2   Among the notable exceptions to this is Marilyn Strathern's *The Gender of the Gift* (1988), which, according to Aletta Biersack, aims 'to use "the analytical categories in the symbolic systems of those studied" ... to develop an "endogenous" analysis of the status of women in Melanesia and the character of Melanesian sociality' (1991: 147).

interlocutors accentuate not human speakership, polyphony, multivocality, dialogism and the partialness of truths, but instead divine speakership, monophony, monovocality, monologism and total truth. In the religious life of the Zambian church with which I am concerned in this article, for example, churchgoers are not particularly interested in what a specific prophet communicates as a human being or in how other churchgoers comment on their prophetic revelations. In the final analysis, they straightforwardly want to learn what is disclosed by the Holy Spirit. Therefore, as concerns representational practices in this church, Archbishop Ngada's 'speaking for ourselves' at times takes the form of a spiritualist 'speaking by itself'.

The vexing question in cases like these is how the appellation of speakership by anthropologists (speaker = human being) is related to the self-appellation of speakership by the anthropologists' interlocutors (speaker = Holy Spirit). In other words, if we concur with Clifford Geertz that the meaning-making of those we study is of crucial importance for anthropology and that anthropologists should cling 'to the injunction to see things from the native's point of view' (Geertz 1984: 124), how do we integrate the ('native') speaker's self-referential positionality in how we reconstruct, translate or evoke what is their meaning-making from the viewpoint thus determined? Or, as Webb Keane has asked in a different thematic context: 'If the agency of others is predicated in part on their own beliefs and on the notions of agency immanent in their practices, how are we, if we are secular scholars, to reconcile their attribution of agency to divine subjects with our desire that they recognize that agency lies within their own hands?' (Keane 1997a: 690).

In considering these questions, one might turn to linguistic anthropology and studies on participation roles and the construction of social personae through language. Research based on the concept of 'voice', for example, 'directs attention to the diverse processes through which social identities are represented, performed, transformed, evaluated, and contested' (Keane 1999: 271). Erving Goffman's renowned decomposition of dyadic models of conversation, on the other hand, differentiates with regard to the notion of 'the speaker' between the animator, who is 'an individual active in the role of utterance production' (Goffman 1979: 17); the author, who is 'someone who has selected the sentiments that are being expressed and the words in which they are encoded' (ibid.); and the principal, who is 'someone whose position is established by the words that are spoken, someone whose beliefs have been told, someone who has committed himself to what the words say' (ibid.). While the animator is an analytical notion, the principal for Goffman represents 'a person active in some particular social identity or role, some special capacity as a member of a group, office, category, relationship, association, or whatever, some socially based source of *self-identification*' (ibid., emphasis added).

With regard to anthropology, however, it can reasonably be maintained that attempts 'to give presence to those who, if at all, are spoken of only in absentia'

(Fabian 2006: 145) usually tolerate only certain types of self-identification while other types become (taciturnly) ruled out. For example, nowadays there is widespread agreement among anthropologists that 'speakers are not unified entities, and [that] their words are not transparent expressions of subjective experience' (Keane 1999: 271). Instead, 'speakers' are mostly thought of as composites characterized either by heteroglossia – that is, 'multiple voices within a single speaker' (ibid.: 272) – or by the fact that 'participation roles entail aspects of a single voice distributed across several speakers' (ibid.). In both cases, the 'I' in discourse and practice is conceptualized as relational, either hybridized or dispersed, and simultaneously dissolved and extended into the social.

In the main I share this theoretical commitment to understanding speakership as a composite and would certainly not want to argue that animator, author and principal are always one (see Goffman 1979: 18). Yet, there exists a problem with this position which clearly comes to the fore in cases of what might be termed 'theoglossia', that is, speech which says of itself that it is a 'monologue of the Divine'. Anthropological selectivity with regard to the question of which appellation of speakership is tolerated and which is ruled out in such cases usually leads to a peculiar inconsistency in ethnographic representations: the propositions made from the interlocutor's 'native point of view' are represented by the anthropologist while the self-referential (divine) positionality, which for the interlocutor is foundational for the represented propositions, is neglected or rejected.

I suggest below that such inconsistencies – following the 'injunction to see things from the native's point of view', while in effect neglecting or rejecting the interlocutors' self-appellation of speakership – have (for good or ill) a certain strategic value for anthropologists because it allows them to deal with conflicting objectives in anthropology, namely to reach propinquity with the life-worlds of interlocutors while at the same time sustaining a distance to them. In other words, the performance of this double gesture provides a strategy for anthropologists to position themselves in the epistemological space between 'us' and 'them', 'ego' and 'alter', or – borrowing terms from linguistics – in the ambiguous space between 'realis modality' and 'irrealis modality'.[3]

Before going more deeply into this issue, let me first pursue an examination of theoglossia in the bureaucracy of the Spirit Apostolic Church, a Pentecostal-charismatic church in the rural areas of southern Zambia that was founded in the early 1990s and nowadays has a membership of more than a thousand, most of whom belong to the Bantu-speaking Tonga (Kirsch 1998, 2008). In this religious community, churchgoers have to assess whether, in specific instances of communal

---

3   In linguistics, 'realis' and 'irrealis' are grammatical modal constructions by which speakers indicate whether something is realistic or hypothetical. According to Suzanne Fleischman, the notion of 'irrealis' signals 'a speaker's lack of belief in or lack of commitment to (a) the reality, realization, or referentiality of an event or sequence of events predicated in an utterance; (b) the realization of an agent's wishes, hopes, or intentions, as expressed in the proposition of an utterance; (c) the authenticity of an utterance or chunk of discourse (i.e. a sequence of utterances); or (d) ... the "canonicity" or normalcy of a discourse or of a communicative situation' (Fleischman 1995: 522).

religious practice, it is a 'human being' (*muntu*) who is speaking or the 'Holy Spirit' (*muya usalala*). As we shall see, ascriptions of speakership to the Holy Spirit are here connected to spiritual epistemologies which, in turn, shape how (written) representations in the name of this speakership are produced and interpreted.

Divine Assignments

The contemporary phenomenon of theoglossia in the bureaucracy of the Spirit Apostolic Church can be said to have as its historical precursor the early Western missionaries' awe in relation to God's lettered words (see also Hofmeyr 2002). For the missionaries, the Bible simultaneously represented the divine assignment for evangelization, the essential script for proselytism, a means for its enactment and the pivotal symbol of self-representation. Translating, printing and distributing literature were among the preoccupations of most mission societies that entered the African continent in the nineteenth and twentieth centuries (Switzer 1984; Etherington 2005). Literacy, in its turn, represented for Protestant missionaries the conditio sine qua non for converting 'pagans' into Christians and for promoting among Africans 'the ascendance of the reflective, inner-directed self: a self, long enshrined in Protestant personhood' (Comaroff and Comaroff 1991: 63).

That the envisaged transformation of African selves was only partially successful becomes evident when examining the literacy practices – that is, 'behaviour and conceptualisations related to the use of reading and/or writing' (Street 1984: 12) – among members of Pentecostal-charismatic churches in the area of my research, the Gwembe Valley in southern Zambia (cf. Colson 1960; Scudder 1962).[4] At present, about a hundred years after Western missionaries had first set up churches and schools in this region (Luig 1997), the majority of people in the Gwembe Valley have acquired at least rudimentary reading and writing skills, and many make use of these skills when visiting one of the numerous Christian denominations in their neighbourhood.

However, the literacy practices pursued in several of these churches differ in significant regards from what the early Western missionaries had envisaged. Most importantly, this difference has to do with notions concerning the spiritual permeability of the human body: In most African-initiated churches, the working of spiritual entities is ascribed an important role. In addition, many of them take it for granted that spiritual entities can take possession of a human being by, for example, entering their body. This idea of the spiritual permeability of the body implies that 'personhood' (Jackson and Karp 1990) might not (only) enshrine a human self but (temporarily also) spiritual entities. Thus, on the one hand, spirits can become part of

---

4   For other works on literacy practices, see, for example, Street (1993, 1995, 2001); Barton (1994); Baynham (1995); Besnier (1995); Barton and Hamilton (1998); Barton, Hamilton, and Ivanic (2000); Wogan (2001); Collins and Blot (2003); Ahearn (2004).

a person's identity, a process that in many cases forms the basis for processes of charismatic legitimation (Kirsch 1998, 2002).[5] On the other hand, the notion of a spiritual permeability of the body imbues religious reading and writing practices with epistemological premises (cf. Street 2003: 1) that in important ways differ from those projected by the early Protestant missionaries. 'Spirituality' – that is, a person's privileged association with the Holy Spirit – in the Pentecostal-charismatic church examined below was seen as a means by which a whole range of religious activities could be successfully accomplished, such as healing and prophecy, but also a divinely ordained reading of the Bible and, most important for what follows, secretarial work.

Overall, in the Spirit Apostolic Church, the conjunction of discourses and practices of spirituality with those of church administration took the form of what I have elsewhere called 'bureaucracy in the Pentecostal-charismatic mode' (Kirsch 2008). This bureaucracy was based on the idea that the work of church secretaries was linked to questions of spiritual agency (cf. Keane 1997b: 65–66; Ahearn 2001: 112–13), with spirituality being seen as either a precondition or a result of secretarial activities.

Bureaucrats in the Pentecostal-charismatic Mode

Besides a variety of other church offices, such as deacon, pastor and treasurer, all congregations of the Spirit Apostolic Church (SAC) had church secretaries (*balembi*). Most of them had been selected from among the ordinary congregation and had then received brief instructions from the former secretary or one of the other church elders. In some cases, they had merely been shown samples of previous secretarial work so that they could understand its overall pattern. Henceforth they were left alone with the task, for none of the branch members usually cared how the secretary carried out his job. Only once a year did the branch secretaries receive any supervision from the general secretary of the church. Having collected the service reports for a whole year, the secretaries sent them to the church's headquarters, where they were examined with a view to their accuracy, handwriting and formal organization. During the General Meeting, which was normally held in July of each year, secretaries were then given feedback and further instructions in how to improve their work.

---

5   Martin Sökefeld has observed, with regard to the anthropological debate on 'non-Western' selves: 'In this debate, the Western self is represented as an instance of the individual's providing it with boundedness, relative autonomy and independence, reflexivity, and the ability to pursue its own goals' (Sökefeld 1999: 418). In conceptualizing 'non-Western' selves, in turn, 'the Western self was taken as the starting point and the non-Western self was accordingly characterized as its opposite: unbounded, not integrated, dependent, unable to set itself reflexively apart from others' (ibid.). My argument concerning the spiritual permeability of human bodies is certainly not intended to resonate with this problematic approach. Although 'individualism' has often been associated with Christianity (Dumont 1985), it is all too clear that in Western Christianity there also exist traditions in which human–spirit relations and the embodiment of spiritual entities are of the utmost importance. Therefore, the characterization above does not pertain specifically to African Christianity. In a similar vein, David Maxwell has recently remarked, with regard to 'African Independent Churches', that 'it is precisely those phenomena in independency which [have often been] interpreted as most exotic or African – prophecy, divine healing, exorcism, glossolalia – which can be shown to be the most Christian part of the churches' (Maxwell 1997: 144).

The selection and training of secretaries was thus an apparently unremarkable and mundane affair. The initial instructions in secretarial tasks were given informally, and supervision by the main board only evolved on a long-term basis. All the same, the question of who might be an appropriate person to act as a secretary involved a series of locally important issues. My interlocutors agreed that some basic literacy skills were indispensable for anyone to be invested with the office. They differed, however, in the extent to which they emphasized reading and writing: whereas some insisted that secretaries should be proficient readers and writers from the start, others maintained that rudimentary literacy skills would suffice at the beginning and that the Holy Spirit would subsequently improve their skills on the job. The latter view agreed with the suggestion made by some that literacy might be acquired through divine guidance. Several of my interlocutors knew of cases in their neighbourhood where somebody who had never attended school suddenly developed the ability to read and write after joining a Christian congregation. In such cases, it was stated, the Holy Spirit had assisted them in becoming proper Christians by providing them with the ability to read the Bible themselves (cf. MacGaffey 1983: 114; Hofmeyr 2002: 449–50). A similar idea was voiced concerning the secretaries of the Spirit Apostolic Church. If someone was truly willing to serve God as a secretary, the Holy Spirit would not let him fail because of a lack of literacy skills; rather, God would help him become a secretary.

In describing the criteria for proper secretarial work, my interlocutors also disagreed over whether, and to what extent, secretaries should already be endowed with spirituality from the start. Some suggested that the office of church secretary was of too low a rank to presuppose spirituality; thus, anyone could initially be invested with the post. However, the very activity of documenting the religious practices of spiritually able church leaders would itself bring the secretary closer to God. Observing and recording spiritually inspired activities would thus increase his personal association with the Holy Spirit and soon make the incumbent a proper – that is, divinely ordained – secretary. Others saw spirituality as a prerequisite for being appointed a church secretary, asserting that only a spiritually able secretary would be able to appreciate the main points (*makani mapati*) of an ongoing religious practice. Ordinary secretaries, I was told, would either write down too much or simply choose the wrong aspects. In order to know what exactly had religious importance at any particular point in time, one had to be endowed with divine power.[6]

There are some parallels here with local discourses on the need for spirituality if one is to preach. Those who interpreted the secretary's career as representing spiritual evolution induced by observing and documenting religious proceedings compared them to members of the laity attentively witnessing sermons and other

---

6   However, similar to what Matthew Engelke has stated for prophets among the Masowe weChishanu Church in Zimbabwe, there was nothing in the demeanor of secretaries 'filled with the Holy Spirit that an outsider would have been able to recognize as possession' (Engelke 2004: 83).

religious activities in order to be spiritualized themselves. The other view, which understood spirituality as a prerequisite for proper secretarial work, drew a parallel with the activities of preachers and prophets. Similar to preachers, who had to be spiritually able in order to select the right Bible verses, selective observation and documentation by church secretaries presupposed the assistance of the Holy Spirit (see also Kirsch 2008). And since this task required one to proceed from a rather diffuse perception of the whole (*kulanga*) to a concentrated focusing (*kubona*) on the significant aspects, the secretary could also be compared to the prophet. This assessment to some extent corresponded with the locally prevailing notion of the verbal inspiration of the Bible. Like the 'authors' of the Old and New Testaments, it was assumed, what the secretary wrote had to be divinely guided.[7]

Other debates in my area of research concerned the topic of God's book in heaven. God was depicted as the primordial bookkeeper, dwelling in heaven with a large bound volume close by him. There were disagreements, however, concerning, first, whether God had already written down everything that will happen in the future or whether he was continuously taking written records of what he observed; and secondly, how the relationship between God's book and the secretaries' writings might adequately be described. Some members of the SAC insisted that God's book was 'closed'; that is, that God had written down everything that would happen on earth a long time ago. The church secretaries thus produced nothing other than an exact copy of what had previously been projected in God's book. God knew beforehand what would happen and how the secretaries would record it. Other members of the SAC considered God's book to be still 'open'; that is, God was said to be continuously monitoring and recording human activities. This interpretation led to two further but different conclusions. For some of my interlocutors, there was an invisible connection between God's book in heaven and the writings of spiritually able secretaries. With the assistance of the Holy Spirit, it was assumed, such secretaries would produce identical documentation to what God was producing in heaven. The monitoring and recording were thus depicted as evolving simultaneously in heaven and on earth. And since the writings in these two dimensions were identical, one knew what was written in God's book by reading the writings of a spiritually endowed secretary. The other conclusion was that the secretaries and their writings were themselves among the objects of God's monitoring. According to this interpretation, God observed and documented how the secretaries were carrying out their task. Whereas the first explanation assumed that spiritually able secretaries would work side by side with God, the latter made

---

7   The notion of 'divine secretaries' is well known from the history of European Christianity. Adriaanse gives an
    example from the Lutheranism and Calvinism of the sixteenth and seventeenth centuries. Here, a new conception
    of divine inspiration had been introduced, which referred less to the inspired contents of the Bible than to 'the way
    in which Scripture had been written down. The humans who had played a role in this putting-on-record had by no
    means acted for themselves. God was the causa principalis of Scripture; they were merely its causa instrumentalis, or,
    to borrow the expression of the Lutheran theologian Joh. Gerhard (1582–1637), "Dei amanuenses, Christi manus
    et Spiritus sancti tabelliones sive notary": "the clerks of God, the hands of Christ and the scriveners or secretaries of
    the Holy Spirit"' (Adriaanse 1998: 322).

commitment and accuracy by secretaries a criterion upon which they would be judged by God on the Day of Judgement. God's book would thus differ from a secretary's writings by including judgements on it.

Divine Representations

Taken together, in the Spirit Apostolic Church (SAC), human agency in the secretaries' representational work was something to be avoided. The secretarial representations of church life were instead expected to adopt the viewpoint of a powerful divine Other. Therefore, in a way comparable to anthropologists who claim to (re)present the 'objectively given' and, in doing so, to incorporate in their writings 'the native's point of view', here it was claimed that secretarial representations depict the 'divinely given' and that they do so because church secretaries act as mediums for 'the spirit's point of view'.

Given these findings, one might expect that there was something gnostic about the secretaries' writings and that the hermeneutics pursued in the SAC may have privileged the 'spiritual sense' over the 'literal'. However, this was definitely not the case. The writings of the secretaries had a spiritual foundation, but they were in no way spiritualistic in nature. First, even those church members who assumed that the office of secretary presupposed spiritual ability did not consider the material products of secretarial work to be endowed with any divine power in themselves. The agendas, reports and lists they drew up were treated like mundane writings. They were not shown any particular reverence, and the reading or consultation of such documents was generally undertaken with a view to their pragmatic value. Secondly, what was actually depicted in the products of secretarial work followed highly conventionalized and formalized patterns.

Let us examine the latter point with a view to a particular type of secretarial writing. Besides being scheduled in writing, the SAC's weekly services were documented in 'Service Reports'. To some extent, these reports resembled the reports of church meetings. Headed by the relevant date, the words 'Sunday Service Report' and occasionally the name of the branch, these reports outlined the course of the service in chronological order. The Sunday service in the church headquarters on 5 May 1999, for example, was documented as follows:

10:16	Choir songs
10:48	Opening song
	~~Gondingo~~
10:55	Prayer
10:54	Gondingo[8]

---

8   *Gondingo* is a type of passionate dancing in front of the altar in which anyone present can participate.

10:57   Thanking time. Only three people given chance to thank our Lord.

11:50   The time was given to Mr [Alaster] the D. Evangelist, who opened the book of Issaiah 66: 10

12:15   The time was given to Mr [Kiran] our G. Secretary who opened the book of second Corinthias 4: 1

12:57   The time was given to our General treasurer Mr [Esnart]. And he opened the Book of 2 Corinthias 9: 1 and verse 8 and verse 9. And the service was ended by G. Secretary.

13:48   The service ended at 13:48
         Attendance is 138
         Money offering is K 1,290[9]

The report was arranged according to the exact times when things occurred. Whereas the scheduling of agendas for church meetings was usually rounded up to the nearest quarter of an hour, in the service reports an attempt was made to record the time accurately. In some cases, the reports had minor inconsistencies in the temporal order; for example, in the case above, the prayer is noted before the *gondingo*, although the time indicated suggests that the order had actually been other way round. Such inconsistencies were mostly due to secretaries' difficulties in simultaneously participating in the service and recording it in writing. If secretaries tried to keep pace with social time, 'mistakes' were almost unavoidable and (idiosyncratic) abbreviations often indispensable. Yet although the reports of Sunday services were therefore provisional in form, they were not corrected or rewritten later on. This is in contrast to the service reports of church meetings, which were occasionally subjected to a considerable *post hoc* reworking.

The crossed-out word 'Gondingo' in the above report at first glance appears to represent another instance of secretarial 'error'. Yet, seen in light of the actual proceedings of the service and of widely shared views of the secretary's role, the peculiarity of this 'mistake' becomes evident. After the opening song had been sung, one of the choir members initiated a *gondingo* by singing the first lines of a popular hymn, soon followed by some other members joining him and dancing. Sitting beside the secretary, I noticed that he wrote down the word 'Gondingo' at this point. It quickly emerged, however, that a majority of the churchgoers were reluctant to join in. Two minutes later, the *gondingo* faded away, and everyone returned to his place. Before starting the next paragraph of his report, the secretary crossed out the word 'Gondingo' which he had previously written down. After the service, a group of church elders assessed the event. They explained to me that the first attempt to start a *gondingo* had lacked the inspiration of the Holy Spirit. The fact that the secretary had eventually omitted it from his report on the

---

9   In this and the following excerpts from the church secretaries' writings in English language, verbatim quotations are not corrected orthographically and 'mistakes' are not indicated, since this would mean submitting their writings a posteriori to orthographic standardization.

service, they asserted, clearly indicated his personal spiritual capacity: any ordinary secretary would not have recognized that this had not been a properly spiritual *gondingo* and would have accordingly recorded it in writing. Knowing what to include and what not to include in a report on a service thus presupposed that one had spirituality.

At their briefest, the Sunday service reports of 1999 took the form of chronological lists in which the kind of activity was merely indicated by one or two words. In other reports – like the one above – some parts of the service were described in complete sentences that reproduced conventionalized formulae – for example, by starting with the phrase 'Time for' (*Chiindi*). Both types of documentation had in common the fact that they usually did not give any indication concerning who had written them. Although the reports frequently mentioned the church offices and personal names of the main actors in the service, those who kept records of the proceedings did usually not record their own names. This self-denial was mostly connected with the view mentioned earlier that secretaries were guided by the Holy Spirit. Since reports of services were widely assumed to be authored by the divine being using the secretaries as its vessel, any secretary adding his own signature would have been dismissed as making a narcissistic and misguided gesture.

All the same, this conception of spiritual authorship was not shared by everybody. As already described, opinions differed when it came to the question of the secretaries' spirituality. Some church elders maintained that being endowed with the powers of the Holy Spirit was no prerequisite for being a secretary. A former General Secretary of the SAC, for instance, clearly distinguished between 'gifts of God' (*cipego caleza*) and secretarial tasks. What is remarkable here is that, in contrast to most other secretaries, he included personal comments when writing reports of church meetings. In May 1993, when describing a baptism, he commented: 'That was a nice day to see those who were sick that they are okay and they began to praise God singing together. The praising of God was forward because some were born again all their different diseases finished'.[10] These personal additions are unusual when compared to the rather depersonalized tone of most other service reports. In imbuing his report with a sermonizing gesture, the former General Secretary was using writing as a means of worshipping God. Occasionally, he even concluded a report of a meeting with the words: 'The End. Amen. Good Night', before placing his signature at the bottom of the page.

These annotations of 1993 were admittedly made in reports of church meetings which, in subsequent years, were also generally more elaborate than the routine Sunday service reports of individual congregations. During church meetings in 1999, it was the General Secretary who was in charge of the reporting. Since he usually did not attend all the services at a meeting lasting several days, he

---

10   Agenda for the Pentecost Meeting in Simanzi, 16 May 1993.

was assisted at times by some of the branch secretaries, who alternated in making records in their own personal school exercise books. At the end of each day, the General Secretary collected the different records in order to collate them into one official report. This process entailed making considerable alterations: hastily taken-down drafts were transformed into carefully phrased stories about what had happened on that particular day. As well as modifications in wording and graphic layout, the initial record of the proceedings was frequently recast so that it approximated to an ideal version of 'how it should have been'.

Whether the former General Secretary's reports of meetings in 1993 had been generated by this sort of (collaborative) writing cannot be determined in retrospect. Yet a comparison between the service reports of the former General Secretary and those of most later secretaries is telling: whereas the former General Secretary often imbued his reports with a personalized undertone, the reports of 1999 tended to be depersonalized. At first sight, this seems to suggest that the SAC had undergone a process of increased formalization in the form of 'institutionalization'. I would argue, however, that there is another way of interpreting this. Denying that secretarial work presupposes spirituality, as the former General Secretary did, went along with claims to authorship and a rather personalized style of writing. Linking secretarial activities to the works of the Holy Spirit, on the other hand, as most later secretaries did, implied a denial of authorship and brought about a rather depersonalized style of writing. Conceptions of spirituality, on the one hand, and conceptions of organizational institutionalization, on the other, therefore agreed in their particular effects, namely the formalized appearance of reports of services.

What was actually depicted in the reports of 1999 thus followed highly formalized and apparently conventionalized patterns. Framed by specifications concerning the beginning and the end of the event, the reports of the weekly services usually recorded the singing of the choir, the 'thanking time', the prayers and sermons, the collection and the *gondingo* dancing. The reports of meetings of the SAC contained the same features, while also dealing with those parts that alone were enacted during the meetings, such as baptism and the allocation of certificates. In addition, both types of reports indicated how many churchgoers had been present during a particular event, as well as the amount of money in the collection. When the service reports were checked by the General Secretary, it was especially these latter features and the themes of the sermons that were examined.

The numbers attending the service were taken as an indication of the evangelical success or failure of the respective branch leaders. If, over time, there was a noticeable falling off in attendance, senior church elders usually increased their supervision. Figures for the amounts received in the collections were added up in the church headquarters in such a way that the amount that had to be passed on from the branches to headquarters was specified. And lastly, the themes of the sermons were checked by the General Secretary in order to determine whether the teaching of the branches was in line with the senior church leaders' expectations.

In most reports, however, the themes of the sermons were merely indicated by mentioning the Bible verses that they had dealt with. The Sunday service report for 14 March 1999 for the congregation of Siamujulu, for example, stated: 'Time was given to Mr. [Obed] the deacon who opened the book of Mathew 16: 24' and 'Time was given to Mr. [Alfeo] Branch Secretary who opened the book of Issaiah 59: 2'. It was not recorded how in particular the preachers had interpreted these Bible verses. Only in rare cases was additional information given. This mostly took the form of short summaries: 'Time was given to the District Evangelist [Kedrick] him he gave … the book from Deut 30: 11–18. This book says obeying these commandments is not something beyond your strength and reach'.[11] Others repeated the headline of the respective chapter in the Chitonga Bible: A preaching was 'from the book of Mat 26: 26 which the headline says 'The paska of Jesus'.[12] Such commentaries represented short annotations rather than detailed descriptions. What was actually said during a sermon was not recorded in detail.

The monitoring of the branches' sermons through the General Secretary thus related almost entirely to the Bible verses indicated, not to how they had been interpreted and commented on. As with numbers attending and money collected, supervision of preaching was reduced very nearly to a list of Bible verses. This had certain parallels in how other religious activities were documented, since it was also unusual to describe the contents of prayers and of the hymns sung by the choirs. The headquarters of the SAC accordingly did not attempt to overcome their (relative) 'ignorance' with regard to the religious practices of the branches. Bible verses served as shorthand symbols that effectively prevented potential conflicts in matters of Biblical interpretation.

Of particular importance, however, is the fact that some features of the services and meetings were omitted altogether. In going through the 'archived' documents for the years 1991 to 1999, I found only rare references to glossolalia or prophesying. Although all the Sunday services of the SAC I attended in 1993, 1995, 1999 and 2001 had been characterized by such Pentecostal-charismatic manifestations of spirituality, they were generally not recorded in the service reports, nor were cases of divinations or cases of spiritual healing. In the case of the Sunday services, this certainly had to do with the fact that the latter activities only took place after the public event had ended – that is, after most participants had left the church. To some extent, divination and healing thus appeared to be detached from the public part of Sunday services. All the same, such activities presupposed the presence of patients, as well as of several witnesses and church elders. They were also considered to be activities of the utmost importance in terms of weekly religious practice and for the church in general. It therefore seems surprising that they were omitted from the Sunday reports, and even more

---

11 Service Report of 9 May 1999, Siamujulu.
12 Report of the Good Friday Meeting in Nanyenda, 3 April 1999.

surprising that prophesies uttered in the course of services were also not mentioned (for an analysis of why this is so, see Kirsch 2008: 227–42).

Up to this point, my considerations have focused on 'representation as praxis' (Fabian 1990) in a religious setting in which secretarial reports are (for the most part) seen to be linked to the speakership of the Holy Spirit. The examination of interactions and processes revolving around the secretarial production of service reports has provided a number of interesting constellations of which, in now winding up my ethnographic examination, I want to highlight two. First, while secretarial work was assumed to require spiritual guidance, spiritual activities like prophecy and healing were normally left out of the records. In other words, the Holy Spirit was understood to author secretarial reports that ruled out the Holy Spirit actually manifesting itself in the writings. Secondly, the above exhibits a fascinating inversion when compared to reflexive discussions in contemporary anthropology: while debates on *Writing Culture* have made clear, among other things, that positivist and objectivist ethnographies are not exempt from exploiting allegorical language (Clifford 1986), spiritual epistemologies in the Spirit Apostolic Church give rise to written representations with a very positivist and objectifying aura about them.

However, as was noted above, cases like the Spirit Apostolic Church also confront anthropology with a peculiar epistemological and representational problem that concerns the ethnographic 'appellation of speakership'. This is discussed in the remainder of this article.

Who Speaks?

There is a passage from a play by Samuel Beckett (1967) which is given a prominent place in Michel Foucault's essay 'What is an Author?' and which states with peculiar ambiguity: "'What does it matter who is speaking", someone said, "what does it matter who is speaking"' (Foucault 1979: 101).

In contemporary anthropology, most agree that it does matter 'who is speaking' and, therefore, most anthropologists consider it important to take account of their interlocutors' status, social positions or subject positions, to mention a few of the terms used. There is less unanimity, however, in how to identify the touchstones of this positionality. How is it informed by, for example, age, class, colour or gender? What role, for instance, do context, situationality, dialogic interaction and intersubjectivity play in setting the (moving) coordinates of those speaking? And how are we to call our interlocutors – social actors, persons, role-takers, selves, subjects, individuals, dividuals, – interlocutors? In short, ethnographic representations of Others who speak with us – 'representation' being here used in the two senses of the word: *darstellen* (re-presenting), and *vertreten* (speaking for) – not only take account of what is spoken but inevitably (although often implicitly) give a definition of what it is that is said to be speaking.

Such specifications are based on epistemological, theoretical and methodological assumptions and have ethico-political implications by, say, stressing either the 'agency' or the 'patiency' of interlocutors or by inadvertently 'assimilating' or 'othering' them. Yet, whatever form these appellations of speakership take, there is always something foundational about them because they specify positionalities from which interlocutors' utterances are said to be coming.[13] For example, it certainly makes a difference whether interlocutors are portrayed as knowing, volitional and intending agents, as representatives of 'a culture' or as subjects nested within certain discursive formations.[14] It makes a difference whether we depict them to be 'egocentric'/'individualistic' or 'sociocentric'/'relational' or to be characterized by a hybrid of both (Mageo 1995: 283). And it makes a difference whether our interlocutors are said to be 'partible' (Strathern 1988) and 'fractal' persons (Wagner 1991) or, instead, to have more or less 'integrated' and 'coherent' (Strauss 1997) selves. Each portrayal lays the groundwork for the interpretation of what is said by interlocutors, but does so in markedly different ways.

With regard to secretarial work in the Spirit Apostolic Church, for example, one can think of several options in naming speakership. Without even attempting to be exhaustive and persuasive, let me briefly and rather crudely rehearse three of them. It would be very plausible to suggest, for instance, that my Zambian interlocutors were not the originators of the discourses and practices described above, because neither the Christian idea of the Holy Spirit nor the bureaucratic genres which they produce originally come from Zambia. Pointing out that my findings reflect processes of transnational diffusion that in Southern Africa began with historic Western mission societies, this line of reasoning could then define my interlocutors to be 'subjects' in the Foucauldian sense of the word. Alternatively, it could be argued, with a view to the reports of church meetings, that the production of these reports entails intertextuality on a medium scale because, as described above, different records of one and the same church service were normally collated into one final (and official) report. On this basis, it could then be concluded – in a somewhat Durkheimian fashion – that this procedure aggregates a variety of 'native points of views' into a collectively composed 'sacred point of view'. And, ending this brief excursion into interpretative options, anthropologists could inquire into how, as intending social actors, church elders

---

13 Of course, this argument owes much to Marcel Mauss, who writes about 'the idea of "person" (*personne*)' and 'the idea of "self" (*moi*)': 'Each one of us finds it natural, clearly determined in the depths of his consciousness, completely furnished with the fundaments of the morality which flows from it' (Mauss 1985: 1).

14 For example, Sherry Ortner remarks, in her critical reading of anthropological writings on 'resistance': 'The whole point of the poststructuralist move is to de-essentialize the subject, to get away from the ideological construct of "that unified and freely choosing individual who is the normative male subject of Western bourgeois liberalism" .... And indeed the freely choosing individual is an ideological construct, in multiple senses – because the person is culturally (and socially, historically, politically, and so forth) constructed; because few people have the power to freely choose very much; and so forth. The question here, however, is how to get around this ideological construct and yet retain some sense of human agency, the capacity of social beings to interpret and morally evaluate their situation and to formulate projects and try to enact them' (Ortner 1995: 186).

establish and stabilize religious authority through discourses and practices of 'bureaucracy in the Pentecostal-charismatic mode'.

There is plausibility in all of these options. Yet, there is also something crucial missing concerning the appellation of speakership. How am I to deal with what I was repeatedly told when doing fieldwork among members of the Spirit Apostolic Church, namely that some of my interlocutors would talk to me not as human beings but as the Holy Spirit? This implied that what I as an ethnographer recorded as versions of the 'natives' points of view' according to the understanding of religious practitioners was at times recounted to me from 'the spirit's point of view'. Should I, one might ask, stick to the injunction 'to see things from the native's point of view' and therefore include the Holy Spirit in my list of interlocutors? Or should I partly suspend this injunction by arguing that these are cases in which 'human beings' are claiming that what they are saying is actually spoken by the 'Holy Spirit'?

Of course, studies of spirit possession (Boddy 1994) and of interactions between 'human host', 'spirit' and 'intermediaries' have for a long time been struggling with the tangled question of what kind of being-ness to attribute to spiritual entities. As is well known, accounts in this regard have included, among other things: the proposition that claims to spirit possession are instrumentalities in power struggles; the idea that spirits are idioms, symbols or symptoms that articulate specific socio-cultural, historical and psychosocial experiences; and the suggestion that they represent dissociated facets of the possessed person's self. To different degrees, these interpretations have taken account of emic explanations in relation to phenomena of spirit possession. When seen as a whole, however, there often remains a certain predicament in analyses of spirit possession which is nicely captured in Erika Bourguignon's suggestion that 'We need to know [emic] explanations, but we cannot stop there; they cannot be our own explanations' (Bourguignon 2004: 558).

The explanatory problem lies in the fact, first, that spirit possession pertains to entities which in many parts of the world are considered to be 'quintessential "others"' (Boddy 1988: 15) and which are nevertheless integral to people's life-worlds. Secondly, this culminates in the fact that, for most anthropologists, this 'integrated Otherness' remains something quintessentially Other. It is arguably for this reason that 'there seems to be an overall agreement [among anthropologists] that there is "something" in possession trance that refuses to be signified. No matter how clever our attempts to break the mystery, something about possession remains enigmatic, unapproachable, resisting the word, displaying the failure of representation' (van der Port 2005: 151).

Certainly, there are anthropologists who criticize their colleagues for the tendency 'to rationalize away the native claim that spirits exist' (Turner 1993: 9) and who insist that anthropological works should appreciate the reality of spirits and take account of them as agencies in their own right. Such criticism recalls what Dipesh Chakrabarty has critically pointed out with regard to the field of history: 'We have two systems of thought, one in which the world is *ultimately*, that is, in the final analysis, disenchanted, and the other in which the humans are not the only meaningful agents. For the purpose of writing history, the first system, the secular, translates the second into itself' (Chakrabarty 1997: 35, original emphasis).

However, it appears to me that, in most ethnographic representations of spirit possession, authors perform a double gesture by, on the one hand, exhibiting spirits' effects on the people and situations studied while, on the other hand, leaving little doubt that, in the final analysis, spirits are not 'really real' (Geertz 2001: 11) for themselves. My examination of above how the Holy Spirit shapes secretarial work in the Spirit Apostolic Church is an apparent illustration of this. Further examples abound, as in Michael Lambek's now classic analysis of Mayotte spirit possession as a system of communication:

> A [the spirit] wishes to send a message to B [the host]. Instead of doing so directly, A passes the message to C (in this case, the anthropologist) who, in turn, passes it on to B. Thus, instead of A ➜ B, we have A ➜ C ➜ B. What is remarkable about this, from the viewpoint of a Westerner, is that A and B are actually the same 'person'. Thus, the process observed is one of 'autocommunication', and the transmission by way of C seems entirely unnecessary. But in the Mayotte view, of course, A and B are separate, discrete individuals. In such a case, transmission via C appears reasonable, even if not, at first sight, most efficient. (Lambek 1980: 321; cf. Lambek 1981)

Another graphic example of the anthropological difficulties involved in dealing with issues of spiritual speakership is a recent article by Adeline Masquelier which has as its protagonists a woman from Niger named Zeinabou and a *zar* spirit named Rankasso. Masquelier writes:

> By 'allowing' *Rankasso* to voice *her* kumya (shame) and articulate verbally the roots of *their* conflict, *Zeinabou* was creating a therapeutic mode of remembering and dealing with a problem *she* could not handle consciously and '*on her own*'. Through an examination of *Zeinabou's* struggles to emancipate *herself* from the various human and spiritual agencies *she* felt controlled by, I explored how the confession '*she*' made while *she* was in the throes of possession provided a critical space of reflexivity and retrospective elaboration at the same time that it authorized further strategies for the redefinition of *her selfhood and subjectivity*. (Masquelier 2002: 60, 71, emphases added).

Appellation of Speakership

Following conventional anthropological reasoning, one can suggest that it is necessary in ethnographic cases like the above to distinguish between the speaker's identity and the self-identification of the speaker. Borrowing terms from linguistics, one would then deduce that (entranced) spirit possession is a case of a 'human being' (realis modality) who claims to speak as a 'spirit' (irrealis modality) from whom enunciations originate (irrealis modality). Reasonings of this kind, which relativize what is ethnographically represented, are common in cultural and social anthropology as in other social sciences and humanities, and there is nothing really problematic about them as long as the irrealis is presented in the form of indirect or reported speech.

However, since there is no epistemological foundation which can help us in making a nonarbitrary decision in this regard, the question remains how to determine which of our interlocutors' self-identifications we treat as realis and which as irrealis. In Masquelier's example above, for instance, what the anthropologist's interlocutor marks to be a speakership in the realis modality – namely that it is a 'spirit' which is speaking – is put into the irrealis modality by the anthropologist. But would – should? – anthropologists do the same if a speaker were to self-identify as, say, a 'member of this or that religious community'?

Of course, anthropologists can refuse to make such decisions by consistently putting all self-identifications either into the realis or the irrealis. Yet, given anthropological conventions, scholars treating all of their interlocutors' self-identifications as realis run the danger of being reproached for credulous naivety and 'going native'; scholars treating them consistently as irrealis, on the other hand, risk being accused of unwillingness to become involved with their interlocutors' social constructions of meaning and reality. It is therefore clear that these two approaches are extremes and that ethnographic representations more commonly combine realis and irrealis modalities. But if this is so, what are the characteristics of such combinations?

As mentioned in the foregoing, I suggest that ethnographic combinations of realis and irrealis are often characterized by an asymmetry in that only specific types of speakership are accepted as realis, while other self-identifications as speakers are disregarded or in effect put into the irrealis. In the latter case, the propositions made from the 'native point of view' are represented by the ethnographer, while the self-referential positionality which, for the speaker, is foundational for the represented propositions is simultaneously neglected or rejected.

I suggest that inconsistencies of this sort are symptoms of an ambiguity that is typical of cultural and social anthropology and that is rooted in its conflicting objectives to participate *and* observe; that is, in its aim to reach propinquity with the life-worlds of our interlocutors while simultaneously sustaining a distance to them. Some strategies in handling these conflicting objectives are well known. One of them is to distinguish distinct phases of the research process, the first being devoted to the anthropologist's 'immersion' into the ethnographic field, the second to a reflexive self-distancing from it. Another strategy – one that is often associated with Evans-Pritchard's (1937) work on witchcraft among the Azande – is to differentiate types of rationality: one type (the Azande's) that is intelligible and rational *if* one accepts certain sociocultural premises, the other (the anthropologist's) that follows objective and universal standards.

My considerations in this article point to the existence of another widespread strategy in dealing with the anthropologists' conflicting objectives as outlined above. This strategy consists, on the one hand, in sticking to the (propinquity-seeking) 'injunction to see things from the native's point of view' while, on the other hand, maintaining a (distance-seeking) viewpoint by excepting the interlocutor's self-identification as speaker from what is reconstructed, translated or evoked in the name of 'the native's point of view'. In other words, this anthropological strategy of balancing propinquity-in-distance, which, depending on the power differentials involved, can have undesirable but also desirable consequences in moral and political terms, means presenting the contents of what is said by interlocutors as realis under the condition that their self-appellation of speakership is treated as irrealis.

A Word in Conclusion

There is a certain danger that anthropologists who aim at giving voice to Others become so preoccupied with notions of multivocality, dialogism and the heteroglossic partialness of truths that they fail to notice that some of these Others are happily seeking monovocality, monologism and the total truth of theoglossia.

In this chapter, I have tried to demonstrate, by way of an example from the anthropology of religion, that there is a peculiar inconsistency between the ethnographic claim to represent the 'native point of view' and certain tendencies in how self-identifications of interlocutors are dealt with by anthropologists. I have rehearsed the argument that this inconsistency has, for good or ill, a certain strategic value for those working in the field of anthropology because it allows them to come to terms with the conflicting objective in anthropology to seek propinquity-in-distance. It helps anthropologists in positioning themselves in the epistemological space between 'ego' and 'alter', and 'realis' and 'irrealis', an ambiguous space that is characteristic for much of cultural and social anthropology.

Given the ethnographic example I have used to set out my argument, the objection might be raised that anthropology is a secular social science which should not (or cannot) subscribe to the idea of nonhuman agency and the reality of spirits. It could also be argued that 'propinquity-in-distance' is plainly fundamental to the social sciences, the humanities and to human heuristics per se. Or one can point out that my own ethnographic representation above is in no way an exception to what I have tried to diagnose in more general terms. In coining the term 'theoglossia', for example, I have conjoined my account of realis

('-glossia') with my agnostic account of irrealis ('theo-'). In doing so, I have striven to retain something of my interlocutors' sense of total truth while indicating that I personally sense this truth to be only partial.

I would not want to counter these objections. If I had subscribed to my interlocutors' self-appellation of spiritual speakership, I certainly would have drafted another representation. If I had done so, it would have been for readers to decide whether or not my self-appellation as 'anthropologist' is acceptable to them. After all, 'our ways of making the Other are ways of making ourselves' (Fabian 1990: 756). But if it is true, as I am inclined to believe, that the epistemological space of cultural and social anthropology unfolds in the middle ground between ego and alter, then it is important to reflect on which strategies anthropologists employ in order to reach and balance this middle ground. This article has attempted to contribute to such reflection by arguing, in a manner of speaking, that Gayatri Spivak's renowned question 'Can the subaltern speak?' (Spivak 1988) should be broadened to include another question; namely, 'How do our representations reflect our interlocutors' self-appellation of speakership?'

References

Adriaanse, Hendrik Johan. 1998. 'Canonicity and the Problem of the Golden Mean', in Arie S. Kooij and Karel van der Toorn (eds), *Canonization and Decanonization*. Leiden: Brill, 313–30.

Ahearn, Laura M. 2001. 'Language and Agency', *Annual Review of Anthropology* 30: 109–37.

———. 2004. 'Literacy, Power, and Agency: Love Letters and Development in Nepal', *Language and Education* 18(4): 305–16.

Barton, David. 1994. *Literacy: An Introduction to the Ecology of Written Language.* Oxford: Blackwell.

Barton, David and Mary Hamilton. 1998. *Local Literacies: Reading and Writing in One Community.* London: Routledge.

Barton, David, Mary Hamilton and Roz Ivanic (eds). 2000. *Situated Literacies: Reading and Writing in Context.* London: Routledge.

Baynham, Michael. 1995. *Literacy Practices: Investigating Literacy in Social Contexts.* London: Longman.

Beckett, Samuel. 1967. *Stories and Texts for Nothing.* New York: Grove Press.

Biersack, Aletta. 1991. 'Thinking Difference: A Review of Marilyn Strathern's *The Gender of the Gift*', *Oceania* 62(2): 147–54.

Besnier, Niko. 1995. *Literacy, Emotion, and Authority: Reading and Writing on a Polynesian Atoll.* Cambridge: Cambridge University Press.

Boddy, Janice. 1988. 'Spirits and Selves in Northern Sudan: The Cultural Therapeutics of Possession and Trance', *American Ethnologist* 15(1): 4–27.

————. 1994. 'Spirit Possession Revisited: Beyond Instrumentality', *Annual Review of Anthropology* 23: 407–34.

Bourguignon, Erika. 2004. 'Suffering and Healing, Subordination and Power: Women and Possession Trance', *Ethos* 32(4): 557–74.

Brettell, Caroline (ed.). 1996. *When They Read What We Write: The Politics of Ethnography*. Westport, CT: Bergin and Garvey.

Carrithers, Michael, Steven Collins and Steven Lukes (eds). 1985. *The Category of the Person: Anthropology, Philosophy, History*. Cambridge: Cambridge University Press.

Chakrabarty, Dipesh. 1997. 'The Time of History and the Times of Gods', in Lisa Lowe and David Lloyd (eds), *The Politics of Culture in the Shadow of Capital*. Durham, NC: Duke University Press, 35–60.

Clifford, James. 1986. 'On Ethnographic Allegory', in James Clifford and George E. Marcus (eds), *Writing Culture: The Poetics and Politics of Ethnography*. Berkeley: University of California Press, 98–140.

Clifford, James and George E. Marcus (eds). 1986. *Writing Culture: The Poetics and Politics of Ethnography*. Berkeley: University of California Press.

Collins, James and Richard K. Blot. 2003. *Literacy and Literacies: Texts, Power, and Identity*. Cambridge: Cambridge University Press.

Colson, Elizabeth. 1960. *The Social Organisation of the Gwembe Tonga*. Manchester: Manchester University Press.

Comaroff, Jean and John L. Comaroff. 1991. *Of Revelation and Revolution: Christianity, Colonialism, and Consciousness in South Africa*. Chicago: University of Chicago Press.

Dumont, Louis. 1985. 'A Modified View of Our Origins: The Christian Beginnings of Modern Individualism', in Michael Carrithers, Steven Collins and Steven Lukes (eds), *The Category of the Person: Anthropology, Philosophy, History*. Cambridge: Cambridge University Press, 93–122.

Engelke, Matthew. 2004. 'Text and Performance in an African Church: The Book, "Live and Direct"', *American Ethnologist* 31(1): 76–91.

Etherington, Norman. 2005. 'The Missionary Writing Machine in Nineteenth-Century KwaZulu Natal', in Jamie S. Scott and Gareth Griffiths (eds), *Mixed Messages: Materiality, Textuality, Missions*. New York: Palgrave Macmillan, 37–50.

Evans-Pritchard, Edward E. 1937. *Witchcraft, Oracles and Magic among the Azande*. London: Oxford University Press.

Fabian, Johannes. 1990. 'Presence and Representation: The Other and Anthropological Writing', *Critical Inquiry* 16(4): 753–72.

————. 2006. 'The Other Revisited: Critical Afterthoughts', *Anthropological Theory* 6(2): 139–52.

Fleischman, Suzanne. 1995. 'Imperfective and Irrealis', in Joan Bybee and Suzanne Fleischman (eds), *Modality in Grammar and Discourse*. Amsterdam: John Benjamins, 519–51.

Foucault, Michel. 1979. 'What is an Author?' in Paul Rabinow (ed.), *The Foucault Reader*. London: Penguin Books, 101–20.

Geertz, Clifford. 1984. '"From the Native's Point of View": On the Nature of Anthropological Understanding', in Richard A. Shweder and Robert A. LeVine (eds), *Culture Theory: Essays on Mind, Self, and Emotion*. Cambridge: Cambridge University Press, 123–36.

———. 2001. *Available Light: Anthropological Reflections on Philosophical Topics*. Princeton, NJ: Princeton University Press.

Goffman, Erving. 1979. 'Footing', *Semiotica* 25(1): 1–29.

Hofmeyr, Isabel. 2002. 'Dreams, Documents and "Fetishes": African Christian Interpretations of The Pilgrim's Progress', *Journal of Religion in Africa* 32(4): 440–56.

Jackson, Michael and Ivan Karp (eds). 1990. *Personhood and Agency: The Experience of Self and Other in African Cultures*. Washington: Smithsonian Institution Press.

Johnstone, Barbara. 2000. 'The Individual Voice in Language', *Annual Review of Anthropology* 29: 405–24.

Keane, Webb. 1997a. 'From Fetishism to Sincerity: On Agency, the Speaking Subject, and their Historicity in the Context of Religious Conversion', *Comparative Studies in Society and History* 39(4): 674–93.

———. 1997b. 'Religious Language', *Annual Review of Anthropology* 26: 47–71.

———. 1999. 'Voice', *Journal of Linguistic Anthropology* 9(1/2): 271–73.

Kirsch, Thomas G. 1998. *Lieder der Macht: Religiöse Autorität und Performance in einer afrikanisch-christlichen Kirche Zambias*. Münster: Lit-Verlag.

———. 2002. 'Performance and the Negotiation of Charismatic Authority in an African Indigenous Church of Zambia', *Paideuma* 48: 57–76.

———. 2008. *Spirits and Letters: Reading, Writing and Charisma in African Christianity*. Oxford: Berghahn Books.

Lambek, Michael. 1980. 'Spirits and Spouses: Possession as a System of Communication among the Malagasy Speakers of Mayotte', *American Ethnologist* 7(2): 318–31.

———. 1981. *Human Spirits: A Cultural Account of Trance in Mayotte*. Cambridge: Cambridge University Press.

Luig, Ulrich. 1997. *Conversion as a Social Process: A History of Missionary Christianity among the Valley Tonga, Zambia*. Münster: Lit-Verlag.

MacGaffey, Wyatt. 1983. *Modern Kongo Prophets: Religion in a Plural Society*. Bloomington: Indiana University Press.

Mageo, Jeannette M. 1995. 'The Reconfiguring Self', *American Anthropologist* 97(2): 282–96.

Malinowski, Bronislaw. 1922. *Argonauts of the Western Pacific: An Account of Native Enterprise and Adventure in the Archipelagoes of Melanesian New Guinea*. London: Routledge and Kegan Paul.

Masquelier, Adeline. 2002. 'From Hostage to Host: Confessions of a Spirit Medium in Niger', *Ethos* 30(1/2): 49–76.

Mauss, Marcel. 1985. 'A Category of the Human Mind: The Notion of Person; The Notion of Self', in Michael Carrithers, Steven Collins and Steven Lukes (eds), *The Category of the Person: Anthropology, Philosophy, History*. Cambridge: Cambridge University Press, 1–25.

Maxwell, David. 1997. 'New Perspectives on the History of African Christianity', *Journal of Southern African Studies* 23(1): 141–48.

Moore, Henrietta and Todd Sanders. 2006. 'Anthropology and Epistemology', in Henrietta Moore and Todd Sanders (eds), *Anthropology in Theory: Issues in Epistemology*. Malden, MA: Blackwell, 1–22.

Morris, Brian. 1994. *Anthropology of the Self: The Individual in Cultural Perspective*. London: Pluto Press.

Ngada, Nbumiso. 1985. *Speaking for Ourselves*. Braamfontein: Institute for Contextual Theology.

Ortner, Sherry. 1995. 'Resistance and the Problem of Ethnographic Refusal', *Comparative Studies in Society and History* 37: 137–93.

Sacks, Harvey, Emanuel Schegloff and Gail Jefferson. 1974. 'A Simplest Systematics for the Organization of Turn-Taking in Conversation', *Language* 50(4): 696–735.

Scudder, Thayer. 1962. *The Ecology of the Gwembe Tonga*. Manchester: Manchester University Press.

Sökefeld, Martin. 1999. 'Debating Self, Identity, and Culture in Anthropology', *Current Anthropology* 40(4): 417–47.

Spivak, Gayatri Chakravorty. 1988. 'Can the Subaltern Speak?', in Cary Nelson and Larry Grossberg (eds), *Marxism and the Interpretation of Culture*. Chicago: University of Illinois Press, 271–313.

Strathern, Marilyn. 1988. *The Gender of the Gift: Problems with Women and Problems with Society in Melanesia*. Berkeley: University of California Press.

Strauss, Claudia. 1997. 'Partly Fragmented, Partly Integrated: An Anthropological Examination of "Postmodern Fragmented Subjects"', *Cultural Anthropology* 12(3): 362–404.

Street, Brian. 1984. *Literacy in Theory and Practice*. Cambridge: Cambridge University Press.

——— (ed.). 1993. *Cross-Cultural Approaches to Literacy*. Cambridge: Cambridge University Press.

———. 1995. *Social Literacies: Critical Approaches to Literacy in Development, Ethnography and Education*. New York: Longman.

——— (ed.). 2001. *Literacy and Development: Ethnographic Perspectives*. New York: Routledge.

———. 2003. 'What's "New" in New Literacy Studies? Critical Approaches to Literacy in Theory and Practice', *Current Issues in Comparative Education* 5(2): 1–14.

Switzer, Les. 1984. 'The African Christian Community and its Press in Victorian South Africa', *Cahiers d'Études Africaines* 24(96): 455–76.

Turner, Edith. 1993. 'The Reality of Spirits: A Tabooed or Permitted Field of Study', *Anthropology of Consciousness* 4(1): 9–12.

van der Port, Mattijs. 2005. 'Circling around the Really Real: Spirit Possession Ceremonies and the Search for Authenticity in Bahian Condomblé', *Ethos* 33(2): 149–79.

Wagner, Roy. 1991. 'The Fractal Person', in Maurice Godelier and Marilyn Strathern (eds), *Big Men and Great Men: Personifications of Power in Melanesia*. Cambridge: Cambridge University Press, 159–73.

Wogan, Peter. 2001. 'Imagined Communities Reconsidered: Is Print-Capitalism What We Think It Is?' *Anthropological Theory* 1(4): 403–18.

6

Interlogue: 'Writing Cultures' and the Quest for Knowledge

Rozita Dimova

❧

It is impossible to overestimate the effect that the volume *Writing Culture* (Clifford and Marcus 1986) has had on shaping my modes of thinking. Serving as a powerful conceptual 'sieve', this book opened up new epistemological horizons, articulating and formulating research questions during and after my doctoral studies. Moreover, the volume has assisted me in applying and questioning theoretical frameworks during my subsequent academic engagements. It was through Clifford and Marcus's ideas that I managed to make sense of my own position, to assess my own academic trajectory, and acknowledge its relevance and value in drawing important theoretical conclusions based on my own involvement with 'the science' of anthropology.

After completing my BA at the Institute of Ethnology in Skopje, Macedonia, I had the extraordinary opportunity to continue my graduate studies at the Department of History at the Central European University (CEU) in Budapest, Hungary. The encounter with historical studies on households in Europe and especially the Balkans – an area where extended households have possibly persisted longer than in other parts of the Western world – left a significant impact on me and drew me into the domain of the politics of knowledge production. Indeed, works by Western anthropologists and family historians on the *zadruga* – the extended household prevailing in the Balkans well into the twentieth century, where several generations live together – were my initiation into the realm of family history and Western social anthropology, and I was genuinely (and innocently) excited, and flattered, by the existence of these studies and by the interest of Western anthropologists in the Balkans and Macedonia. But

I was also puzzled by the fact that I had neither read nor heard anything on *zadruga* in Macedonia and the Balkans during my BA studies or during fieldwork for my BA thesis in northern Macedonia, although I carried out research in several households where three generations lived under the same roof. Moreover, some of these books argued that the *zadruga* was most prevalent in Macedonia (Mosely 1976; Kaser 1997). I assumed, however, that my ignorance and the absence of any literature on this topic was due to the isolation of the Institute for Ethnology in Skopje, which, when I was a student there, belonged to the Department of Geography and the Faculty for Natural Sciences and was marked by a complete absence of comprehensive literature and competent teachers. The people in the remote mountainous village where I had carried out my research claimed that they had neither heard the term nor had they seen these 'specific' families although most of the households in the village were definitely extended, with two or three generations living together. I assumed that they where detached from 'civilization', and that *zadruga* probably did not reach their world or they were not able to recognize that type of family.

My encounter with Maria Todorova's book *Balkan Family Structure and the European Pattern: Demographic Developments in Ottoman Bulgaria* (Todorova 1993) provided me with important answers to this dilemma. Her fierce critique of the ideology and politics underlying the production of knowledge on the Balkans in the domain of history and family studies, and the invention of *zadruga* as an ideological construct, revealed how a region can be represented in academic discourse. After attending a conference in Budapest in May 1994, at which Maria Todorova suggested additional references on *zadruga* written by anthropologists and ethnographers, I was determined to pursue further the issue of *zadruga* and its reality or even non-existence. This propelled me to apply for a scholarship for the M.Phil. programme at the Department of Social Anthropology at Cambridge University, U.K., which, after reading the works of Peter Laslett and his Cambridge Group for the History of Population and Social Structure, seemed a perfect place to continue my investigation and explore the ideology behind the *zadruga* phenomenon. The critical sprouts planted by Maria Todorova's rigorous work resulted in my attempt to write my MA thesis at CEU comparing the *zadruga* in Macedonia with the Hungarian joint family. At Cambridge, similarly, I wrote an M.Phil. thesis on women in the extended-family *zadruga*. I mention these two texts because they are part of the context of my own quest for answers into the questions that were raised by my encounter with literature on the Balkans and Macedonia written by foreign scholars.

In addition to realizing my inability to write well, draft an argument and engage different readings on a topic (given that during the BA programme in Skopje the students were never encouraged to write and most of our exams were oral), the Cambridge period involved a painfully uncomfortable encounter with ethnographies written in the British social anthropology tradition, which struck me in terms of their detailed descriptions as well as their overwhelming neglect of the larger context. After undergoing an intensive period of questioning the Western construction of the Balkans and the *zadruga*, and rereading the powerful work of Todorova, writing an essay on the details of sacrificial rites among the Lugbara and Azande, as described by Middleton (1960) and Evans-Pritchard (1976), without being encouraged to question the wider context by my structural-functionalist tutor, was painful indeed.[1]

After arriving at Stanford in 1997 to continue my doctoral studies, and encountering the introduction to *Writing Culture*, assigned in one of the required core courses on anthropological theory and methods, I felt pieces of puzzle were finally coming together. By revealing the power of language in how we write about cultures, how we represent different people, and where we stand in the process of representation, I realized that language had a much deeper role in the process of anthropological research and should not be treated merely as a tool with which we describe our observations.

Clifford's argument is that the old tradition and ideology had crumbled and given rise to a new way of looking at 'culture', a way based on new assumptions that culture is a composition of 'seriously contested codes and representations'. Such an argument made perfect sense in revealing that the poetics and politics of writing are inseparable, that anthropological science is part of historical and linguistic processes, and that written cultural descriptions should be viewed as 'properly experimental and ethical' (Clifford 1986: 2). Authorial authority becomes a thing of the past and writing involves an invention of cultures.

The subsequent courses I attended and the assigned books that I read – ones which developed the arguments laid out in *Writing Culture* – further pushed me to pay close attention to the process of writing, but also to identify the need to be attentive to power relations among the people where I conducted research, and to contextualize my own position and understand the dynamics generated by the interaction of different agents in the field.[2] The attitudes of people in my field site at the time I began fieldwork in Macedonia in June 1999 were marked by deep anti-American feelings following the three-month NATO bombardment of Serbia. The daily flights of military jets traversing the territory of Macedonia encouraged many people to detest the imperial role of the U.S. in world politics and condemn its hypocritical global political stance. This factor came to constitute an important analytical category in my field research and also shaped much of how I proceeded with my work during the writing-up period. Fieldwork and the analysis accompanying the writing-up period opened up a whole new way of addressing issues relevant to the people I worked with and for my own concerns as a 'native' anthropologist studying in the U.S. As Rosaldo has observed:

---

1   The M.Phil. programme at Cambridge at the time when I studied was structured in such a way that each student was allocated a tutor and the essays written throughout the year were read and marked by the assigned tutor alone. With all due respect, a significant number of the lecturers (and a couple of the professors too) were forerunners in introducing new theoretical streams into social anthropology as a discipline.
2   See, e.g., Lorde (1984), Rich (1986), Gilroy (1993) and Hall (1999).

The transformation of anthropology showed that the received notion of culture as unchanging and homogeneous was not only mistaken but irrelevant ... Marxist and other discussion groups sprang up. Questions of political consciousness and ideology came to the foreground. How people make their own histories and the interplay of domination and resistance seemed more compelling than textbook discussions of system maintenance and equilibrium theory. Doing committed anthropology made more sense than trying to maintain the fiction of the analyst as a detached, impartial observer. (Rosaldo 1989: 36)

I believe that the power of the ethnographic text to become a social critique of the differential access to (and the distribution of) power remains the most significant contribution of *Writing Culture* and the volumes that followed its publication (see especially Marcus and Fischer 1986). Understanding one's own position, the relationship towards different hierarchies of power, the politics embedded in the production of knowledge and the importance of emotions in writing an anthropological account, have indeed shifted the way in which one's personal experience is present in ethnographic writing and have questioned prevailing academic canons. Anthropological writing, probably more than any other academic discipline, had been entangled in the skirmishes of postmodern (and other) discussions about 'the crisis of representation and the imperialism of knowledge' (Stockton 2002). The legitimacy of the field – which rested on the premise that the writer is an objective transcriber of other cultures, without taking into account the force of their own subjectivity – has been challenged and the issue of objectivity has been complicated by criticisms from within (by those who argued that an anthropologist is a detached observer with a capacity to provide an objective grasp of a particular culture) and outside the discipline of anthropology (other disciplines which were firmly rooted in positivistic paradigms). Such criticism calls into question not only the history of the field but also the very premises that authorize it (ibid.).

Despite criticism of the new way of doing anthropology – classifying it mainly as an experimental and postmodernist genre or confined primarily to the domain of writing, hence utterly detached from the people anthropologists study – the discipline has undergone an evident shift.[3] I would argue that the liberating impact of politicizing the discipline and expanding its analytical repertoire by including race, ethnicity, gender and other categories that address minority issues (or positioning identity politics at the core of anthropological inquiry) was cardinal. Although one could argue that these analytical categories existed prior to *Writing Culture*, the discussions (and reactions to it) triggered by the book marked 1986 as a year when identity politics became indispensable in

---

3   See, e.g., Hastrup (1987, 1992a, 1992b), Olivier de Sardan (1992) and Richardson (1996).

anthropological analysis. This trend had also been occurring within many other disciplines in the social sciences and the humanities, introducing the political dimension into academia by transforming the previous tradition of area studies, to a large extent a cold-war phenomenon. The transformation of academia, however, was quickly assimilated by the changing nature of the post-cold war logic of late capitalism, which has become reflexive and able to incorporate the critics directed at it without being really affected or destabilized.

The politicization of the domains of minority issues has initiated a process of the depoliticization of economy, has paved the way for late capitalism (especially its U.S. version) to integrate multiculturalism and rests on political correctness and difference instead of the previous 'melting pot' ideology. By politicizing identity, especially ethnicity and gender, late (transnational or post-Fordist, according to Harvey 1990) capitalism, personified in large transnational corporations, has been preventing a politicization of economy and hence has been preventing any successful (unified) struggle along class lines effective enough to transgress or subvert the late capitalist 'tolerant' society. The Left has been gradually been losing its power to launch effective criticism and has become unable to provide any transgression of reflexive liberal-democratic late capitalism (or second modernity; see Žižek 1999: 357). Multiple voices (ethnic, gay, religious minorities, and so on) have been demanding their rights at the same time revealing that the social sciences, critical theory (including critical anthropology emerging after 1986) have been complicit in giving the contemporary capitalist regime its reflexive nature, where the distinction between the Left and the Right is very blurred, and where explicit critique easily loses its potential to initiate real political change. Many of us are now faced with the question of how to proceed and how to address issues of social inequality and justice without fuelling the late-capitalist regime that rests on the power of critical and multiple voices. It seems that we are facing another crossroads: as in the late 1980s and early 1990s, when anthropologists tried to articulate new, more relevant ways of *writing cultures* in the post-cold war world, we should now again rethink the link between the experimental and the ethical maybe by strategically reclaiming authorial authority and by going back to the founding 'fathers' of the social sciences who recognized the centrality of class and economy as crucial and to, and part of implementing, real social change.

References

Clifford, James. 1986. 'Introduction: Partial Truths', in James Clifford and George E. Marcus (eds), *Writing Culture: The Poetics and Politics of Ethnography*. Berkeley: University of California Press, 1–26.

Clifford, James and George E. Marcus (eds). 1986. *Writing Culture: The Poetics and Politics of Ethnography*. Berkeley: University of California Press.

Evans-Pritchard, Edward E. 1976. *Witchcraft, Oracles, and Magic among the Azande*, rev. edn. Oxford: Clarendon Press.

Gilroy, Paul. 1993. *The Black Atlantic: Modernity and Double Consciousness*. Cambridge, MA: Harvard University Press.

Hall, Stuart (ed.). 1999. *Representation: Cultural Representations and Signifying Practices*. London: Sage.

Harvey, David. 1990. *The Condition of Postmodernity: An Enquiry into the Origins of Cultural Change*. Oxford: Blackwell.

Hastrup, Kirsten. 1987. 'The Reality of Anthropology', *Ethnos* 52(3/4): 287–300.

———. 1992a. 'Out of Anthropology: The Anthropologist as an Object of Dramatic Representation', *Cultural Anthropology* 7(3): 327–45.

———. 1992b. 'Writing Ethnography: State of the Art', in Judith Okely and Helen Callaway (eds), *Anthropology and Autobiography*. London: Routledge, 116–33.

Kaser, Karl. 1997. 'Family and Kinship in the Balkans: A Declining Culture?' *Ethnologia Balkanica* 1: 150–55.

Lorde, Audre. 1984. *Sister Outside: Essays and Speeches*. Trumansburg, NY: Crossing Press.

Marcus, George E. and Michael M.J. Fischer. 1986. *Anthropology as Cultural Critique: An Experimental Moment in the Human Sciences*. Chicago: University of Chicago Press.

Middleton, John. 1960. *Lugbara Religion: Ritual and Authority among an East African People*. London: Oxford University Press.

Mosely, Philip. 1976. *Communal Families in the Balkan: The Zadruga*. Notre Dame, IN: University of Notre Dame Press.

Olivier de Sardan, Jean-Pierre. 1992. 'Occultism and the Ethnographic "I": The Exoticising of Magic from Durkheim to "Postmodern" Anthropology', *Critique of Anthropology* 12(1): 5–25.

Richardson, Miles. 1996. 'Blurring the Line Between Fact and Fiction', *American Anthropologist* 98(3): 623–24.

Rich, Adrienne. 1986. *Blood, Bread, and Poetry: Selected Prose.* New York: Norton.

Rosaldo, Renato. 1989. *Culture and Truth.* Boston: Beacon Press.

Stockton, Sharon. 2002. 'The Multiple Discourses of Anthropology: Ethnographic Reportage, Theoretical Critiques, and Classroom Pedagogy', *American Behavioral Scientist* 45(7): 1103–24.

Todorova, Maria. 1993. *Balkan Family Structure and the European Pattern: Demographic Developments in Ottoman Bulgaria.* Washington, DC: American University Press.

Žižek, Slavoj. 1999. *The Ticklish Subject.* London: Verso.

7

Language Matters:
Reflexive Notes on Representing
the Irish Language Revival
in Catholic West Belfast

Olaf Zenker

Since the inception of anthropology as a modern discipline, ethnography has been its core business. Ethnography has thereby been linked from early on to both what 'natives' say and to what they do. Hence, in *Argonauts of the Western Pacific*, one of the classics of modern anthropology, Bronislaw Malinowski (1922: 1–25) characterized the work of an ethnographer as entailing the 'collection of ethnographic statements' as well as the observation of 'types of behaviour'. Methodologically, this required a prolonged period of fieldwork, participant observation and sufficient familiarity with the local vernacular. Based on this ethnographic method, ethnographic texts on 'their' lives became possible. Ethnographic facts thus emerged quite self-consciously at the intersection of representing and non-representing practices of both the 'natives' and the ethnographer. Yet the textual focus of such classical ethnography, trying to 'grasp the native's point of view' (ibid.: 25) in 'their' linguistic expressions and behaviour, confined the ethnographer's linguistic expressions and behaviour to the realm of ethnography as methodology. In other words, language mattered, and it mattered a lot indeed; but it was 'their' language that mattered and hence needed to be acquired for ethnography as a methodology to work. As to 'ethnographies as texts' (Marcus and Cushman 1982), however, 'our' language was not a matter of interest, but rather the insignificant means to convey 'their' reality. As it is well known, *Writing Culture* (Clifford and Marcus 1986) engendered a debate radically questioning such a position and highlighting instead the poetics and politics entailed in any act of representation. Now 'our' language mattered, and it mattered very much indeed.

In this chapter,[1] I explore some ways, in which both 'their' language practices and my own can be seen to matter, and I reflect on how the relationship between these two matters can be conceptualized. I will do so firstly by describing and analysing an empirical case from the North of Ireland[2] concerning the Irish language revival in Catholic West Belfast since the mid twentieth century, in which 'their' language has become an issue of contestation for the local actors themselves. I will focus, particularly, on two interrelated, yet somewhat conflicting levels: on the one hand, the ways in which and the extent to which the Irish language has been practised in local daily life; and, on the other hand, the ways in which the Irish language itself has been locally represented. In a second step, I will reflect both on the insights gained from this empirical example and on some of my own assumptions that have been implied in the process of representing this case study. Drawing on philosophies of ordinary language, particularly those of Ludwig Wittgenstein and John L. Austin, I will suggest that the ethnographic enterprise can and should be understood as an act of cultural translation, based on symmetrical mechanisms and means of representation, between two different 'language-games'. Aside from existing differences between everyday and scientific language usages, to which I refer briefly, this symmetry consists mainly in the mutual constitution of meaning and truth in the actual use of language, the simultaneous production and observation of facts at the intersection of words and the world, and the inevitable striving for truth and plausibility within factual representations. Against this backdrop, I will argue that language – the 'words' – do indeed matter in the sense that better and more reflexive representations require a sufficiently sensitive language competence in *both* 'their' and 'our' language-games. At the same time, however, 'the world' also needs to be confronted persistently with 'their' as well as 'our own' alleged truths, so that the combination of these two endeavours ultimately produces truer and more plausible representations.

❦

---

1   Apart from its presentation at the workshop 'Beyond *Writing Culture*' at the Max Planck Institute for Social Anthropology, Halle/Saale, in 2006, this text, in an earlier German-language version with the title 'Fakten schaffen durch Sprache', was also presented at the annual meeting of the Max Planck Society in 2005 in Rostock-Warnemünde, specifically in the symposium of the Humanities Section 'Die Konstruktion der Fakten durch die Sprache'. For constructive comments on both occasions, I am indebted to various workshop participants and critical readers, most notably Vincent Crapanzano, Frank Donath, Markus Höhne, Thomas Kirsch, Karsten Kumoll, Boris Nieswand, Stephen Reyna, Richard Rottenburg, Günther Schlee and Julia Zenker.

2   In the politicized Northern Irish context, the use of words referring to the region is itself a matter of dispute, purportedly reflecting one's own ideological position on the conflict. In this text, I thus use the terminology of my Irish Catholic Nationalist/Republican informants in Catholic West Belfast, who prefer terms such as 'the North of Ireland', 'the six counties' or the 'occupied counties' to 'Northern Ireland' or 'the province'.

Before turning to the Irish language revival in Catholic West Belfast, let me situate the ethnographic case in a wider context. Until the present day, the society of the North of Ireland has remained, by and large, deeply divided, despite some fundamental political changes. The latter include the de facto end during the 1990s of more than twenty years of violent conflict, the Good Friday Agreement of 1998, the decommissioning in 2005 of what the Independent International Commission on Decommissioning (IICD) then described as 'the totality of the IRA's arsenal' (IICD 2005), and the subsequent cooperation between the Democratic Unionist Party (DUP) and Sinn Féin in a devolved assembly since 2007. This persisting social divide can be characterized in terms of three dichotomies pertaining respectively to religious background, ethnic identity and political aspirations. The first dichotomy separates members of the local population into those with 'Catholic' versus 'Protestant' backgrounds. The second dichotomy distinguishes between those who see themselves as 'Irish,' who are mostly Catholic, and those who see themselves as 'British,' who are mostly Protestant. The third involves a distinction between most local Irish, who can be described as 'Nationalist/Republican' and who aspire to a united Ireland, and the majority of local British 'Unionists/Loyalists', who advocate the maintenance of the United Kingdom with Great Britain. Despite a degree of cross-cutting, there is a far-reaching homology between 'Catholic,' 'Irish' and 'Nationalist/Republican,' on the one hand, and 'Protestant,' 'British' and 'Unionist/Loyalist,' on the other (see Trew 1998; Coulter 1999: 10–22; Zenker 2006).

In cities like Belfast or Derry, this social divide finds expression in a pronounced residential segregation. As data from the last Northern Ireland Census of 2001 indicates, West Belfast consists predominantly of a Protestant area to the North and a larger Catholic area to the South.[3] Given the long history of violence, Catholic and Protestant West Belfast have, to a considerable extent, been physically divided by protection walls, or so-called 'peace lines'. Although interaction across this social and geographical divide has increased somewhat in the course of the peace process (and while exceptions obviously do exist), social contact and close personal relations are still more common among people with the same religious and ethno-political background. For this reason, it is not surprising that during the fourteen months of ethnographic fieldwork I

---

3   The delineation of 'West Belfast' based on the Northern Ireland Census 2001 is somewhat ambiguous. Belfast is officially subdivided into the four Parliamentary Constituencies 'Belfast East', 'North', 'South' and 'West'. However, in the 2001 Census the constituency 'Belfast West' consisted of seventeen electoral wards, four of which at its most south-western extent did not belong to Belfast but to nearby Lisburn on the level of Local Government Districts (NISRA 2006: Look-up Table (Ward to Parliamentary Constituency) KS). In other words, only thirteen of the seventeen wards of the constituency 'Belfast West' also belonged to the local government district of Belfast. Taking these thirteen wards as an approximation for 'West Belfast', it can be observed that the three northernmost wards were predominantly Protestant, whereas the remaining ten wards to the south were basically Catholic in the sense that in each case more than 80 per cent of the respective ward populations had either a Protestant or Catholic religious background. See NISRA (2006: Table KS07b), which details 'Community Background: Religion or religion brought up in' at ward level.

undertook in Catholic West Belfast in 2003/4, during which I focused particularly on the relationship between the Irish language and ethnicity, almost all my informants were Irish Catholic Nationalists or Republicans.

I now turn towards the Irish language itself. Irish may be described as one of six Celtic languages, which, taken together, form a branch within the Indo-European language family, along with other branches, such as the Germanic languages, including English, to which Irish is only distantly related (see Hindley 1990: 3; Murchú 2000; Price 2000; Schrijver 2000). Historically, Irish constituted the mother tongue of most of Ireland's inhabitants, but it was increasingly replaced by English as the dominant first language during Ireland's long colonial history and especially during the nineteenth century. While small areas inhabited by native Irish speakers, so-called Gaeltachts, still exist along the west coast of the island, the Irish language continues to be threatened with extinction. This general trend has been somewhat slowed, though not really reversed, by cultural revivalist movements since the late nineteenth century. These included most prominently the activities of the Gaelic League and the language policies of the new Irish state in the South after partition in 1922, although the latter's perseverance and commitment to the Irish language seems to have rather weakened in the course of the past century (see Hutchinson 1987; Hindley 1990; Purdon 1999; Murchú 2000).

Against this background, it is not particularly surprising that the Irish language was no longer practised to a significant extent in Catholic West Belfast during the first half of the twentieth century. However, a triangulation between historical sources, observational and interview materials that were generated during my fieldwork, as well as the historical[4] and ethnographic[5] literature, suggests that this local situation has changed quite significantly since the mid twentieth century. During the 1950s, and especially the 1960s, a fairly successful local language revival took off, and it has, by and large, been gaining momentum ever since. Although a detailed description and disentanglement of the variously interrelated strands within the language scene of this period cannot be provided here, it seems evident that the success of the local language revival has been due mainly to two factors: first, the establishment of a quite effective language supply by a relatively small circle of committed language activists; and second, the increasing local demand for practising the language, which – although in divergent, conflicting and sometimes contradictory ways – has been stimulated by the political conflict and resulting social tensions in the North of Ireland.

One particularly consequential development within the local language scene was the establishment of Ireland's first urban Gaeltacht in Catholic West Belfast

4   See especially Hindley (1990), Andrews (1997, 2000a, 2000b), Mac Póilin (1997, 2003a, 2003b, 2006), Mac Corraidh (2006) and De Brún (2006).
5   See especially Maguire (1991), Kachuk (1993, 1994), O'Reilly (1996, 1997, 1999), McCoy (1997a, 1997b, 2006) and Nig Uidhir (2006).

during the 1960s. In founding their own small Gaeltacht neighbourhood, where Irish has been spoken as the everyday language ever since, a small group of language enthusiasts gave the Irish language a permanent physical location and place of concentration, which, subsequently, could serve as a point of departure for further developments (see Maguire 1991; Nig Uidhir 2006). Given that the families within this urban neo-Gaeltacht raised their children with Irish as their first language, education through the medium of Irish became the next pressing issue. Hence, the same Irish speakers also founded and ran the first Irish-medium school in the North of Ireland despite the disapproval of the Northern Irish educational authorities and their refusal for more than a decade to support the school financially. Initially the school only catered to children from the urban Gaeltacht itself, but after a few years it was also opened to those pupils from surrounding neighbourhoods, who had acquired some basic Irish in a specifically designed language-immersion nursery that had also been established within this community of Irish speakers. The Irish-medium school and nursery were later to function as models for many other educational institutions throughout the whole North of Ireland (see Mac Corraidh 2006). Within the wider network of these same language activists, additional initiatives appeared over the years, including a bookshop, an Irish-medium newspaper, drama groups, an Irish-medium pirate radio station and Irish-medium TV production companies. Apart from the emergence of a plethora of Irish-language projects and organizations, the foundation of a local Irish language, culture and arts centre in 1991 proved to be of particular importance, because it provided a focal point for regular and continual Irish-medium interactions in Catholic West Belfast, which, previously, had been dispersed.

Corresponding to this expanding infrastructure of language supply, there has also been a growing demand for Irish language activities. Since the 1970s, thousands of locals started learning Irish, for example, in evening classes, which began to mushroom in social clubs, schools, pubs, parish halls and private houses in Catholic West Belfast, or during increasingly long terms of imprisonment (see Feldman 1991: 204–45; Kachuk 1993: 152–258; O'Reilly 1999: 17–31). Many Republicans within the IRA and its political wing, Sinn Féin, who had hitherto not ascribed much importance to the Irish language, also started promoting it in the 1980s. This development was fostered, first, by the use of Irish among Republicans in prison (see McKeown 2001), most prominently perhaps by the instigator of the hunger strike of 1981 and, subsequently, the iconic martyr, Bobby Sands; and, second, by the establishment in 1982 of Sinn Féin's Cultural Department, which also started promoting and lobbying for the language. In addition, more and more parents in Catholic West Belfast also wished their children to be educated in Irish-medium schools. This has led to an explosion of Irish-medium education, especially since the 1990s. Thus, according to The Council for Irish-medium Education (Comhairle na Gaelscolaíochta 2004), at the time of my fieldwork there were thirteen Irish-medium nursery, primary and secondary schools with a total of 1,349 pupils in Catholic West Belfast alone, as compared to twenty such schools in the whole of Belfast and sixty-nine in all of 'Northern Ireland'. And as data from the last Northern Ireland Census indicates, in 2001 in Catholic West Belfast a total of 15,244 persons out of 55,008 local residents 'aged three and over' claimed to have 'some knowledge of Irish'. This adds up to a considerable 27.7 per cent of the local population in Catholic West Belfast, as compared to only 13.6 per cent in the local government district of Belfast and a mere 10.4 per cent within the whole of 'Northern Ireland'.[6]

These census figures of self-ascribed language competence should, of course, be taken with a grain of salt. What Máiréad Nic Craith observes with regard to the Northern Ireland Census of 1991 – when, after a vigorous campaign, a question regarding the Irish language appeared again in the census after a hiatus of eighty years and for the first time since the foundation of the Northern Irish state (see Nic Craith 1999: 496–97) – is also valid for the current data: individuals' perceptions of their own language competence vary quite considerably, making it difficult to evaluate the overall response. Conscious or unconscious attitudes towards language may well 'interfere with the legitimacy of self-ascription', thereby leading either to an underestimation or – as is more likely in the politicized Northern Irish context – an overestimation of the Irish language competence of participants in the census (ibid.: 496; see also Nic Craith and Shuttleworth 1996; Mac Giolla Chriost n.d.). Nevertheless, these figures may still be understood to point towards a dramatic increase in the actual practice of the Irish language within Catholic West Belfast and beyond.

As I could observe during fieldwork, while learning Irish myself, the language was locally practised at different levels of fluency and to varying extents in a broad range of contexts, which included, aside from informal communication with relatives and friends, Irish-language meeting places, organized Irish-medium events and activities, companies and voluntary groups providing products and services through the medium of Irish, organizations promoting and lobbying for the language, adult Irish language classes as well as the whole Irish-medium educational sector. Needless to say, however, the Irish language still remained, and continues to remain, a minority phenomenon, encountered only in selected places and within special circles.

So far, I have concentrated on the ways in and the extent to which the Irish language has been practised in Catholic West Belfast. Turning now to the question of how the Irish language has been locally represented, I must emphasize that my characterization of these language practices is itself to a large extent based on local

---

6   'Catholic West Belfast' refers here to ten of the thirteen electoral wards on the local government level in West Belfast at the time of the Northern Ireland Census of 2001, in which more than 80 per cent of the residents had a Catholic religious background. For the various figures for people 'aged three and over', who claimed to have 'some knowledge of Irish', see Northern Ireland Statistics and Research Agency (NISRA) 2006: Table KS24 ('Knowledge of Irish'), various levels.

representations. While this observation sounds a note of caution, I am confident that the preceding sketch of local language practices in Catholic West Belfast during the second half of the twentieth century is sufficiently accurate, reflecting the largely uncontroversial, matter-of-fact self-understanding of local informants.

What was controversial locally can be summarized with reference to three contested issues. First, a few language purists argued that what had happened in Catholic West Belfast did not actually count as a 'real' Irish language revival. Orienting themselves towards what they saw as the 'true' Irish, as it has been spoken in the historical Gaeltacht areas in Donegal, these critics tended to ridicule the local language practices by characterizing them as 'broken Irish'. 'Broken Irish', in the sense of a polluted and degenerated form of Irish, heavily modelled on overly literal and, hence, 'false' translations from English into Irish, had increased in local practice, these purists argued, but 'true Irish' had not. Hence, calling this local development an Irish language 'revival' was, at best, misleading and, at worst, legitimizing ex post facto the introduction of malapropisms into an already endangered, yet precious language. The second contested issue centred on the question whether the success of the Irish language revival, as most local actors would call it, was to be attributed primarily to the language activists, whose language supply, especially through Irish-medium education, has been particularly effective; or whether this revival is, rather, a consequence of the political conflict in general and of the role of Republican prisoners in particular in increasing the demand for the language. This leads to the third contested issue, namely the question of whether or not Sinn Féin and Republicans generally have hijacked the Irish language for political purposes. The answers to these questions obviously varied among my informants, but usually depended on their more general attitudes towards the Irish language, to which I now turn.

During my fieldwork, three basic positions regarding Irish could be discerned among local Irish speakers (see also Kachuk 1993; O'Reilly 1997, 1999). A small group, consisting mainly but not exclusively of language lobbyists, argued for a 'rights' position, depicting the Irish language as an issue of 'human', 'civil' or 'minority rights' that were above narrow political concerns such as the constitutional status of the North of Ireland. From this perspective, the language was sometimes viewed as a precious object of culture in danger being lost. It is important to note, however, that in this context the term 'culture' was used to refer not to a distinctive 'ethnic culture,' one typically associated with Irishness (as in the following two positions), but to an overarching 'human culture', the diversity of which needed to be protected as an end in itself through a kind of cultural environmentalism. In contrast, for those holding the second, 'ethnicist' position, Irish represented a fundamental, yet largely lost, element of their own 'Irish culture and identity'. However, ethnicists argued for a strict separation between the Irish language and political concerns with unifying Ireland. These actors were, therefore, suspicious of any public involvement of Republican politicians, whom they accused of 'hijacking' the language, abusing it as a means for their ultimately purely political ends. Those associated with a third 'nationalist' position shared with ethnicists the conviction that the Irish language was an important cultural element of Irishness, which had to be reappropriated. Yet they rejected the suggestion that they or their allies had 'hijacked' the language, while arguing that by speaking Irish, one already was and should be engaged in the political struggle for decolonizing the island of Ireland and, thus, liberating it from its external British oppressors.

Despite some important differences, the ethnicist and nationalist positions – which, to my knowledge, have been far more pervasive than the rights position within the language scene of Catholic West Belfast – have at least one important feature in common; namely, the representation of Irish as 'our own native language'. This notion, which I encountered again and again in conversations with locals, seems to have become both widespread and relevant in Catholic West Belfast only since the 1970s, although the close link between Irish and Irishness had already been propagated in nationalist discourses since the late nineteenth century (see, e.g., Hutchinson 1987; Hindley 1990: 21–42; Kachuk 1993: 112–51; O'Reilly 1999: 32–48; Andrews 2000a, 2000b).

Among the various factors that ultimately contributed to this change in local representations, one aspect stands out: the conflict in the North of Ireland of recent decades, which broke out in 1969 after the local civil rights movement was met with violence by Protestants and the state. Looking back, many Catholics in West Belfast told me that they had 'always felt being Irish'. However, 'the Troubles' – as the conflict is locally known – brought a new sense of identity to the fore, as the Catholics of West Belfast increasingly came to understand the local discrimination and violence in terms of the oppression of 'Irish' people by agents of 'British colonialism' and 'imperialism'. From such a perspective, an end to discrimination and violence could only be achieved by removing 'the Brits' and uniting Ireland. Given the growing sense of their own Irishness, many local Catholics also started to engage with their own history and 'Irish culture'. In this process, they were increasingly confronted with the contradiction between the high relevance of the Irish language in representations of Irishness and its low profile in daily life. Many reacted to this inconsistency between representations and practices, by changing their language practices: they started learning their 'own native language'. Most of my ethnicist and nationalist interlocutors described this as the attempt to 'repossess' or 'reappropriate' their 'own mother tongue' in order to 'feel whole' or to 'reassert' their sense of Irishness.

❧

As this empirical case of the Irish language revival shows, language mattered a lot in Catholic West Belfast. It was both a significant medium and object of local representation. Through their linguistic representations, local Catholics not only generally reproduced the means for intelligible and meaningful signification; they also used them in particular ways to project a specific world-view, in which their experiences of discrimination and violence could be understood as the result of an ethno-nationalist conflict between the dominating British state and the dominated Irish people. Within these linguistic representations, language – more precisely, a particular language – also turned into an important object of representation, when locals defined their sense of Irishness through including Irish as their 'own native language', despite knowing that this representation actually was, and had been for a considerable time, largely counter-factual for most Irish people in Catholic West Belfast and beyond.

On a more general level, this last point indicates that the inscription of meanings into the world through conventionalized language usage does not simply produce facts; rather, it creates a framework in which questions regarding the truth of factual statements can be meaningfully asked and answered in the first place. In other words, conventionalized language usage produces the possibility for something to become representable as a fact and for statements related to such potential facts to be evaluated as more or less true in a given context. By borrowing from ordinary language philosophy, we can reframe this idea in terms of a Wittgensteinian 'language-game' (Wittgenstein 1953). Wittgenstein uses the notion of language-games for a broad variety of linguistic activities or phenomena, ranging from simple usages 'by means of which children learn their native language' (ibid.: §7) to what we would now call 'illocutionary speech acts' (see Austin 1962; Searle 1969), such as 'giving orders' or 'reporting an event', and to the larger 'whole', consisting of 'language and the actions into which it is woven' (Wittgenstein 1953: §23 and 7). A detailed exploration of the nuances in and facets of Wittgenstein's usage of the term 'language-game' lies beyond the scope and purpose of this chapter and has of course been extensively addressed in the exegesis of Wittgenstein's later work.[7] Here, it suffices to emphasize that one unifying idea behind his use of the term consists in bringing into 'prominence the fact that the *speaking* of language is part of an activity, or a life-form' (ibid.: §23, original emphasis). For our current purposes, it is useful, however, to restrict the use of the term to sociolects or linguistic varieties; that is, to forms of conventionalized language usages that are mutually intelligible and meaningful within, and somewhat characteristic of, a given social group.[8]

Drawing on the thoughts of John L. Austin – another philosopher of ordinary language and a contemporary of Wittgenstein – and paraphrasing his definition of 'truth' (Austin 1979: 122), we can say that an individual statement within a language-game is true if the specific state of the world referred to correlates sufficiently with those types of the world to which the conventionalized use of the

---

7   See especially Kripke (1982), as well as the four interrelated volumes by Baker and Hacker (1980, 1985) and Hacker (1990, 1996).

8   On the concepts 'sociolect' and 'linguistic variety' within sociolinguistics, see Ager (1999: 817), Cheshire and Bell (2003), Christian (2003: 85), Crystal (2003), Macaulay (2006: 484) and Mesthrie (2006: 474).

words within this individual statement usually refers. According to this understanding, a statement is thus true if the particular use of its constituent words sufficiently corresponds to the latter's conventionalized uses, which – as Wittgenstein (1953: §43) suggests – are their meanings. The meaning of a proposition is hence its true statement, which is equivalent to Wittgenstein's observation in the *Tractatus* that 'to understand a proposition means to know what is the case, if it is true' (Wittgenstein 1922: §4.024). In short, meaning and truth can be seen to be mutually constitutive in the linguistic practice of language-games. And in this process, any specific state of the world acquires the potential to turn into a 'fact', which – as Austin characterizes it – involves 'both words and world' (Austin 1979: 124): it consists, on the one hand, of a state of affairs about which, on the other hand, a (purely conventional) statement is a truth.[9]

That the 'truth' of statements within language-games indeed matters empirically is easily demonstrated with regard to the widespread representation in Catholic West Belfast that 'Irishness entails speaking one's own native language'. Many local Catholics started to learn the Irish language precisely because they realized that the linguistic construction of their own Irishness was simply not true with regard to this particular representation. Thus, by modifying their language practices, they changed the actual facts in a way that increasingly turned their own representations of Irishness into true statements. In the case of the Irish language revival in Catholic West Belfast, language can thus be seen to matter on two different levels: Within their language-game, local Catholics have created potential meanings of possible facts through their conventionalized language usage at the level of representations. In addition, they have increasingly switched their language usages from English to Irish at the level of representable practices in order to produce a state of the world that can be represented within their language-game by the sufficiently true statement that 'Irishness entails speaking one's own native language'.

So far, I have been exclusively concerned with the ways in which 'their' language practices can be seen to matter. I have thereby *not represented* my own language practices, but I have *performed* them. And what I was thereby trying to demonstrate was my attempt to conceptualize 'their' language practices in terms of the very same conditions that I assume to be at work when representing 'their' case through my own language practices. In other words, in representing the local language-game in Catholic West Belfast, I have simultaneously invited you – the reader – to participate in another language-game – in 'our' language-game of English-medium social science. Based on our conventionalized language usage, we

---

9   See also Davidson (1967).

can thereby hope to achieve a sufficient consensus about what might have been the case in Catholic West Belfast according to our language-game, if my representations are true. By treating my representations as if they were true, you have been able to understand them without either knowing or necessarily agreeing that they actually are true. Thus, we might argue whether they are sufficiently true or whether there are other representations within our language-game that are truer for this empirical case. Yet neither you nor I nor local actors in Catholic West Belfast can, thereby, avoid producing representations that equally claim to be true in the sense of exhibiting a sufficient correlation between individual statement and conventionalized language usage. This, of course, also applies to representations altogether rejecting the notion of truth in the evaluation of representations. We are, thus, left in a situation in which various statements within a language-game necessarily compete to be the truest representation of a particular state of the world, and this competition is also shaped by presumptions about their generalized plausibility. By plausibility, I mean the compatibility of the particular representation at issue with other representations also deemed to be true within one's own world-view or theoretical approach.

This struggle for true and plausible representations seems to be conditioned, on the one hand, by social processes shaping the actual act of representation itself. Such processes include, among others, the social conventions of language use within particular language-games and prevalent 'regimes of truth' in their historical embeddedness in given power structures (see Foucault 1980). Yet the struggle for true and plausible representations must, on the other hand, also be conditioned by states of the world itself. As Austin reminds us, there is hereby no reason why this 'world' should not be conceptualized to 'include the words, in every sense except the sense of the actual statement itself which on any particular occasion is being made about the world' (Austin 1979: 121). Both the conditions of the actual statement of 'the words' and of 'the world', to which these stated words refer, have thus to be acknowledged. If it were only the world that mattered, no dissent would be possible; if it were only the discursive construction without an external referent that mattered, language use itself would be impossible.

If we bend these general observations back to the issue of ethnographic representation, it becomes evident that both 'we' (ethnographers) and 'they' (e.g., Catholics of West Belfast) seem to be left in symmetrical spaces between words and the world, where we are all united in our inevitable search for truth and plausibility when engaging in factual representations. From such a perspective, ethnography can be characterized as aiming at a cultural translation between two different language-games, which are symmetrical in that, apart from the common search for truth and plausibility, in each, truth and meaning are mutually constitutive, so that facts may be seen to reside at the intersection of their respective words and the world. Such an approach leads to two reflexive acknowledgements: first, the need to develop a sufficiently sensitive language competence in both language-games; and second, the need to confront persistently 'their' as well as 'our' own factual statements with the world in order to produce greater plausibility or, as Stephen Reyna puts it in his contribution to this volume, 'harder truths'. To sum up: within the anthropological endeavour of ethnography, language does indeed matter in that its usage within different language-games does provide and shape the necessary backgrounds, against which respective questions about the truth of statements concerning the world can only be posed meaningfully, answered sufficiently and translated approximately. But this is only half of the story: the improvement of one's language competence and linguistic reflexivity in both settings also needs to be supplemented with systematic and more encompassing confrontations of one's alleged truths with the world.

❦

Back in West Belfast, I have argued that many local Catholics have started learning the Irish language in order to make their representation true that 'Irishness entails speaking one's own native language'. Obviously, this has not been the case for all local Catholics. On the contrary, the majority of locals continue to have no knowledge of Irish. Although I regularly encountered a certain sense of guilt among non-speakers when talking about the Irish language, I also met many locals who regarded the acquisition of Irish as superfluous. Some represented the Irish language as an historical relict that was no longer necessary for being truly Irish. Others simply ignored the inconsistency between their representations of Irishness and their lack of actual language practices.

This last observation may seem surprising, but perhaps only to those who expect everyday life in West Belfast to function according to the same strictness of truth and plausibility that can be expected to characterize the work of social scientists. If this is not the starting point, then it is rather the quite strenuous attempts by members of a local minority to achieve a more consistent Irish identity through learning the language that need to be explained. I have characterized a few processes that might help shed light on this phenomenon, but much more would have to be said in order to develop a deeper understanding of such 'identity work'.[10] In this contribution, however, I have been more concerned with showing that both 'their' and 'my' language practices can be seen to matter in symmetrical ways: both 'they' and 'I' are engaged in language-games that function according to rules of truth and plausibility. This basic observation holds true, even though everyday actors, such as my informants in Catholic West Belfast, often produce their own facts in order to turn preconceived opinions into true statements – behaviour that is illegitimate within the sciences. This basic observation also holds true, even though the rules of truth and plausibility are

10   On this issue, see Zenker (2008).

often less relevant (yet not categorically different) in daily life than in science, as the common disregard for inconsistencies between representations of Irishness and actual language practices in West Belfast shows.

This last point can also be made in the following way: 'our' scientific language-games and 'their' everyday language-games are also fundamentally asymmetrical, insofar as scientific communication is fundamentally constituted and set apart through its principal concern with the truth value of its representations (Luhmann 1984, 1990), while 'their' language usages may equally pursue communicative functions other than the referentiality of truth and plausibility (a theme that Vincent Crapanzano explores in his contribution to this volume). However, this asymmetry, which is based on additional communicative functions within language-games in everyday situations, actually enhances, rather than undermines, the scientific search for true and plausible representations by extending the scope of its potentially relevant facts. In other words, acknowledging the potential relevance of communicative functions beyond referential truth in everyday communication does not negate the symmetrical relationship between truthful communication in both daily and scientific language-games, nor does it call into question the heightened relevance of truth in scientific representations. On the contrary, it makes scientific representations about the world – in this case, the functionalities of communicative acts – truer and more plausible.

By highlighting the ways, in which 'our' language potentially matters when representing ethnographic others, the *Writing Culture* debate challenged us to think about the nature of knowledge and representation, about the interrelation between representing and the represented, and suggested alternative modes of writing as the reflexive way forward in the pursuit of 'our' ethnographic endeavour. In this chapter, I have suggested that we borrow from ordinary language philosophy in order to conceptualize the ethnographic process as an encounter of two language-games which are symmetrical in their respective mutual constitution of meaning and truth, in their production-cum-observation of facts at the intersection of words and the world, and in their common search for truth and plausibility in factual representations. From this perspective, ethnography turns into an act of cultural translation, in which language matters to the extent that a sufficient competence in both 'their' and 'our' language-game is necessary in order approximately to understand and translate – that is, represent in 'our' language-game – what they mean when making certain moves in 'their' language-game. At the same time – and this puts the matter of language as the medium of representation in its place – such a cultural translation also entails a commitment continually to confront 'their' as well as 'our' own factual statements with the world itself (which may include the matter of language as a relevant object of representation) in order to produce truer and more plausible representations. From such a viewpoint, what matters in our attempts to produce more reflexive ethnographic representations is hence less the change in 'our' rhetoric that was suggested in *Writing Culture*, than the continual attempt to produce representations that are – as Sperber (1993) puts it – 'true-to-life' in accounting for, rather than copying, the original (including the latter's own attempts to be 'true-to-life').

I recognize, of course, that such an approach can hardly claim much originality. It stands in a long tradition, which conceives and critically reflects upon 'cultural translation' as the primary task of ethnography (see, e.g., Lienhardt 1954; Needham 1972; Asad 1986; Pálsson 1994; Budick and Iser 1996; Clifford 1997; Crapanzano 2001; Jordan 2002; Maranhão and Streck 2003; Rottenburg 2003; Rubel and Rosman 2003). Yet, as one positions oneself within the field of anthropology, especially with regard to the contested interrelation between epistemology and representational practice, it is perhaps not so much originality but rather the truth and plausibility of the occupied position itself that matters.

References

Ager, Dennis Ernest. 1999. 'Sociolinguistics', in Adam Kuper and Jessica Kuper (eds), *The Social Science Encyclopedia*, 2nd edn. London: Routledge, 817–18.

Andrews, Liam S. 1997. 'The Very Dogs in Belfast Will Bark in Irish: The Unionist Government and the Irish Language 1921–43', in Aodán Mac Póilin (ed.), *The Irish Language in Northern Ireland*. Belfast: Ultach Trust, 49–94.

———. 2000a. 'Northern Nationalists and the Politics of the Irish language: The Historical Background', in J.M. Kirk and D.P. Ó Baoill (eds), *Language and Politics: Northern Ireland, the Republic of Ireland and Scotland*. Belfast: Cló Ollscoil na Banríona, 45–64.

———. 2000b. 'Unionism and Nationalism and the Irish Language, 1893–1933', Ph.D. dissertation. Belfast: Queen's University Belfast.

Asad, Talal. 1986. 'The Concept of Cultural Translation in British Social Anthropology', in James Clifford and George E. Marcus (eds), *Writing Culture: The Poetics and Politics of Ethnography*. Berkeley: University of California Press, 141–64.

Austin, John L. 1962. *How to do Things with Words*. Oxford: Clarendon Press.

———. 1979. 'Truth', in John L. Austin, *Philosophical Papers*, 3rd edn. Oxford: Oxford University Press, 117–33.

Baker, Gordon P. and Peter Michael S. Hacker. 1980. *Wittgenstein: Understanding and Meaning; Volume 1 of an Analytical Commentary on the Philosophical Investigations*. Oxford: Blackwell.

———. 1985. *Wittgenstein: Rules, Grammar and Necessity; Volume 2 of an Analytical Commentary on the Philosophical Investigations*. Oxford: Blackwell.

Budick, Sanford and Wolfgang Iser (eds). 1996. *The Translatability of Cultures: Figurations of the Space Between*. Stanford, CA: Stanford University Press.

Cheshire, Jenny and A. Bell. 2003. 'Register and Style', in William J. Frawley (ed.), *International Encyclopedia of Linguistics, Volume 3*, 2nd edn. Oxford: Oxford University Press, 454–59.

Christian, D. 2003. 'Social Variation: Social Dialects', in Willaim J. Frawley (ed.), *International Encyclopedia of Linguistics, Volume 4*, 2nd edn. Oxford: Oxford University Press, 85–88.

Clifford, James. 1997. *Routes: Travel and Translation in the Late Twentieth Century.* Cambridge, MA: Harvard University Press.

Clifford, James and George E. Marcus (eds). 1986. *Writing Culture: The Poetics and Politics of Ethnography.* Berkeley: University of California Press.

Comhairle na Gaelscolaíochta. 2004. *Bunachar sonraí gaelscoileanna 2003–04 / Irish-Medium School Database 2003–04.* Belfast: Comhairle na Gaelscolaíochta.

Coulter, Colin. 1999. *Contemporary Northern Irish Society: An Introduction.* London: Pluto Press.

Crapanzano, Vincent. 2001. 'Transfiguring Translation', *Semiotica* 128(1/2): 113–36.

Crystal, David. 2003. 'Sociolect', in David Crystal (ed.), *A Dictionary of Linguistics and Phonetics*, 5th edn. Oxford: Blackwell, 422.

Davidson, Donald. 1967. 'Truth and Meaning', *Synthese* 17: 304-23.

De Brún, Fionntán (ed.) 2006. *Belfast and the Irish Language.* Dublin: Four Courts.

Feldman, Allen. 1991. *Formations of Violence: The Narrative of the Body and Political Terror in Northern Ireland.* Chicago: University of Chicago Press.

Foucault, Michel. 1980. 'Truth and Power', in *Power/Knowledge: Selected Interviews and other Writings, 1972–1977*, (ed.) C. Gordon. New York: Pantheon, 109–133.

Hacker, Peter Michael S. 1990. *Wittgenstein: Meaning and Mind; Volume 3 of an Analytical Commentary on the Philosophical Investigations.* Oxford: Blackwell.

———. 1996. *Wittgenstein: Mind and Will; Volume 4 of an Analytical Commentary on the Philosophical Investigations.* Oxford: Blackwell.

Hindley, Reg. 1990. *The Death of the Irish Language: A Qualified Obituary.* London: Routledge.

Hutchinson, John. 1987. *The Dynamics of Cultural Nationalism: The Gaelic Revival and the Creation of the Irish Nation State.* London: Allen and Unwin.

IICD. 2005. *Report of the Independent International Commission on Decommissioning.*

Jordan, Shirley Ann. 2002. 'Ethnographic Encounters: The Processes of Cultural Translation', *Language and Intercultural Communication* 2(2): 96–110.

Kachuk, Patricia M.C. 1993. 'Irish Language Activism in West Belfast: A Resistance to British Cultural Hegemony', Ph.D. dissertation. Vancouver: University of British Columbia.

———. 1994. 'A Resistance to British Cultural Hegemony: Irish Language Activism in West Belfast', *Anthropologica* 36: 135–54.

Kripke, Saul A. 1982. *Wittgenstein on Rules and Private Language: An Elementary Exposition.* Cambridge, MA: Harvard University Press.

Lienhardt, Godfrey. 1954. 'Modes of Thought', in Edward E. Evans-Pritchard, Raymond Firth and Edmund Ronald Leach (eds), *The Institutions of Primitive Society: A Series of Broadcast Talks.* Oxford: Basil Blackwell, 95–107.

Luhmann, Niklas. 1984. *Soziale Systeme: Grundriss einer allgemeinen Theorie.* Frankfurt am Main: Suhrkamp.

———. 1990. *Die Wissenschaft der Gesellschaft.* Frankfurt am Main: Suhrkamp.

Mac Corraidh, Seán. 2006. 'Irish-Medium Education in Belfast', in Fionntán De Brún (ed.), *Belfast and the Irish Language.* Dublin: Four Courts, 177–83.

Mac Giolla Chriost, Diarmait n.d. 'The Irish Language and the Northern Ireland Census 1991', unpublished manuscript. Dublin: Trinity College.

Mac Póilin, Aodán (ed.), 1997. *The Irish Language in Northern Ireland.* Belfast: Ultach Trust.

———. 2003a. 'The Irish Language in Belfast After 1900', in Nichoals Allen and Aaron Kelly (eds), *The Cities of Belfast.* Dublin: Four Courts Press, 127–51.

———. 2003b. 'The Irish Language in Belfast Until 1900', in Nicholas Allen and Aaron Kelly (eds), *The Cities of Belfast.* Dublin: Four Courts Press, 41–61.

———. 2006. 'Irish in Belfast, 1892–1960: From the Gaelic League to Cumann Chluain Ard', in Fionntán De Brún (ed.), *Belfast and the Irish Language.* Dublin: Four Courts, 114–35.

Macaulay, Ronald K.S. 2006. 'Sociolect / Social Class', in Keith Brown (ed.), *Encyclopedia of Language and Linguistics, Volume 11*, 2nd edn. Amsterdam: Elsevier, 484–89.

Maguire, Gabrielle. 1991. *Our Own Language: An Irish Initiative.* Clevedon: Multilingual Matters.

Malinowski, Bronislaw. 1922. *Argonauts of the Western Pacific: An Account of Native Enterprise and Adventure in the Archipelagoes of Melanesian New Guinea.* London: Routledge and Kegan Paul.

Maranhão, Tullio and Bernhard Streck (eds). 2003. *Translation and Ethnography: The Anthropological Challenge of Intercultural Understanding.* Tucson: University of Arizona Press.

Marcus, George E. and Dick Cushman. 1982. 'Ethnographies as Texts', *Annual Review of Anthropology* 11: 25–69.

McCoy, Gordon. 1997a. 'Protestant Learners of Irish in Northern Ireland', in Aodán Mac Póilin (ed.), *The Irish Language in Northern Ireland.* Belfast: Ultach Trust, 131–69.

———. 1997b. 'Protestants and the Irish Language in Northern Ireland', Ph.D. dissertation. Belfast: Queen's University Belfast.

———. 2006. 'Protestants and the Irish Language in Belfast', in Fionntán De Brún (ed.), *Belfast and the Irish Language.* Dublin: Four Courts, 147–76.

McKeown, Laurence. 2001. *Out of Time: Irish Republican Prisoners, Long Kesh, 1972–2000.* Belfast: Beyond The Pale.

Mesthrie, Rajend. 2006. 'Society and Language: Overview', in Keith Brown (ed.), *Encyclopedia of Language and Linguistics, Volume 11*, 2nd edn. Amsterdam: Elsevier, 472–84.

Murchú, Máirtín Ó. 2000. 'Irish', in Glanville Price (ed.), *Encyclopedia of the Languages of Europe*. Oxford: Blackwell, 243–50.

Needham, Rodney. 1972. *Belief, Language and Experience*. Oxford: Blackwell.

Nic Craith, Máiréad. 1999. 'Irish Speakers in Northern Ireland, and the Good Friday Agreement', *Journal of Multilingual and Multicultural Development* 20(6): 494–507.

Nic Craith, Máiréad and Ian Shuttleworth. 1996. 'Irish in Northern Ireland: The 1991 Census', in Máiréad Nic Craith (ed.), *Watching one's Tongue: Aspects of Romance and Celtic Languages*. Liverpool: Liverpool University Press, 163–75.

Nig Uidhir, Gabrielle. 2006. 'The Shaw's Road Urban Gaeltacht: Role and Impact', in Fionntán De Brún (ed.), *Belfast and the Irish Language*. Dublin: Four Courts, 136–46.

NISRA. 2006. 'Northern Ireland Census 2001 Output'. Retrieved 6 June 2006, from http://www.nisranew.nisra.gov.uk/Census/Census2001Output/index.html.

O'Reilly, Camille. 1996. 'The Irish Language – Litmus Test for Equality? Competing Discourses of Identity, Parity of Esteem, and the Peace Process', *Irish Journal of Sociology* 6: 154–78.

———. 1997. 'Nationalists and the Irish Language in Northern Ireland: Competing Perspectives', in Aodán Mac Póilin (ed.), *The Irish Language in Northern Ireland*. Belfast: Ultach Trust, 95–130.

———. 1999. *The Irish Language in Northern Ireland: The Politics of Culture and Identity*. Basingstoke: Palgrave Macmillan.

Pálsson, Gísli (ed.). 1994. *Beyond Boundaries: Understanding, Translation and Anthropological Discourse*. Oxford: Berg.

Price, Glanville. 2000. 'Celtic Languages', in Glanville Price (ed.), *Encyclopedia of the Languages of Europe*. Oxford: Blackwell, 83–84.

Purdon, Edward. 1999. *The Story of the Irish language*. Dublin: Mercier Press.

Rottenburg, Richard. 2003. 'Crossing Gaps of Indeterminacy: Some Theoretical Remarks', in Tullio Maranhão and Bernhard Streck (eds), *Translation and Ethnography: The Anthropological Challenge of Intercultural Understanding*. Tucson: University of Arizona Press, 30–43.

Rubel, Paula G. and Abraham Rosman (eds). 2003. *Translating Cultures: Perspectives on Translation and Anthropology*. Oxford: Berg.

Schrijver, Peter. 2000. 'Indo-European Languages', in Glanville Price (ed.), *Encyclopedia of the Languages of Europe*. Oxford: Blackwell, 239–42.

Searle, John Roger. 1969. *Speech Acts: An Essay in the Philosophy of Language*. London: Cambridge University Press.

Sperber, Dan. 1993. 'Interpreting and Explaining Cultural Representations', in Gísli Pálsson (ed.), *Beyond Boundaries: Understanding, Translation and Anthropological Discourse*. Oxford: Berg, 162–83.

Trew, Karen. 1998. 'The Northern Irish Identity', in Anne J. Kershen (ed.), *A Question of Identity*. Aldershot: Ashgate, 60–76.

Wittgenstein, Ludwig. 1922. *Tractatus Logico-Philosophicus*. New York: Harcourt, Brace and Company.

———. 1953. *Philosophical Investigations*. Oxford: Blackwell.

Zenker, Olaf. 2006. 'De Facto Exclusion through Discursive Inclusion: Autochthony in Discourses on Irishness and Politics in Catholic West Belfast', *Paideuma* 52: 183–95.

———. 2008. 'Irish/ness Is All Around Us: The Irish Language and Irish Identity in Catholic West Belfast', Ph.D. dissertation. Halle/Saale: Martin Luther University Halle-Wittenberg.

8

Ethnographic Cognition and *Writing Culture*

Christophe Heintz

❧

One of the best ways to pursue and go beyond the programme of *Writing Culture* (Clifford and Marcus 1986), I suggest, takes as its point of departure the cognitive anthropology of anthropology, because situating *Writing Culture* with regard to this field of research can contribute to its further development.[1] It is, after all, sensible to start the anthropological study of anthropology with an analysis of its own cultural productions: ethnographic texts. The analyst can thus identify the relevant properties of such cultural products and track down their causes. These causes include in particular the cognitive processes of working ethnographers.

Starting with textual analysis, I will argue that some of the rhetorical conventions that are viewed critically by contributors to *Writing Culture*, rather than being misleading, actually serve to inform the reader about the cognitive genesis of the ethnography. The information conveyed when complying with these conventions enables readers to evaluate the reliability of ethnographic accounts and anthropological analyses.

---

1   I thank the editors of this volume for their open-mindedness to a not very orthodox view on *Writing Culture*. Olaf Zenker's invitation to participate in the workshop 'Beyond *Writing Culture*' forced me to consider seriously the work of the *Writing Culture* movement and postmodernist anthropology more generally. I am very grateful to him for that, as well as for his encouragement and editorial work. Ironically, it is he who reminded me to include acknowledgments (a case of distributed cognition). The chapter benefited from comments at the 'Beyond *Writing Culture*' workshop and from an informal presentation at the Institut Jean-Nicod, Paris. The comments and criticisms of Dan Sperber, Hugo Mercier and Anikó Sebestény have been most useful. The general project of doing a cognitive anthropology of anthropology began during my stay at the Max Planck Institute for Social Anthropology in Halle (Saale), and I benefited from numerous discussions whilst there. It is, however, Monica Heintz who enabled me to get an insider's view into ethnographic and anthropological practices. I tend to think that she is the one to blame if my views are erroneous.

Following on from this, I specify some of the cognitive processes at work in the production of ethnographies. These include, for example, a reflexive and critical cognition that is distributed among the community of anthropologists, and also 'mind-reading' – a cognitive process, much studied by cognitive psychologists, that enables ethnographers to make sense of the behaviour of indigenous people[2] by attributing mental states to them (beliefs, intentions, desires, feelings).

Writing Culture and the Cognitive Anthropology of Anthropology

Writing Culture *as a Project in Naturalized Epistemology*

The core project of *Writing Culture* (Clifford and Marcus 1986) consists in adopting a reflexive attitude with regard to the production of ethnographic writings. There is no doubt that a reflexive attitude is worth pursuing as part of any scientific enterprise; what could be seen as controversial, in *Writing Culture*, is the content of those reflections. James Clifford, in his introduction, foresaw that the authors of the contributions to the book would be 'accused of having gone too far' (Clifford 1986a: 25). Indeed, many anthropologists are weary of the ever-present reflexivity of postmodern writing, which results in ethnographies in which self-contemplation takes precedence over information about the life of the indigenous people. Such criticisms pertain to the way in which specific prescriptions made by the authors of *Writing Culture* have been applied by others. The *Writing Culture* movement has also been viewed as a critique of an over-confident positivism, which was initially justified and beneficial but is now no longer fruitful. Criticisms of this type pertain to the epistemic evaluations of the ethnographic project of the contributors to *Writing Culture*.

The way to refute, counterbalance and/or update the ideas announced in *Writing Culture* is, nonetheless, to continue thinking about what ethnographic writings are, could be and should be, and to continue developing the reflexive project of *Writing Culture*. Indeed, nobody would claim that a full understanding of the complex social and cultural processes that yield ethnographies has yet been achieved. In this sense, the anthropologists involved in the *Writing Culture* project, which is understood as a reflection on ethnographic practices, have not gone 'too far'.

The reflexive project of *Writing Culture* includes three programmes of research. First, there is a descriptive programme which attempts to bring into the open the

---

2   By 'indigenous people' I mean the people belonging to the culture being studied. 'Indigenous people' has no
     further connotation in my usage of the word. It can be people in an African small-scale society, stockbrokers in
     New York, scientists in a lab, and so forth. In the anthropology of anthropology, the indigenous people are the
     anthropologists themselves.

ways in which ethnographers explain other cultures in written texts. With *Writing Culture*, a set of largely unquestioned social phenomena comes under scrutiny: the book analyses the work of the ethnographer, their social relations with the people about whom they write, the rhetorical conventions they use, and their epistemological beliefs. Secondly, there is an evaluative programme, which consists in assessing the value, scientific or otherwise, of ethnographers' productions. Biases, such as those resulting from the cultural constellations and power relations that emerged during the history of colonialism, are denounced. The authors of *Writing Culture* also reveal the 'masking' in ethnographic descriptions and the 'mystifications' they entail, qualifying ethnographic truths as 'inherently partial' (Clifford 1986a: 7). Finally, a normative programme, which proposes or prescribes methods for producing better ethnographic representations. In particular, the contributors of *Writing Culture* advocate the production and use of new rhetorical conventions.

In *Writing Culture*, as in many critical enterprises, these three programmes are strongly interconnected and not explicitly distinguished. It is fruitful, however, to distinguish between them, first, so that one can specify the programme that one is pursuing in developing further the project of *Writing Culture*; and, second, so that one can show how one intends to relate the three programmes to one another. For instance, 'logical positivists' conceived of epistemology as an a priori reflection on science and its method. They conceived of the normative programme as being independent of the empirical analysis of actual scientific practices. By contrast, 'naturalized epistemology' puts the descriptive programme prior to the evaluative and normative programmes. From this perspective, epistemology is based on empirical investigations about how knowledge is produced, which subsequently inform prescriptive reflections.[3]

A similar view of the relation between description and prescription is present, although less explicitly, in critical theory in literary studies, from which *Writing Culture* takes its inspiration. The authors who contributed to *Writing Culture* endeavour to describe and criticize ethnographic practices before proposing some new practices, such as self-consciousness and new rhetorical devices. Clifford's work (e.g., Clifford 1982, 1986b) is a case in point. His first action is to analyse the rhetorical devices that were used in major ethnographic writings. He then denounces the mystifying effects of these devices, such as unjustified attributions of authority. Finally, he proposes some new rhetorical tools, such as polyphonic writing, for achieving the goal of ethnography. For Clifford, an attack on the book *Writing Culture* for its relativism should 'make clear why close analysis of one of the principal things ethnographers do – that is write – should not be central to evaluation of the results of scientific research' (Clifford 1986a: 24). Here again, the project is presented as being based on empirical analysis, followed by evaluation. The distinction between programmes is made for methodological

---

3   On 'naturalized epistemology', see Kornblith (1987).

purposes. The goal is to obtain descriptions that are as independent as possible from various possible normative ideas of science,[4] while normative epistemology should be as realistic as possible – adapted to actual practices and to the possibilities of implementation.

A consequence of this hierarchical organization of epistemological thinking, from the descriptive to the normative, is that if the description is flawed then the evaluations are likely to be wrong and the prescription inappropriate. A good way, therefore, to critically develop the issues raised by *Writing Culture* further is to start with the descriptive programme. Indeed, it may be noted that most attacks on the *Writing Culture* movement have not fully addressed the descriptions of ethnography that can be found in the book, but, rather, have focused on the particular applications of methodological advice. Finally, describing socio-cultural phenomena ought to be what anthropologists do best. Describing ethnography fits squarely within the traditional tasks of anthropologists of science. It is an anthropology of anthropology, a genuinely reflexive project.

The Study of Ethnographic Practices

Anthropology itself has been studied from a historical point of view by historians and anthropologists themselves (e.g., Kuper 1983, 1999; Stocking 1992; Spencer 2000); from a philosophical point of view, especially regarding the question of rationality (Wilson 1970; Hollis and Lukes 1982); and from a methodological point of view by those authoring research guides on anthropological methods. Spencer (2000) shows how the community of British anthropologists defines anthropology during the course of events such as research seminars. This shows that the reflexive attitude can be found in many anthropological activities. Since any discipline is to a large extent auto-constitutive, it is bound to declare, more or less explicitly, what it is and what its aims are. Nonetheless, the anthropology of anthropology is far from constituting a systematic and productive field of research.

Ethnographic practices and the making of anthropological knowledge are themselves socio-cultural phenomena that deserve the anthropologist's attention. One specific contribution of *Writing Culture* to reflexive anthropology is its detailed description and analysis of written representations as cultural products. The focus on texts is justified, because writing is constitutive of the ethnographer's work; it is always present, and the ethnographic enterprise importantly relies on the written mode of communication. Among the many processes and properties of scientific communication, it is mainly the 'rhetorical conventions' used by ethnographers that are analysed in the contributions to *Writing Culture*.

---

4   This methodological point is distinct from the beliefs that scientific descriptions are de facto independent from values.

One way to go 'beyond *Writing Culture*', as the editors of this volume advocate, is to further the study of texts through the study of the causes and effects of the properties that textual analyses have revealed. In the introduction to *Writing Culture*, Clifford says that 'ethnographic writing is determined in at least six ways: (1) contextually ... ; (2) rhetorically ... ; (3) institutionally ... ; (4) generically ... ; (5) politically ... ; (6) historically' (Clifford 1986a: 6). Mind and cognition are absent from this list, and yet they are important determining factors: how and what people communicate depends on what they think, which in turn depends on their cognitive abilities. Against the assumption that the ethnographer's mind furnishes nothing but the locus where social and cultural determinations come together to influence the ethnographer's behaviour, findings from cognitive psychology suggest that the specifics of the human mind do impinge significantly on ethnographic production. In this chapter, I will describe some of the cognitive aspects of human communication and the cognitive abilities with which humans come to understand the intentions of others.

The approach I advocate consists in situating the production of public representations – ethnographies in our case – within the chain of production of representations and their cognitive effects. I propose using the approach of cultural epidemiology (Sperber 1996) to study ethnographers' practices and beliefs and the cognitive causal chain that produces ethnographies and ethnographic knowledge. The underlying pattern for thinking about ethnography in *Writing Culture* seems to be the simplistic chain shown below, upon which power relations and other macro-social events may subsequently be imposed:

fieldwork ➔ ethnographic data gathering ➔ ethnographic description

Instead, I suggest investigating the details of the processes through which representations are created and transformed, going from minds to the environment, through behaviour such as speaking or writing, and back again into other minds. This approach should serve to restore to cognitive processes their proper role in the production of the public representations being investigated. While *Writing Culture* has limited its analysis to the contingencies of language, rhetoric, power and history, I propose that the thinking processes by means of which ethnographers produce ethnographies and understand the ethnographies of their colleagues be taken into consideration. This approach implies looking at the infra-individual level, eventually making reference to the properties of the human mind. I illustrate this approach below, where I argue that ethnographers in the field rely significantly on their cognitive abilities when they attribute intentions to others.

In cognitive anthropology and socio-cognitive research, emphasis falls not only on the infra-individual level but also on the transmission and transformation of representations in the environment and through social interactions. In other words, cognitive processes are not restricted to working brains; rather, cognition, as cognitive anthropologist Ed Hutchins (1995) puts it, is distributed. Let us call 'ethnographic representations' those representations that have a significant role in the causal cognitive chains that lead to the production of published ethnographies. An epidemiological approach in the anthropology of anthropology would consist in tracking down ethnographic representations, from the perceptions of the anthropologist in the field to the dissemination of a published ethnography in the scientific community, and, thus, specifying the flow of these representations and the transformations they undergo. There is a rich set of cognitive processes at work in making sense of indigenous people's behaviour. These processes are implemented in the field, at the ethnographer's home university, when they are reading field notes, when they are phrasing the account for communicating with their colleagues, when the account is understood (or not), when feedback is given, when reviewers comment on texts, and when texts are edited. This incomplete list of the events that make up the cognitive causal chains that produce ethnographic knowledge shows that ethnographic cognition implies distributed cognition. I will return to distributed reflexive cognition as an important process that finds expression in ethnographies. In this epidemiological theoretical framework for reflexive anthropology, analysis of ethnographic texts has its own place: it is a key public representation that carries information, as I will argue, about the socio-cognitive causal chains of which it is an output.

To date, there are relatively few published contributions to the cognitive anthropology of anthropology, and even these are not always presented in these terms. Paulo Sousa's paper (Sousa 2003) is a remarkable case, as it is a self-declared work in the cognitive anthropology of anthropology, attempting to explain the history of the anthropology of kinship. In the last section, I will briefly refer to the work of Maurice Bloch (1998) and Dan Sperber (1996: 32–55), which I will relate to the approach and findings of *Writing Culture*. Now, however, I turn directly to a discussion of the work of Pierre Bourdieu, which will allow me to specify my understanding of the place of *Writing Culture* and textual analysis in the cognitive anthropology of anthropology. I will show that Bourdieu's understanding of the *Writing Culture* movement could be more charitable, and that the limits of his own reflexive project are in some senses similar to the limits of the *Writing Culture* approach: neither gives sufficient attention to the specifics of ethnographic cognition.

Bourdieu Versus the Writing Culture *Movement?*

Bourdieu describes his programme of 'participant objectivation' as cognitive anthropology of anthropology, or more precisely as 'reflexive cognitive anthropology' (Bourdieu 2003: 285). What is especially 'cognitive' in this sociology-cum-anthropology of science? Bourdieu refers to Durkheim's research programme in the sociology of knowledge (Durkheim 1912), which involves uncovering the categories of thoughts and their social origins. Applying this to the academic community, Bourdieu speaks of the 'academic transcendentals' in order to designate the categories of professorial understanding: for instance the classificatory schemata that French teachers implement in assessing students. He is, thus, applying his theory of habitus (Bourdieu 1977) to French academia.

Assessing the extent to which Boudieu's work may be deemed a contribution to the cognitive anthropology of anthropology would require questioning the truth of the psychological assumptions that are developed in his theory of habitus. Here, it suffices to note that the theory of habitus is, understandably, not informed by current theories in cognitive psychology. Like many theorists in the social sciences, Bourdieu often assumes that the human mind is a blank slate upon which culture and society write. He attempts to decipher what is being written on the blank slate in terms of habitus, but the specificity of the human mind is not given its proper role. Consequently, Bourdieu's reflexive cognitive anthropology departs far less from the project of *Writing Culture* than he suggests. The two projects remain fundamentally similar: the goal, in each case, is to reveal the epistemologies underlying ethnographic texts and the social context in which they arose.

Bourdieu (2003) insists on the importance of scientific analysis of the socio-cultural conditions of ethnographic knowledge production, and, indeed, he has dedicated much of his work to the study of the 'academic world' (Bourdieu 1975, 1976, 1982, 1984, 1997, 2001, 2003, 2004). His inaugural lecture at the Collège de France (Bourdieu 1982), for instance, is a sociological analysis of inaugural lectures at the Collège de France, viewed as academic rituals and institutions. In his book, *Homo academicus*, Bourdieu attempts to 'unveil and divulge ... the objective structures of a social microcosm to which the researcher himself belongs, that is, the structures of the spaces of positions that determine the academic and political stances of the Parisian academics' (Bourdieu 2003: 284). When applied to the social scientist himself – and, thus, also to the ethnographer – the programme is called 'participant objectivation'. It consists in the objectivation of the ethnographer, viewed as an objectifying agent.

Attempting to clarify his programme, Bourdieu spends some time distinguishing it from the *Writing Culture* movement. Unfortunately, he employs a dismissive tone, rather than a well argued refutation of the points of *Writing Culture*, as is evident in the following quotation:

> [R]eflexivity as I conceive it does not have much in common with 'textual reflexivity' and with all the falsely sophisticated considerations on the 'hermeneutic process of cultural interpretation' and the construction of reality through ethnographic recording. Indeed, it stands opposed at every point to the naïve observation of the observer which, in Marcus and Fisher (1986) or Rosaldo (1989) or even Geertz (1988), tends to substitute the facile delights of self-exploration for the methodological confrontation with the gritty realities of the field. This pseudo-radical denunciation of ethnographic writings as 'poetics and politics' to borrow the title of Clifford and Marcus's (1986) edited volume on the topic, inevitably leads to the 'interpretive scepticism' to which Woolgar (1988) refers and nearly manages to bring the

anthropological enterprise to a grinding halt (Gupta and Ferguson 1997). But it does not suffice either to explicate the 'lived experience' of the knowing subject, that is, the biographical particularities of the researcher or the Zeitgeist that inspires his work ... or to uncover the folk theories that agents invest in their practices, as the ethnomethodologists do. For science cannot be reduced to the recording and analysis of 'pre-notions' (in Durkheim's sense) that social agents engage in the construction of social reality; it must also encompass the social conditions of the production of these pre-constructions and of the social agents who produce them. (ibid.: 282)

I want to defend the *Writing Culture* authors from Bourdieu's attack by suggesting that there is no qualitative difference between their research and his. Both are engaged in a descriptive reflexive project. In contrast, one may renew and improve reflexive research in anthropology by taking the results of cognitive science seriously and using them as a basis for understanding ethnographic practices.

Bourdieu's first criticism is directed against the scepticism induced by *Writing Culture*. Arguably, it is valid to dismiss an assertion, not on the basis of its content but on the basis of its epistemic consequences; but the point is that *Writing Culture* does not necessarily lead to destructive scepticism. A radically sceptical attitude is arrived at only if, after the descriptive analysis, one pursues an evaluative programme leading one to conclude that viable criteria of scientific investigation – for example, an idealistic positivist model of science – are unattainable. Although such thoughts are lurking in *Writing Culture* – for instance, when Clifford laments that only partial truths can be obtained in ethnography – (Clifford 1986) – the authors of the volume do attempt to propose new modes of scientific knowledge production, rather than dismissing the ethnographic project altogether.

Bourdieu's second criticism concerns the scientific status of the targeted reflexive enterprises. He provides a well detailed analysis of the 'social conditions' that determine academics' pre-notions, and his analyses are developed using the explanatory power of sociological tools and concepts. In *Homo academicus*, for instance, Bourdieu includes a number of graphs and statistical data – an ostensibly scientific approach that the authors of *Writing Culture* did not consider. Bourdieu's contribution to the sociology of the social sciences puts more emphasis on scientific analysis than does *Writing Culture*. However, it remains the case that both Bourdieu's project and the *Writing Culture* project are reflexive in a way that gives prevalence to the analysis of the making of science. The textual analysis of *Writing Culture* is no less empirical than Bourdieu's clearly sociological analysis: textual analysis takes texts as cultural objects, describes their properties and studies their causes and effects.

The third attack on the *Writing Culture* programme addresses the substitution of 'the facile delights of self-exploration for the methodological confrontation with the gritty realities of the field'. Self-consciousness is not the only proposal of

Writing Culture – there is also, for example, the advocacy of polyphonic writing – but it is admittedly among the most prominent effects of *Writing Culture* on anthropological practice. Independent of the value of these self-exploring works for the advancement of anthropology in general, I think that these works can provide valuable information for the development of the anthropology of anthropology. Finding ways to exploit these works, rather than just dismissing them, is an important step in going 'beyond *Writing Culture*'. In Bourdieu's work one can observe that the more reflexive he gets, for example, the more he focuses on his own practice as a sociologist and anthropologist, the closer he comes to the self-exploratory texts of the *Writing Culture* movement.[5]

The 'study of the social conditions of the production of pre-construction', which is how Bourdieu characterizes his own reflexive research programme, is already present in *Writing Culture*. While the emphasis is on textual analysis, it aims at understanding the social and cultural origins and effects of rhetorical devices. Presenting the *Writing Culture* volume in the introduction, Clifford explains as follows: 'Most of the essays, while focusing on textual practices, reach beyond texts to contexts of power, resistance, institutional constraint, and innovation' (Clifford 1986a: 2). For instance, the underlying epistemology of the anthropologist is shown to justify the rhetoric of scientific authority, which itself reinforces the epistemology. The effects of colonialism on ethnographic practice are also analysed. As defined by Clifford, the programme of *Writing Culture* sounds quite rich, while we might wonder whether Bourdieu's programme ever reaches beyond the study of institutions and their modes of constraint. A more modest criticism of *Writing Culture* can be formulated, however. Its strength, which is the focus on texts, is also one of its weaknesses, for the analysis of the contextual determinations of ethnographies remains incomplete.

One of the reasons why Bourdieu does not manage to 'go beyond' the *Writing Culture* movement is that he explains the behaviour of ethnographers only with reference to the social conditions in which they are embedded. When it comes to the analysis of the behaviour of an individual scientist such as himself, Bourdieu inevitably ends up – despite his denials – in an autobiographical mode: the search for the cause of his own habitus consists in retracing his own life. If, in contrast to Bourdieu, one abandons the erroneous blank slate image of the mind, then one opens up the investigation of a whole range of determinants of the behaviour of the ethnographer: those that derive from the specific nature of the human mind. Self-exploration is then relegated to one factor of explanation, which must be understood in conjunction with what is known of human cognition: that is, taking into account the results of psychology and cognitive science. Another

---

5 Bourdieu's *Esquisse pour une auto-analyse* (Bourdieu 2004) includes a warning that takes the whole second page of the book: 'Ceci n'est pas une autobiographie', and the first pages insist on the aim of the scientific, sociological, objectivation of oneself. Yet, Bourdieu recalls in detail his past in the boarding school, at the École Normale Supérieure; his talks with his father; and includes sentences such as 'I have to confess that …', or 'I remember very well that …'

point that limits Bourdieu's analysis concerns his understanding of the social phenomena involved in ethnographic cognition, confined as it is to the transmission of values, practices and more generally habitus. However, the production of ethnographic writing involves socially implemented cognitive processes that are highly relevant for understanding ethnographies. Bourdieu's analysis must be enriched with the idea of distributed cognition.

From Texts to Thoughts: Referring to the Cognitive Genesis of Ethnographies

I argue in this section that some rhetorical conventions used in ethnographies provide information about the cognitive means that ethnographers have employed in acquiring ethnographic information and in formulating theories. These rhetorical conventions are used to communicate relevant information to the reader for assessing and understanding the truths of ethnographic descriptions. I review three such rhetorical conventions. The following two conventions are well described in *Writing Culture*: the autobiographical section at the beginning of ethnographies; and the absence of the author in the main body of texts. I also point out a third convention: the use of acknowledgements. One of my goals here is to relate the textual approach of *Writing Culture* to the cognitive anthropology of anthropology.

Why We Write and Read Acknowledgements

Here is a quotation from *Writing Culture*:

> I would like to thank the members of the Santa Fe seminar for their many suggestions incorporated in, or left out of, this Introduction. (I have certainly not tried to represent the 'native point of view' of that small group.) In graduate seminars co-taught with Paul Rabinow at the University of California at Berkeley and Santa Cruz, many of my ideas on these topics have been agreeably assaulted. My special thanks to him and to the students in those classes. At Santa Cruz, Deborah Gordon, Donna Haraway, and Ruth Frankenberg have helped me with this essay, and I have had important encouragement and stimulus from Hayden White and the members of the Research Group on Colonial Discourse. Various press readers made important suggestions, particularly Barbara Babcock. George Marcus, who got the whole project rolling, has been an inestimable ally and friend. (Clifford 1986a: 26)

You will have recognized this usually small part of academic texts, written in smaller characters and occupying a relatively modest place within the written artefact, most often in an endnote. These are the acknowledgements. As modest as their positioning may appear to be, acknowledgements form a genuine part of academic texts. They can be the subjects of textual analysis, as they constitute a genuine literary convention in the academic world. I am not aware that this convention has been studied by the authors of the *Writing Culture* movement, but acknowledgements provide a rich source of information on their favourite topics, such as power relations.

The acknowledgements quoted above are James Clifford's, located at the end of his introduction to *Writing Culture*. The passage in question is rather long, when compared to acknowledgements in most articles, and it contains many names; but it is relatively short for the acknowledgment section of a book – it is in between. Not everything can be done in an acknowledgement section. Jerry A. Fodor, a philosopher of mind, allows us to see the conventional and very formal aspects of the acknowledgment section by mocking it. After telling the usual story of how his book arose in a series of lectures, and so forth, and after acknowledging the feedback given to him by his peers, he continues, saying: 'Not one red cent was contributed to the support of this work by: The MacArthur Foundation, the McDonnell Pugh Foundation, the National Science Foundation, or the National Institutes of Health. The Author is listed alphabetically' (Fodor 2000: ix). Are acknowledgements purely formal artefacts with no genuine function other than allowing the author to express their debts – as if repaying these debts were a pressing desire that authors indulge in, and that editors and readers put up with? What do we learn from Clifford's acknowledgements? Why did he write them? Why did he think it important to include this boring list of names in his text? Having perused a large number of acknowledgements, Cronin et al. (1993) find that people or institutions are acknowledged for their moral support; their financial support; for having provided access (to facilities, data, etc.); for clerical support; and for peer-interactive communication. In general, the result is a somewhat cryptic but sufficiently informative description of the processes through which the article or book has been produced. The above acknowledgements are a case in point. We learn especially how much James Clifford's ideas have been discussed: with the participants of the Santa Fe seminar; with some graduate students at Berkeley and Santa Cruz; and particularly with Paul Rabinow. The list then continues with people who have had an impact on the written article itself. Being mentioned in acknowledgements is not only pleasurable, because it is a token gesture from the author, but it is also a way in which one can acquire prestige and power. The case of the funding bodies makes the point apparent. The more a funding body is acknowledged in important and valued texts, the more prestigious it becomes. But an inverse flow of prestige is also occurring: acknowledgements are rhetorical devices that confer authority to the author who acknowledges. Acknowledging the contribution of some authoritative person or institution is also appealing to this source of authority as a guaranty of quality. Often, the acknowledgements boast of a network of colleagues, as if one were aligning one's allies in order to impress those readers who may wish to criticize the text. This is the case in *Writing Culture*, in which seven out of the ten contributions (excluding the preface and afterword) include acknowledgements, all containing a list of the names of authorities in some relevant field. A social networking analysis of acknowledgements, questioning for instance the social conditions of reciprocity, would not be out of place in a study within the anthropology of anthropology. And a few, quite informative, studies on acknowledgements can be found in literature from the field of bibliometrics (Cronin 1995, 2004). In sociology journals, three quarters of the articles include acknowledgements and more than half include acknowledgements, which attest to interactive communication among peers. Among those acknowledged, only a very few are frequently included. The analysis revealed no relation between citation frequency and the frequency of being acknowledged (Cronin et al. 1993).

What would the *Writing Culture* movement do and say about the literary convention of acknowledgements? The convention of acknowledgments could, for instance, be denounced: they introduce power relations among academics as tools of persuasion; they are irrelevant to the object of the text; they appear as mystifying rhetorical devices, hypocritically put in a modest place in the text, but they are still meant to be read and still exert their influence on most readers. Pursuing this trend, one could suggest creating some new conventions of acknowledgement, or advocate their total elimination. However, a more descriptive analysis may be needed before evaluations and prescriptions can be recommended. Maybe some fieldwork would help. Do anthropologists read acknowledgements? What information do they expect to find in them? There seem to be multiple reasons for maintaining this literary convention: authors do derive some pleasure in acknowledging the contributions of friends and colleagues; and saying thanks already lightens the burden of the debt. Funding bodies, also, do insist that they are mentioned in acknowledgements.

Yet, an important reason why the practice of acknowledgment perdures can be traced to the expectations of the readership. In 2002, when one of my informants took her viva for the Ph.D. degree at Cambridge, her two examiners complained that she did not include acknowledgements in her thesis. The examiners wondered, at first, why she did not comply with the literary convention of writing acknowledgements, and then they explained that this omission prevented them from knowing who – in other words, which schools of thought and which institutions – had influenced her doctoral work.

For Davis and Cronin, 'acknowledgements necessarily imply a high degree of social interaction', and they suggest 'significant intellectual indebtedness', especially when they refer to peers in academic life: 'through their use of acknowledgements as tokens of intellectual indebtedness ("super-citations"), authors seem to conform to a normative behaviour that may be peculiar to a given field or closely related fields' (Davis and Cronin 1993: 592). Davis and Cronin think that acknowledgements are so revealing of academic life that they suggest using the number of occurrences of names in acknowledgement sections for research assessment procedures. The fact is that attestations of peer-interactive communication are very useful for understanding the cognitive processes through which texts are produced. Acknowledgements communicate something to the reader. They inform them about the cognitive processes that brought about the text and that are distributed among several anthropologists and experts. When Fodor mocks acknowledgements, he reserves his sarcasm for the funding bodies rather than for the peers with whom he actually interacted. Fodor would not want to damage his academic social network; furthermore, information about this network is relevant to the reader. Situating the author socially helps make sense of the text; it is as informative as reading the bibliography. Thus, acknowledgements refer to a key practice in science – anthropology included – which consists in communicating, discussing, arguing and evaluating the thoughts of others as well as one's own. Acknowledgements tell the readers that the article or book went through the argumentation and the critical processes that are part of scientific practices.

Why the Ethnographer Appears Where They Do

Taking acknowledgements as an illustration, I have started from a textual convention, first asking what reason authors could have for complying with the convention. I have then concluded that acknowledgements communicate something about the cognitive processes that result in the text, and I have suggested that information about these processes helps the reader to make sense of the text and evaluate the arguments. Conventional references within ethnographic texts to the ethnographer themselves also bear witness to cognitive processes involved in text production. Both the inclusion and the exclusion of references to the author in ethnographies are denounced in *Writing Culture* as mystifying literary conventions, contributing to the 'textual construction of anthropological authority'. In the words of Rabinow, 'Clifford ... argues that ... anthropological authority has rested on two textual legs: An experiential "I was there" establishes the unique authority of the anthropologist; its suppression in the text establishes the anthropologist's scientific authority' (Rabinow 1986: 244).

I maintain that these conventions are less mystifying than Clifford and other authors of *Writing Culture* pretend. They refer in fact to actual cognitive processes upon which ethnographic writing is based. The reader is not a naive child being mystified by deceptive rhetorical devices. Social anthropologists are convinced by a text because the rhetorical conventions that it displays correspond to two types of cognitive processes – interpretation during fieldwork and explanatory reflection in the academic world – that are themselves taken as warrants of good ethnographic thinking.[6]

---

6   Absent from Clifford's analysis of the rhetorical means through which Malinowski's authority is established in *Argonauts of the Western Pacific*, remarks Roth (1989: 557), 'is what makes a claim to authority socially acceptable'. The analysis of what is communicated by rhetorical conventions should take into account how the readers react to the conventions in question. This is what I will now attempt to do.

Respecting the new conventions issuing from *Writing Culture* makes ethnographies harder to read, often awfully boring and difficult to mine for theoretical elaboration. In this sense, it is perhaps the mode of writing of participants in the *Writing Culture* movement (rather than the project itself) that really annoys readers such as Bourdieu. Why, however, are traditional conventions more successful than the conventions advocated by the authors of *Writing Culture*? Why does polyphonic writing have so little appeal, while good old-fashioned descriptions of cultural phenomena, without any details about what the ethnographer feels, are still able to satisfy the majority of anthropologists, despite the criticism of Clifford and his colleagues? One answer is that the corresponding conventions are not, and have never been mystifying. They are understood to be expressive of the way ethnographies are produced and of the cognition involved in their production, and rightly so. A second, complementary answer for explaining the success of established conventions is that they favour scientific communication in one way or another. It is relevant to recount one's own adventures and situation at the beginning of an ethnography, and less relevant in the rest of the book.

One reason why the presence of the ethnographer in ethnographies is fruitfully limited to introductory chapters comes from the remarks made above: the writing of ethnography is, to a large extent, not the product of a single isolated author, but involves collaborative thinking. In anthropology, collaborative thinking is most apparent in departmental seminars. What anthropology *is*, as Spencer (2000) shows, is specified, communicated and learned during departmental seminars, which often impart tacit knowledge about how anthropology must be done. Departmental seminars are places of important social interaction where ideas are discussed and where cognition is distributed among the participants. In seminars, critiques include questions of clarification, attempts to make the anthropological literature relevant (for theory, regional studies, or the speaker's own field data), theoretical pointers about how to deal with the data, and suggestions that help either in applying theories in order to understand events or in using the data to formulate or refine theories. This latter type of comment shows that anthropology always consists of engaging in dialogue with other anthropologists, not only with nearby colleagues but also with the discipline's classical authors. When writing, one addresses the scientific community. Often, one attempts to answer questions previously asked or to refute or confirm arguments made by others. With reference to quantum mechanics, Mara Beller (2001) has drawn attention to and analysed this dialogical aspect of scientific practices.

Ethnographies are not written in the field. They are written in an academic setting – back at the ethnographer's home university, where they reflect on their fieldwork experience. They reflect by entering into a critical dialogue with both the literature in anthropology and with their colleagues. This dialogue is so intrinsic to the writing process that it is possible to say that the cognitive processes of writing ethnographies are always distributed among anthropologists. It is this reflexivity and the process of distributed critical thinking that renders the reference to the ethnographer in the field irrelevant, if not misleading, in the main part of ethnographic texts.

Ethnographies are not facsimiles of some unrealistic scientific ideals. They are to be understood as a means of scientific communication. So the question concerning the presence of the ethnographer in the main part of any ethnography is: what more could be communicated by providing further autobiographical details? The answer is that further information about the ethnographer is irrelevant, because ethnographies are meant to be answers to questions about cultures asked by members of the community of anthropologists. Simply said, ethnographies address an audience that is presumably not so very interested in the life of the ethnographer.

Admittedly, however, the absence of the ethnographer conveys a sense of scientific objectivity, but this conveyed meaning is mystifying only to the extent that science and objectivity are understood in an ultra-positivistic way. I doubt that this is usually the case. Only positivist philosophers ever thought that scientific descriptions could be pure data unspoiled by the person gathering it. For practising scientists, objective knowledge is, rather, knowledge that has gone through the process of critical assessment and that has been confronted with the ideas of other scientists. Objective knowledge is not subjective impression or opinion, because the authors have thought twice and had the help of others before writing. The hypothesis that anthropologists do not tend to interpret the absence of the ethnographer in ethnography as a sign of ultra-positivist objectivity seems to be more plausible than the idea that they were mystified before *Writing Culture* appeared in libraries.

Clifford (1982, 1986b) also remarks that (classical) ethnographies do contain a section dedicated to autobiographical information. While the bulk of their descriptions do not refer to their fieldwork experience, ethnographers often begin their ethnographies by describing how they arrived in the field, under which conditions they lived, how they interacted with the natives, and so on. Clifford and other authors of *Writing Culture* see in that textual convention yet another rhetorical way of imposing scientific authority (e.g., Crapanzano 1986; Rosaldo 1986). The underlying meaning of the autobiographical section is, they suggest: 'I have been there, so I know'. If many anthropological readers have found the ethnographer's claim to have 'been there' so convincing, one may, once again, pose the following question: Is it really because it is mystifying, or is it simply because it is convincing? And since ethnographers make the effort to write this autobiographical section and readers make the effort to read it, would it not be because it is in some way relevant?

The autobiographical section of an ethnography describes the conditions under which the ethnographer has interpreted indigenous people's behaviour. It provides insight into the cognitive processes of the ethnographer in the field, which they put to work in living and socializing with indigenous people and which eventually furnish the most fundamental thoughts for writing ethnographies. Knowing the conditions under which the ethnographer has produced these fundamental thoughts and formulated their basic interpretations of indigenous people's behaviour is highly relevant to the academic reader. By revealing these conditions, introductory information about the ethnographer's arrival and experiences in the field enables the reader to assess the ethnographer's ability to interpret. The autobiographical section, therefore, has a function similar to the acknowledgement section: it reveals the cognitive processes contributing to the production of the ethnography; it is a trace of, and a reference to, the making of ethnographies.

But what are these cognitive processes? How do ethnographers benefit from their time as participant observers and draw information for writing their future ethnographies? One needs to answer such questions in order to understand the relationship between ethnographies and the particular experiences that ethnographers have had in the field. But while sociology and the cognitive science of science provide some insight into reflexive processes in the academic setting, the literature in science studies says nothing about participant observation. In anthropology, there are manuals on participant observation, rich in methodological advice on practical matters, but the thinking processes of the participant observer are normally not addressed. The authors who have contributed most to our understanding of what happens in the head of the ethnographer are Maurice Bloch (1991, 1998) and Dan Sperber (1996: 32–55). I will now briefly review their ideas in relation to *Writing Culture*.

Cognizing Culture

Bloch's (1991) reflections on participant observation begin with a radical critique of the role usually given to verbal statements in anthropology. What is said is important to the extent that it gives some information about what is thought by the indigenous people, but the connection is far from immediate. What is said does not simply reflect what is thought. This is so since, the cultural knowledge of the indigenous people is not necessarily 'language-like'. Bloch points to the importance of tacit knowledge, and draws on connectionists theories in cognitive science, which assert that mental representations do not have the same structure as language. Non-linguistic knowledge can be rendered into language, but this process changes its character. Therefore, most of the informants' discourse will be *post-hoc* rationalizations and should be considered as such.

Bloch's contentions go strongly against the method of polyphonic writing. He argues that what people say is just one aspect of their behaviour and that reporting their statements in isolation can be misleading. What can the ethnographer do if the situation is as Bloch describes it? The answer lies, according to Bloch, in participant observation, since long-term presence within a community enables the ethnographer to acquire this cultural, non-linguistic knowledge:

> I believe that anthropologists who have done prolonged fieldwork have always obtained the basis of their knowledge about the people they study from informal and implicit co-operation with them, whatever they might have pretended. I am fairly sure that the way I proceed in giving an account of the Malagasy culture I study is by looking for facts, and especially for statements, that *confirm* what I already know to be right because I know how to live efficiently with these people. (ibid.: 194)

According to Bloch, the rendering of this cultural knowledge in ethnographies is based on introspection. Once knowledge is acquired by the ethnographer through continuous and intimate contact with those they study, it is possible to retrieve this knowledge through introspection and express it in written words.

I suggest that a specific cognitive ability is at work when 'cognizing culture': mind-reading, which is the ability to attribute desires, beliefs and intentions to others. The consequent account of the ethnographer's cognitive processes is, then, somewhat different from Bloch's. Rather than using introspection to retrieve and express the knowledge acquired during participant observation, ethnographers use the knowledge acquired in the field to inform their mind-reading abilities in order to formulate better interpretations of, and accounts for, the behaviour of indigenous people (including oral communication).

Much of participant observation consists in making sense of other people's behaviour. Attributing beliefs, feelings and inferences to other people is a day-to-day cognitive practice for the anthropologist observing and interacting with people in the field. Therefore, exploring the cognitive bases of the practice of participant observation requires giving an account of the cognitive processes that enable anthropologists to attribute beliefs, intentions and feelings to others, and, thus, to make sense of their behaviour. The ability to ascribe mental states to others is, in fact, shared by all members of the human species and is used successfully everyday in making sense of other people's behaviour. When dealing with the simplest of social interactions, we constantly reason about other's thoughts, motives and feelings. Mind-reading is also put to work in understanding what speakers mean by what they say (Sperber and Wilson 1986). Anthropologists' communication is no exception and also involves mind-reading. In seminars in departments of social and cultural anthropology, it is not uncommon to hear someone ask, 'what do you mean by …' It is a request for further specification of what the speaker had in mind, what exactly they wanted to convey.

Participant observation, I contend, relies quite fundamentally on the specifically human ability to ascribe mental states to others, or what has been dubbed 'mind-reading'. The mind-reading ability, also called Theory of Mind, has been much studied in cognitive psychology (e.g., Nichols and Stich 2003). There are, incidentally, different accounts of introspection in the psychological literature: according to the 'theory theory' of mind-reading, introspection is the application of mind-reading abilities to oneself – in which case introspection would have a less important role in ethnographic thinking than Bloch has hypothesized. According to the 'simulation theory' of mind-reading, we attribute intentions, beliefs and desires to others by 'imagining' we are in their situation ('putting oneself in their shoes') and then retrieving the result through introspection. From this perspective, introspection is indeed a cognitive process at the heart ethnographic thinking, but it serves, I maintain, not to retrieve tacit knowledge but to make sense of others by simulating what they might think and feel.

Saying that cognition in the field implicates human cognitive abilities is not a strong assertion; it is merely a reminder that ethnographers are, after all, human beings. What is of greater consequence is the assertion that one particular cognitive ability – mind-reading – is central to participant observation and at the heart of ethnographic thought. The use the participant observer makes of their mind-reading ability constitutes a central characteristic of anthropology. Once the pervasive and inevitable role of mind-reading in ethnography is recognized, new epistemological questions arise. Can we trust our mind-reading abilities when doing anthropology? Under what conditions? If mind-reading is as pervasive as has been claimed, what conception do we have, or should we have, of the ethnographer as a data collector? With Bloch (1991), I maintain that the acquisition of tacit, cultural knowledge is necessary for understanding other cultures. Contrary to Bloch, I do not think that culture is absorbed in the brain, and then exposed in ethnographies through introspection. What happens, rather, is that cultural knowledge informs mind-reading. Mind-reading abilities are more reliable when the person has learned how people normally behave, how people usually express their beliefs, feelings and desires, and about the circumstances of their lives, all of which provide the ethnographer with information about what is considered to be important, what is at stake.

The traditional justification for fieldwork is that the fieldworker can testify: they have observed, and they can tell their community what they have seen. *Writing Culture* shows that this traditional account does not stand up under close analysis. For instance, Clifford states: 'The specific accounts contained in ethnographies can never be limited to a project of scientific description so long as the guiding task of the work is to make the (often strange) behavior of a different way of life humanly comprehensible' (Clifford 1986b: 101). I suppose that what he means is that there cannot be a description that does not deeply involve ethnographic thinking, interpretation or mind-reading cognition. The ethnographer necessarily and automatically puts their mind-reading abilities to work in order to make sense of indigenous people's behaviour. I also hypothesize that mind-reading abilities attain a significant degree of reliability only after minimal enculturation. Consequently, fieldwork is not bound merely to impartial, external observation; fieldwork is understood as social and cognitive training for developing mind-reading abilities appropriate to the cultural environment. One can, indeed, dispense with a naive view of testimony, understood as the presentation of data unspoiled by interpretation, as the participants in the *Writing Culture* movement argue. There remains, however, the possibility of rethinking the ethnographer's testimonial work as warranted by the cognitive training of their mind-reading ability that is provided by long-term fieldwork. This, in turn, also makes it possible to rethink the process of attributing authority to the ethnographer. In *Writing Culture*, Mary Louise Pratt writes as follows:

> Fieldwork produces a kind of authority that is anchored to a large extent in subjective, sensuous experience. One experiences the indigenous environment and lifeways for oneself, sees with one's own eyes, even play some roles, albeit contrived ones, in the daily life of the community. But the professional text to result from such an encounter is supposed to conform to the norms of a scientific discourse whose authority resides in the absolute effacement of the speaking and experiencing subject. (Pratt 1986: 32)

My point, however, is that the subjective, sensuous experiences, while being part of the cognitive training of the participant observer, are irrelevant as such. Most of the time, they do not even need to be conscious and can rarely be expressed linguistically. What is important is that they inform mind-reading, which can then result in plausible interpretations of indigenous people's behaviour. It is these interpretations that will constitute the core of any given ethnography. The effacement of the speaking and experiencing subject is a consequence of a double cognitive process. To begin with, mind-reading makes a detour around personal feelings (that have previously informed it) and automatically provides interpretations of other's behaviour; then, following that, distributed critical thinking comes into play during the writing up of ethnographies. However, the autobiographical introduction in ethnographies remains relevant, because it informs the reader of the conditions under which the author has trained their mind-reading abilities. It is valuable information for evaluating the ability of the ethnographer to provide a reliable interpretation of indigenous people's thoughts and desires.

Unfortunately, there is little work in cognitive psychology on the role of enculturation in mind-reading.[7] In ethnographic fieldwork, the process of enculturation is experienced by adults, rather than by children who are born into the community under investigation. Fieldworkers learn through participant observation – that is, through actual social interactions with indigenous people. Could the autobiographical, self-conscious work of postmodernist ethnography help in analysing how enculturation informs mind-reading? If so, it would contribute both to cognitive psychology and to our understanding of ethnographic cognition. We might, for example, gain insights comparable to those provided by Ellingson (1998), who shows in great detail how experiencing fear and pain is a necessary prerequisite for understanding the behaviour and thoughts of those others who have experienced similar fears and pains.

Finally, let us reflect on the role that mind-reading abilities have or should have in ethnographic and anthropological cognition. This is what Sperber does in his essay, 'Interpreting and Explaining Cultural Representations' (1996: 32–55).[8] Sperber recognizes the necessity of interpretation in anthropology, but wonders about the extent to which anthropological explanations should be informed by it. Interpretation is necessary, because it is the means of making sense of others' behaviour: 'we are all producing explicit interpretations when answering questions such as: what did he say? What does she think? What do they want? In order to answer such questions, we represent the content of utterances, thoughts, or intentions by means of utterances of similar content' (ibid.: 34). I have called this kind of interpretive activity 'mind-reading'. Sperber agrees that mind-reading should enter into ethnographic thinking. His doubts concern the extension of interpretation or mind-reading into domains that are beyond their natural grasp. If the cognitive function of mind-reading abilities is to interpret people's behaviour, can interpretation be applied fruitfully to other phenomena? Sperber concludes as follows: 'In anthropology, however, what gets interpreted is often a *collective representation* attributed to a whole social group ... The lack of a clear methodology makes it difficult to evaluate, and hence to exploit, these interpretations' (ibid.: 35). In other words, reading the minds of individual people is generally reliable, but attempting to apply mind-reading to social groups can lead to nonsense: whole groups do not really have minds that can be read.

My goal is not to tackle the epistemological and methodological problems that Sperber raises, but to show that opening descriptive analysis to the cognitive processes involved in ethnographic production gives rise to new and interesting questions and addresses some of the concerns of the authors of *Writing Culture*.

Conclusion

In a departmental seminar, held by Richard Rottenburg at the Martin Luther University in spring 2005, Akira Okazaki asked the participants why they had chosen to study anthropology. Most of them answered that they wanted to discover other cultures, but one student answered that he wanted to know himself better. This was a departmental seminar, and, as we now know, departmental seminars are contexts within which anthropology is continually defined and redefined. Okazaki was very pleased with this particular student's answer; and,

---

7   But see Lilliard (1998), along with the comments; and Chiu et al. (2000).
8   I have singled out this essay, but the idea is present in all of his criticisms of interpretive generalizations.

indeed, it is possible to view anthropology as a way of delving further into self-consciousness. One postmodern trend is to understand anthropology as a therapeutic enterprise directed largely towards achieving self-awareness. From this perspective, going abroad for fieldwork may be comparable to lying on the psychoanalyst's sofa. I have argued, however, that this is not the understanding of anthropology that is proposed in *Writing Culture*. Going beyond *Writing Culture* implies continuing the reflexive project that is advocated by the authors of that book in order to produce better knowledge about social and cultural phenomena. One fruitful way to continue this project, I have suggested, is to go beyond the theoretical limits of *Writing Culture* by studying anthropological cognition.

Clifford noted in *Writing Culture* that 'Much of our knowledge about other cultures must now be seen as contingent, the problematic outcome of intersubjective dialogue, translation, and projection' (1986b: 109). Doing cognitive anthropology of anthropology means engaging the details of these contingencies, which implies analysing the cognitive practices of ethnographers. I have suggested that anthropological cognition is human cognition – that is, it is based on the fundamental abilities that characterize the human mind – in the cultural milieu of anthropology. I have identified two cognitive processes at the heart of ethnographic cognition: first, the distributed cognitive processes of critical reflexive thinking; and second, mind-reading, the basis for interpreting culturally situated events that include human behaviour. Of course, there are many more cognitive events that are implicated in the making of ethnographies. For instance, mind-reading is also at work during social interactions among social anthropologists, and cognition is also distributed among the indigenous people. However, the cognitive processes that I have specified play a role that is reflected in some rhetorical aspects of ethnographies. The ethnographer appears in ethnographies at the beginning, because this appearance lets the reader know that the author has been in position to make sense of indigenous people's behaviour. Later references to the life of the ethnographer in the field are irrelevant to most readers, who want to know about the cultural phenomena being investigated. I therefore contend that this rhetorical convention results from social anthropologists' belief that participant observation is the best means to understand indigenous people's behaviour. Drawing on cognitive psychology, I have argued that what really grounds such beliefs is the fact that ethnographers' mind-reading abilities, which they put to work to make sense of indigenous people's behaviour, become more reliable after some kind of enculturation.

Ascribing beliefs to social anthropologists – the indigenous people of the reflexive enterprise in anthropology – is a way of making sense of some of their cultural practices, such as the ones implemented in writing ethnographies. For instance, I hypothesize that social anthropologists are keen to have at least some minimal information about the distributed reflexive processes to which the ethnographer's ideas were subjected – which is one of the reasons why acknowledgements are often included in books and papers. But my main contention in this chapter is that the reflexive enterprise that was begun in *Writing Culture* is best pursued by developing further the cognitive anthropology of anthropology, which implies gathering information about anthropologists' behaviour. And, by the way, did you read the acknowledgments that I wrote?

References

Beller, Mara. 2001. *Quantum Dialogue: The Making of a Revolution.* Chicago: University of Chicago Press.

Bloch, Maurice. 1991. 'Language, Anthropology and Cognitive Science', *Man* 26(2): 183–98.

———. 1998. *How We Think They Think: Anthropological Approaches to Cognition, Memory, and Literacy.* Boulder, CO: Westwiew.

Bourdieu, Pierre. 1975. 'La spécificité du champ scientifique et les conditions sociales du progrès de la raison', *Sociologie et Société* 7(1): 91–118.

———. 1976. 'Le champ scientifique', *Actes de la recherches en sciences sociales* 2–3: 88–104.

———. 1977. *Outline of a Theory of Practice.* Cambridge: Cambridge University Press.

———. 1982. 'Leçon sur la leçon', *Leçon inaugurale au College de France* (no. 90). Paris: Éditions de Minuit.

———. 1984. *Homo academicus.* Paris: Éditions de Minuit.

———. 1997. *Les usages sociaux de la science: pour une sociologie clinique du champ scientifique.* Paris: INRA Éditions.

———. 2001. *Science de la science et réflexivité.* Paris: Éditions Raisons d'Agir.

———. 2003. 'Participant Objectivation', *Journal of the Royal Anthropological Institute* 9(2): 281–94.

———. 2004. *Esquisse pour une auto-analyse.* Paris: Éditions Raisons d'Agir.

Chiu, Chi-yue, Michael W. Morris, Ying-yi Hong and Tanya Menon. 2000. 'Motivated Cultural Cognition: The Impact of Cultural Theories on Dispositional Attribution Varies as a Function of Need for Closure', *Journal of Personality and Social Psychology* 78(2): 247–59.

Clifford, James. 1982. *Person and Myth: Maurice Leenhardt in the Melanesian World.* Berkeley: University of California Press.

———. 1986a. 'Introduction: Partial Truths', in James Clifford and George E. Marcus (eds), *Writing Culture: The Poetics and Politics of Ethnography.* Berkeley: University of California Press, 1–26.

———. 1986b. 'On Ethnographic Allegory', in James Clifford and George E. Marcus (eds), *Writing Culture: The Poetics and Politics of Ethnography.* Berkeley: University of California Press, 98–121.

Clifford, James and George E. Marcus (eds). 1986. *Writing Culture: The Poetics and Politics of Ethnography.* Berkeley: University of California Press.

Crapanzano, Vincent. 1986. 'Hermes' Dilemma: The Masking of Subversion in Ethnographic Description', in James Clifford and George E. Marcus (eds), *Writing Culture: The Poetics and Politics of Ethnography.* Berkeley: University of California Press, 51–76.

Cronin, Blaise. 1995. *The Scholar's Courtesy: The Role of Acknowledgements in the Primary Communication Process.* London: Taylor Graham.

———. 2004. 'Bowling Alone Together: Academic Writing as Distributed Cognition', *Journal of the American Society for Information Science and Technology* 55(6): 557–60.

Cronin, Blaise, Gail McKenzie, Lourdes Rubio, and Sherrill Weaver-Wozniak. 1993. 'Accounting for Influence: Acknowledgements in Contemporary Sociology', *Journal of the American Society of Information Science* 44(7): 406–12.

Cronin, Blaise, Gail McKenzie and Michael Stiffer. 1992. 'Patterns of Acknowledgements', *Journal of Documentation* 48(2): 107–22.

Davis, Charles H. and Blaise Cronin. 1993. 'Acknowledgements and Intellectual Indebtedness: A Bibliometric Conjecture', *Journal of the American Society for Information Science* 44(10): 590–92.

Durkheim, Émile. 1912. *Les formes élémentaires de la vie religieuse: Le système totémique en Australie.* Paris: Felix Alcan.

Ellingson, Laura. 1998. '"Then You Know How I Feel": Empathy, Identification, and Reflexivity in Fieldwork', *Qualitative Inquiry* 4(4): 492–514.

Fodor, Jerry. 2000. *The Mind Does Not Work That Way.* Cambridge, MA: MIT Press.

Hollis, Martin and Steven Lukes. 1982. *Rationality and Relativism.* Cambridge, MA: MIT Press.

Hutchins, Ed. 1995. *Cognition in the Wild.* Cambridge, MA: MIT Press.

Kornblith, Hilary. 1987. *Naturalizing Epistemology.* Cambridge, MA: MIT Press.

Kuper, Adam. 1983. *Anthropology and Anthropologists: The Modern British School.* London: Routledge.

———. 1999. *Among the Anthropologists: History and Context in Anthropology.* London: Athlone.

Lilliard, Angeline. 1998. 'Ethnopsychologies: Cultural Variations in Theories of Mind', *Psychological Bulletin* 123(1): 3–32.

Nichols, Shaun and Stephen Stich. 2003. *Mindreading: An Integrated Account of Pretence, Self-Awareness, and Understanding Other Minds.* Oxford: Oxford University Press.

Pratt, Mary Louise. 1986. 'Fieldwork in Common Places', in James Clifford and George E. Marcus (eds), *Writing Culture: The Poetics and Politics of Ethnography.* Berkeley: University of California Press, 27–50.

Rabinow, Paul. 1986. 'Representations are Social Facts: Modernity and Post-Modernity in Anthropology', in James Clifford and George E. Marcus (eds), *Writing Culture: The Poetics and Politics of Ethnography.* Berkeley University of California Press, 234–61.

Rosaldo, Renato. 1986. 'From the Door of His Tent: The Fieldworker and the Inquisitor', in James Clifford and George E. Marcus (eds), *Writing Culture: The Poetics and Politics of Ethnography*. Berkeley: University of California Press, 77–97.

Roth, Paul A. 1989. 'Ethnography without Tears', *Current Anthropology* 30(5): 555–69.

Sousa, Paolo. 2003. 'The Fall of Kinship: Towards an Epidemiological Explanation', *Journal of Cognition and Culture* 3(4): 265–303.

Spencer, Jonathan. 2000. 'British Social Anthropology: A Retrospective', *Annual Review of Anthropology* 29: 1–24.

Sperber, Dan. 1996. *Explaining Culture: A Naturalistic Approach*. Oxford: Blackwell.

Sperber, Dan and Deirde Wilson. 1986. *Relevance: Communication and Cognition*. Cambridge, MA: Harvard University Press.

Stocking, George W. 1992. *The Ethnographer's Magic and Other Essays in the History of Anthropology*. Madison: University of Wisconsin Press.

Wilson, Bryan Ronald. 1970. *Rationality*. Oxford: Blackwell.

9

Hard Truths: Addressing a Crisis in Ethnography

Stephen P. Reyna

✿

This essay [1] was written in the twentieth year after publication of *Writing Culture* (Clifford and Marcus 1986), a text believed by many to offer a decisive break with a moribund modern anthropology through the offer of a literarily enriched postmodern ethnography. The passage of time offers commentators something of a vantage point to contemplate the significance of *Writing Culture*. I wish to use this vantage point to identify one of *Writing Culture*'s epistemological consequences and, in so doing, to suggest a way of going beyond it. The consequence in question is a negative one, that *Writing Culture* exacerbated a crisis in ethnography. Further, I suggest a way of ameliorating this crisis. Argument proceeds in three stages. First, it is shown that there *is* an epistemological crisis in ethnography heightened by *Writing Culture*. This crisis is that ethnographers make their texts in ways largely indifferent to questions of truth. Second, a pragmatic notion of approximate truth is developed. Third, in conclusion, it is argued that approximate truths are hard ones whose forging can ameliorate ethnography's crisis. In order to illuminate the crisis in ethnography, let us turn to the notion of agnosognosia.

1   Originally presented at the workshop 'Beyond *Writing Culture*: Current Intersections of Epistemologies and Practices of Representation', 28–29 September 2006 at the Max Planck Institute for Social Anthropology, Halle/Saale, Germany. I am indebted to the spirited comments of various workshop contributors as well as to the editorial acumen of Olaf Zenker and Karsten Kumoll.

Agnosognosia

agnosognosia, a useful psychiatric term for a lack of awareness of one's own condition.

—Ian McEwan (2005: 74)

Reader, study the curious lexeme agnosognosia. We shall bring it into the analysis following explication of *Writing Culture*'s treatment of truth. There were nine contributors to *Writing Culture* – James Clifford, George E. Marcus, Mary Pratt, Vincent Crapanzano, Renato Rosaldo, Steven A. Tyler, Talal Asad, Michael Fischer and Paul Rabinow. They did not agree on all matters, and Clifford in his introduction carefully stated that the volume's essays did 'not represent a tendency or perspective' (Clifford 1986: 4). However, this did not dissuade outside commentators from the belief that theirs was a common project. Perhaps, at the core of this project, as Clifford put it in his introduction to the volume, was a sense of 'crisis in anthropology' (ibid.: 3); posing the question, what is this crisis? Marcus and Fisher, in *Anthropology as Cultural Critique* (Marcus and Fisher 1986), a companion volume to *Writing Culture*, appeared to answer this question when they stated, 'The crisis arises from uncertainty about adequate means of describing social reality' (ibid.: 8). This meant that the crisis was epistemological, because if you could not represent reality you could not know it. A second view *Writing Culture*'s contributors shared was that in some way ethnography would resolve this crisis. After all, as Marcus put it, ethnography was the 'heart' of anthropology (Marcus 1994: 42). Further, Tyler stressed 'Evocation – that is to say "ethnography" – is the discourse of the post-modern world, for the world that made science, and that science made, has disappeared, and scientific thought is now an archaic mode of consciousness surviving yet in a degraded form' (Tyler 1986: 123). A third shared aspect of *Writing Culture*'s project was an interest in the application of literary approaches in anthropology. As Marcus explained it, the task of *Writing Culture*'s authors was 'to introduce a literary consciousness to ethnographic practice' (Marcus 1986: 262).

Such consciousness raising meant that the heavy epistemological lifting in *Writing Culture* was concerned, as the sub-title of the volume made clear, with the 'poetics' of ethnography. Nowhere in *Writing Culture* is it explained how poetics is employed. However, implicit in its textual usage is an Aristotelian constructivist interpretation. Aristotle in his *Poetics* defined poiesis as the 'activity of creating or making' (Runes 1962: 241). So for Clifford, 'Ethnographic writings can properly be called fictions in the sense of "something made or fashioned," the principal burden of the word's Latin root, *fingere*' (Clifford 1986: 6). Something made is something constructed, and such a constructivism appeared to offer *Writing Culture*'s authors a way out of the 'crisis of anthropology'. This was to analyse how ethnographies were made; that is, to study their poetics, especially their 'conventions of ethnographic writing' (Marcus 1986: 163).

Because humans have limited resources to do things, if resources are expended upon one endeavour, others suffer. This situation is conceptualized as opportunity cost in economics. There were opportunity costs to *Writing Culture*'s authors' expenditure of intellectual resources upon the project of establishing a literary ethnography. One of these was an indifference to establishing true ethnography; that is, to establishing ethnographies whose accounts could be judged as to how well they exhibited truth. The index of *Writing Culture* indicates that 'true' is mentioned seven times (Clifford and Marcus 1986: 304).[2] These citations reveal *Writing Culture*'s contributors' opinions about truth. The first of these is articulated by Tyler, who suggests that ethnography, which he equates with evocation, is 'beyond truth' (Tyler 1986: 123). The point here is that truth is irrelevant to ethnography and so does not need to be considered. Tyler simply asserts his position. Argument by assertion is argument without warrant. It commits a fundamental fallacy of argument; to wit, arguing without argument – with the fallacy being that saying it is so does not make it so.

The second of the *Writing Culture*'s contributors' attitudes towards truth was advocated by Rabinow who advanced a Foucault/Hacking line; namely, that 'the production of truth is epiphenomenal to something else' (Rabinow 1986: 240). The 'something else' is a Foucauldian regime of truth or, as Rabinow explains Hacking, a 'style of thinking', both of which establish statements as truth or false. Foucault's and Hacking's positions are complex and contested. Rabinow's explication of them neither explicates the complexities, nor warrants why they win the contest as the way to proceed on matters of truth. Rabinow's approach exhibits a fallacy of argument termed 'begging the point'. Such arguments provide reason for knowing why X is true, when what one is arguing for is Y. Certainly, it is correct that at different times and places different cultural, political and economic regimes will influence what is believed to be true. For example, due to the regime of truth in Nazi Germany, opinion had it that 'the Jews were an inferior race' (X). However, regime-of-truth arguments, while they may tell you something about what people believe to be true, beg the point of providing warrant for whether or not what people believe to be true, is true (Y).

A third attitude towards truth exhibited by *Writing Culture* authors was articulated by both Clifford and Crapanzano, who asserted truths to not be 'the whole truth' (Crapanzano 1986: 53) but, rather, 'inherently partial' (Clifford 1986: 7). Certainly, truths can be partial – or, as I would prefer to term it, approximate – but the problem with Clifford's and Crapanzano's position is that though they assert truth's partiality they do not warrant it. They provide no consideration of what a partial truth might be or how to construct one. Hence, there was indifference in *Writing Culture* of the need to make truths. One can go further.

---

2   In fact, I noted two other places where it was mentioned: on pages 123 and 130.

I believe that for the most part anthropologists have been on the extreme fringe of twentieth century arguments raising scepticism concerning the possibility of truthful knowing (Reyna 2004). For example, I know of no instance where an anthropologist takes an influential defence of truth – say Alston's (1996) alethic realist approach – and states what might constitute a justified argument against it; and, then, makes that argument. Most anthropologists seem unaware of what the various positions were that led to scepticism in the first place – for example, Duhem's views on underdetermination, Wittgenstein's on epistemic relativism, or Kuhn's on incommensurability. So they seem even less aware that these views have been critiqued (Kitcher 1995; Zammito 2004; Boghossian 2006) and that what is really needed are critiques of the critiques of epistemic scepticism. *Writing Culture*, then, was not so much a radical mutation in the anthropological epistemology as a culmination of a trend, a trend distinguished by neglect for the truth of ethnographic statements. Now it is time to return to the crisis of anthropology.

A 'crisis in anthropology' was signalled in *Writing Culture* in the mid 1980s, which its authors hoped to resolve by raising the 'literary consciousness' of ethnography. Many cultural anthropologists sought to participate in this project, because it was regarded as a 'watershed' volume (James, Hockey and Dawson 1997: 1). So in the years that followed, as Hüwelmeier observed, the example of *Writing Culture* focused many ethnographers' attention upon 'a search for a new ethnographic style' (Hüwelmeier 2000: 45), heavy on 'literary consciousness', indifferent to truth. Then, nearly two decades after the publication of *Writing Culture*, Marcus announced something truly horrific: ethnographies were 'objects of aestheticism and often summary judgment and evaluation', 'judged quickly,' used 'to establish reputation, and, then ... often forgotten' (Marcus 2002: 3). An intellectual discipline whose chief contribution is 'often forgotten' is, indeed, in crisis. Which poses the question, why are ethnographic texts 'forgotten'? Now it is time to introduce agnosognosia into the analysis.

Ethnography may be 'fiction', 'something made'. But what gets made in ethnographies are texts. These texts contain statements about social and cultural actualities. It is better that statements about reality be truer. After all, untrue actualities are about what is not, and who is interested in what is not. To make this point, consider the statement, 'the Bush II regime does not make war'. This is untrue, so who needs to know it. Remember that agnosognosia means a 'lack of awareness of ones condition', and *Writing Culture*-inspired ethnography is unaware of any imperative to work towards truth. Bluntly put, *Writing Culture*-inspired ethnographers become epistemological dodos sticking their heads in the sands of unwarranted, fictional statements. This, then, is the true crisis of ethnography, and the remainder of this chapter seeks to ameliorate it. It does so by suggesting how to develop what many call approximate truths (Laymon 1985; Niiniluoto 1987; Resnik 1992; Weston 1992), but which I ultimately prefer to call hard truths.

Formulating Approximate Truths

The view of approximate truth developed below is influenced by William James and Charles Peirce, two of pragmatism's founders, and so it is broadly speaking pragmatic. The concern is not with the question, 'what is truth', but with, 'what do you have to do to formulate more accurate and reliable statements about reality' because, practically speaking, more accurate and reliable statements are approximately truer than less accurate and reliable ones. The statements I am interested in are generalizations, or sets of generalizations – sometimes structured as deductions (as in some economic theory), or at other times as concatenations (as in Darwinian evolutionary theory) – that explain realities observed in nature (it being understood that social and cultural realities are just as much part of nature as physical or biological realities). Generalizations are judged to be 'approximately true' if they can confront reality and be shown to reliably and accurately picture it, even though the exact truth of that reality remains a mystery. Approximate truths are partial ones in the sense that they are not attempts to know the whole truth, or, in nineteenth-century positivist terms, the absolute truth. They are only true in so far as their accuracy and reliability is known. Thus, such a view of truth is post- (at least nineteenth-century) positivist. Key to understanding the present approach to approximate truth is grasping what is meant by confrontation, then accuracy, and finally reliability.

The notion of confrontation is not one of different thinkers with different theoretical positions in aggressive competition (Reyna 2001). Rather, it is confrontation between different ideas about reality with reality. Generalizations are a particular symbolizing of reality defined by their structure, whose parts are concepts and whose relations are relationships between concepts. Generalizations state that certain things go on in reality. Confrontation occurs when observation produces perceptions of reality that may, or may not be, what the generalizations state should go on. A confrontation is said to show the truth of a generalization if what is perceived to go on is what the generalization states will go on. Consider, for example, the generalization, 'military occupation of a people frequently leads to resistance by that people'. There are two concepts in this generalization – 'occupation' and 'resistance' – which exhibit one relationship, the former concept leading to the latter. If it is perceived that the U.S. occupies Iraq and that there is both Sunni and Shi'ite resistance to this, then it can be said that the generalization has confronted perceptions of the world, and what is perceived to occur is what the generalization states will occur. If this is the case, then it is said that the generalization has been verified, confirmed or validated, and is approximately true for this one instance of confrontation. A brief word is in order about why the notion of validation is to be preferred to those of confirmation or verification.

Validation, confirmation and verification have tended to be roughly equated. However, confirmation seems inappropriate because of its popular connotations. It has too final a ring. If you are a Catholic, you get confirmed, and it's over and done with. If a theory has been confirmed, it is over and done with; it is true. The same objection applies to the term 'verification', which has often been understood 'as complete and definitive establishment of truth' (Carnap 1953: 48). The problem, as Carnap observed, is '*no complete verification is possible*' (ibid.: 49, original emphasis). This is the case because verification involves a finite number of confrontations of perceptions of reality with particular generalizations of reality. However, reality is effectively infinite, which means that confrontations only occur for small chunks of reality, so there are huge chunks of it hurtling through space and time that go unconfronted. So the less absolute term 'validation' seems preferable, because it implies that a theory can be validated as approximately true, even though it has not been confirmed or verified as the truth. Specific confrontations that lead to validation will be said to have their histories. Confrontation, in this optic, is about establishment of validation histories. Such histories are what need to get made to construct approximate truths. However, before continuing, let us consider falsification, a condition for validation.

Falsification is associated with Karl Popper, and his views might be interpreted as relaxing the need to validate, which I do not believe to be the case. Let us understand how such a misconstrual might have arisen. The concept of falsifiability was developed to address what Popper believed was a flaw in the validation of theory. The weakness was that, 'it is easy to obtain confirmation, or verification, for nearly every theory – if we look for confirmation' (Popper 1963). This is problematical because if every theory has its validation, every theory is true, which is untrue. Now the preceding seems to suggest that Popper was recommending falsification over validation. This, I believe, was not Popper's intent. Popper developed the notion of falsifiability because, as he later recalled, he 'wished to distinguish between science and pseudoscience', which meant he sought 'a criterion for the scientific character or status of theory' (ibid.). Falsifiability was this criterion. A generalization pictures reality in a certain manner. By virtue of its picturing in one manner, reality should not turn out to be pictured in some other manner. If reality does turn out some other way, alien to how it is pictured in the generalization, then the generalization's picture is false. It has been falsified. Thus, the criteria of falsifiability are: Firstly, if a generalization can be compatible with some perceptions of reality, and incompatible with other observations, then it is falsifiable. And secondly, if a generalization is compatible with all perceptions of reality then it is unfalsifiable. The point here is that validation is not possible unless falsification is possible. Thus, the set of all confrontations of falsifiable generalizations that results in some information bearing upon validation may be said to be a validation history.

Let us make clear what happens during confrontation. This involves recognizing a difference between observational and theoretical concepts, a distinction originally made by Carnap (1966). Observational concepts are those that can be immediately apprehended following brain processes that produce perception. Look at a couple whose lips are touching. You see they are kissing. 'Kissing' is an observational concept. Theoretical concepts are apprehended as a result of the application of cognitive rules to the observational concepts which raise the abstraction and generality of these latter concepts. Sense the couple kissing; apply the rule 'people kissing are intimate', and discover that the kissing couple are exhibiting intimacy. 'Intimacy' is a more theoretical concept than kissing.

Generalizations may be imagined to make pictures. The first picture is that of theoretical, the second that of observational, concepts. Theoretical concepts picture reality abstractly. Observational concepts picture it in terms of what the abstractions will mean in terms of perceptions of reality. Sense organs make observations of reality and, as a result, perceptions are formed. It is possible to confront these perceptions with observational concepts. Confront the perception of a 'barking thing,' assign it the observational concept of 'dog'. Further, it is possible to confront observational terms with the more abstract pictures of theoretical concepts. To illustrate, consider the more theoretical generalization: 'The closer the kinship between persons, the greater their altruism'. 'Kinship' and 'altruism' are more abstract concepts; 'father' and 'son' are more observational forms of close kinship; while 'giving food' and 'not giving food' are more observational forms of altruism. The theoretical picture here is of 'a positive relationship between close kinship and altruism'. The observational picture of this theoretical picture is of 'sons give food to fathers'. If it is detected that the observational picture, produced by reality, is the same as that imagined by the theoretical picture, then it can be said that the theoretical picture is validated by reality because what is theorized to go on in reality is perceived to go on there. If such a confrontation can be established, the generalization is said for that set of observations to be validated. If no such a confrontation can be established, then, it is falsified. Validation histories are records of confrontations made. Validation histories can be evaluated in terms of their accuracy and reliability. Why these are important for approximate truth and how they are recorded is discussed next.

Accuracy and Reliability

Truth for us is simply a collective name for verification processes … pursued because it pays to pursue them. Truth is made.

—William James (1968: 143)

William James in the above quotation essentially asserts: Give up on ultimate truths in favour of believing that statements are as true as the verification or, as I prefer, validation processes which make them. This shifts the chore in truth-making to developing validation processes. Different disciplines exploring different realities develop different techniques for validating their generalizations. However, to be useful these techniques need to satisfy two epistemological conditions. They need to be able to make the different confrontations in a validation history as accurate and reliable as possible. I begin by discussing accuracy.

Accuracy

Accuracy is not about how well generalizations correspond to reality. It is about the capacity of concepts to observe reality in confrontations. The greater the usability of concepts by observers making observations, the greater their accuracy. Blur is bad for accuracy. This is because blur reduces accuracy, making it difficult to connect observational pictures with theoretical pictures of reality. 'Blur' epistemically is a situation either, firstly, where there are no clear instructions tying theoretical to observational concepts or, secondly, where theoretical as well as observational concepts are in some way obscure. The 'tying' of theoretical to observational terms refers to the existence of rules that specify when an observational term is an instance of a theoretical term; and vice versa, when a theoretical term is a general category of an observational term. Instructions specifying what observational concepts correspond to what theoretical concepts are called 'correspondence rules' by Carnap (1953). A 'wife', for example, is an instance of a 'kinsperson' because of the rule, 'kinspersons are those able to show consanguinity or affinity to each other'. Conversely, a 'kinsperson' is a general category included in which are 'wives' because of the rule, 'wives are specific instances of the general category of persons exhibiting consanguinity and affinity'. A concept is 'obscure' when it is unclear what perceptions qualify as instances of it. For example, the notion of 'God' is obscure because nobody knows what qualifies as a perception of 'Her', 'Him' or 'It'. Untied and obscure concepts mean that the observer does not know what a generalization should do to their perceptions that will validate or falsify it. They are all a blur, which is why they are inaccurate.

Concepts are often left untied in the heat of high theorizing. Consider for example the postmodern notion of rhizome. Gilles Deleuze and Felix Guattari developed this concept in *A Thousand Plateaus* (1987) by taking a well known term from plant biology and pressing it into service in social theory. They explain rhizome as follows:

> Let us summarize the principal characteristics of a rhizome: unlike trees or their roots, the rhizome connects any point to any other point, and its traits are not necessarily linked to traits of the same nature; it brings into play very different regimes of signs, and even non-sign states. The rhizome is reducible neither to the One nor the multiple. It is not the one that becomes Two or even directly three, four, five, etc. It is not a multiple derived from the One, or to which One is added (n+1). It is composed not of units but of dimensions or rather directions in motion. It has neither beginning nor end, but always a middle (*milieu*) from which it overspills.

It constitutes linear multiplicities with n dimensions having neither subject nor object, which can be laid out on a plane of consistency, and from which the One is always subtracted (n-1). (ibid.: 19)

This definition of rhizome works as follows. The first five sentences in the definition tell readers what the rhizome is not, thereby providing them with no information as to what perceptions qualify as instances of the concept. The sixth sentence asserts something about the rhizome. It is 'linear multiplicities with n dimensions having neither subject nor object'. These can be 'laid out on a plane of consistency' where 'the One' is always subtracted '(n-1)'. But these sentences contain no correspondence rules telling analysts what realities might indicate an observational term that corresponds to the theoretical term 'rhizome'. A person who wishes to use the concept of rhizome is given no instructions as to what observational concept(s) correspond to these 'linear multiplicities' where 'the One' is 'subtracted'. Consequently, the concept of rhizome is inaccurate because its component concepts are untied, which means it is impossible to guess what in the world Deleuze and Guattari are talking about.

Let us consider two major contributors to obscurity. These are vagueness and ambiguity. C.S. Peirce proposed what has become a central understanding of vagueness, stating, 'A proposition is vague when there are possible states of things concerning which it is intrinsically uncertain whether, had they been contemplated by the speaker, he would have regarded them as excluded or allowed by the proposition' (Peirce 1902: 748). For example, consider the observational concept 'tall'. Now it is intrinsically uncertain whether a person 6'1" is tall or whether a person 6' 2" is tall.

A second sort of obscurity is due to ambiguity. This is where there are two or more clearly different senses of a concept and, hence, potential confusion as to which sense applies. For example, the word 'funny' in English can mean either a 'person who is humorous' or a 'person who is a bit crazy', and sometimes it is hard to distinguish an amusing person from one who is wacko. Many common cultural concepts are both vague and ambiguous. For example, the English kin term 'child' is ambiguous between 'offspring' and 'immature offspring'. Further, the latter reading of 'child' is vague because it is uncertain when an offspring ceases to be immature. Let me illustrate the sort of problems that can arise when vagueness and ambiguity are ignored.

Consider the generalization proposed in Kant's *Perpetual Peace* (1795) that, 'democracies do not fight other democracies' (Kant 1957: 67–110), widely accepted as true in mainstream U.S. social science (Lake 1992; Mintz and Geva 1993), including anthropology (Ember, Ember and Russett 1992).[3] However, the concept 'democracy' is ambiguous and vague: ambiguous because the term is subject to numerous definitions; vague because, as with tallness, the conditions

---

3　There are, however, some negative views on this matter: see, e.g., Layne (1992).

that divide democratic from non-democratic governments are indefinite. Let us consider certain problems that arise from the concept's ambiguity. Two general and different definitions of democracy exist. Under the first, a polity is democratic if it has a voting system for major offices; while under the second, a polity is democratic if all its citizens have more or less equal influence over its decisions.

A problem arises for the generalization that 'democracies do not fight each other' with the former understanding of democracy, because in 1954 and 1970 the U.S. government covertly used violence against the governments of Guatemala and Chile. So, when voting is made an observational concept that indicates the existence of democracy, the validation history is that democracies fought each other in 1954 and 1970. In these confrontations, the observations falsify the generalization. However, if democracy is defined in terms of the equal ability of citizens to influence decisions, then there is a body of findings indicating that the U.S. is oligarchic (Mills 1956; Palast 2003; Domhoff 2006). If this is the case, then the same confrontation yields a different observation regarding the generalization, because now a non-democracy (the U.S.) wars against democracies (Guatemala and Chile). This finding validates the generalization but is the opposite finding of the previous confrontation, using a different understanding of democracy. Ambiguity allows for different findings when the same reality is confronted with different meanings of a term.

Cultural anthropologists seem mesmerized by vague and ambiguous concepts. Terms like deconstruction, imaginary, polyphonic and genealogy float in their texts like algae in mud puddles. I am not proposing to drain the puddles. Rather, I am suggesting that when such terms are employed it is important to specify if it is in the strict sense of their creators; if these senses are ambiguous and vague; and, if so, to offer unambiguous and non-vague alternatives. This means, for example, if the concept of deconstruction is used it is important to specify whether it is used in a pure Derridian sense, or whether it is used, as is occasionally the case, as a synonym for 'criticism'. If it is used in the strict sense of Derrida, it is important that the user show the term to be accurate. This is especially the case because Derrida, when asked about the definition of deconstruction responded, 'I have no simple and formalizable response to this question. All my essays are attempts to have it out with this formidable question' (Derrida 1985: 4). However, the task of making accurate concepts is important because approximately truer generalizations are more accurate ones cleared of blur resultant from untied and obscure concepts. Let us turn in the next section to investigating the role of reliability in making approximate truth.

Reliability

Other things being equal, provided that there is accuracy, a generalization is approximately truer the more reliable it is. The higher a generalization's total ladder score and positivity ratio in its validation history, the greater its reliability. The notions of evidential ladder, total ladder score, positivity ratio and validation universe need to be explained in order to grasp this assertion. However, their explication depends upon a further exposition; that of Peirce's views upon the role of common sense in truth because in his view reliability is just a matter of common sense.

Common sense

Peirce wrote an article entitled 'How to Make Our Ideas Clear' (1878) proposing, 'the opinion which is fated to be ultimately agreed to by all who investigate is what we mean by truth' (Peirce 1958b: 133). So truth is what is 'agreed to' by those 'who investigate'. This view is clarified by considering letters from a correspondence Peirce had towards the end of his life with Lady Viola Welby, who shared his interest in semiotics. In a 1909 letter he explained that reality 'is such that whatever is true is not true because some individual person's thought or some individual groups of persons' thoughts attributes its predicate to its subject, but is true, no matter what any person or groups of persons may think *about it*' (Peirce 1958c: 419; original emphasis). There appears to be a contradiction in Peirce's views on truth. He wrote in 1878 that truth was what was 'agreed to' by those 'who investigate'. However, three decades later, he informed Lady Welby that something was true 'no matter what any ... groups of persons may think'. How does one resolve the apparently contradictory statements of 1878 and 1909?

One interpretation returns to other, earlier statements in which Peirce talks of both truth and agreement. These statements can be found in his 'Critical Discussion of Berkeley's Idealism' (1871). Here Peirce said, 'There is, then, to every question a true answer, a final conclusion, to which the opinion of every man is constantly gravitating. He may for a time recede from it, but give him more experience and time for consideration, and he will finally approach it' (Peirce 1958a: 81–82). This quotation asserts that a person will find truth given 'more experience and ... consideration'. A few sentences on he introduces 'final agreement' into his argument, stating:

On many questions the final agreement is already reached, on all it will be reached if enough time is given. The arbitrary will or other individual peculiarities of a sufficiently large number of minds may postpone the general agreement in the opinion indefinitely; but it cannot affect what the character of that opinion shall be when it is reached. The final opinion, then, is independent ... of how you, or I, or any number of men think. (ibid.: 82)

Peirce's position, if one puts the two previous quotations together, is that given 'enough time', there will be 'final agreement' concerning truth of what a group of individuals' 'experience' and give 'consideration', posing the question: What is this 'agreement'? This question is answered in the paragraph following that of the previous quotation, where Peirce says,

> to assert that there are external things which can be known only as exerting a power on our sense, is nothing different from asserting that there is a general *drift* in the history of human thought which lead it to one general agreement, one catholic consent. And any truth more perfect than this … is a fiction of metaphysics. (ibid.: 82, original emphasis)

Thus, Peirce's understanding of agreement is not some gentleman's conspiracy, where the truth is anything a community confabulates. Rather truth is what a particular community, that of 'investigators', is 'fated' to believe following their investigations. Fate is not understood here as superstition or chance. Rather it is 'that which is sure to come true'; as Peirce reminds us, for example, 'We are all fated to die' (Peirce 1958b: 133). Ultimately, knowledge of what is fated is through 'experience and … consideration'. One investigator has 'experience and … consideration' of one reality, and observes that something always happens there. Another investigator has 'experience and … consideration' of the same reality, and observes the same something happens. Still other investigators have the same 'experience and … consideration' of the same reality, and the same something happens. This is Peircian agreement: investigators' concurrence that the same somethings occur in the same experienced realities.

Agreement may be conceptualized as common sense because, according to Peirce, each individual investigator, experiencing the same reality, comes up against the same 'external things' that exert 'a power' over the 'sense'. The implication here is that given 'enough time' investigators will recognize that the same 'external things' have the same 'power' over 'sense'. One person observing another for 'enough time' senses that the other will die. A second person, observing someone for 'enough time' senses that someone will die. Every person who observes every other person for 'enough time' eventually senses it. The agreement here comes from observations that produce common senses; and this 'common sense' is agreement about that which is fated to occur. We die. Reliability concerns how often something said to happen actually happens. What is supposed to happen with a car is that it drives. If it breaks down a lot, it does not drive as much. It is unreliable. Thus, the more that investigators' confrontations share a common sense of how 'external things' produce other 'external things', the more reliable is their knowledge. Otherwise put, a generalization's reliability is a matter of common sense. Approximate truths, once the best accuracy possible has been achieved, are generalizations with the most common sense and, hence, reliability.

Peirce talked only in the broadest sense of how investigators achieved such agreement. I suggest below that common sense will be about 'getting high'. This high has nothing to do with elevating euphoria and everything to do with total ladder scores on evidential ladders and positivity ratios on validation histories. Recall that a validation history is a record of investigators' confrontations of a generalization with reality. Such a history is based upon 'validation episodes', a particular instance of the confrontation of a generalization with the reality to which it pertains. Specifically, then, a validation history is the record of all the validation episodes made by investigators bearing upon a particular generalization. Recall further that reliability is how much it is that investigators of a generalization have a common sense that the validation is, or is not, validated. Reliability of validation histories can be established in two ways. The first establishes how much data there is bearing upon the validation of a specific validation episode. Evidential ladders and total ladder scores are used to establish this information. A second way that reliability can be evaluated is to record how many positive validation episodes there are in different validation episodes of a validation history, with the positivity ratio a statistic summarizing the ratio of positive to total validation episodes. Let us consider evidential ladders and total ladder scores.

Evidential ladders and total ladder scores
Researchers might be thought of as climbing a stepladder when they acquire more positive evidence validating a generalization. An 'evidential ladder' has steps concerning how much of the reality pictured in a generalization is observed in a confrontation. Specifically, the steps of the ladder involve five criteria for evaluating the amount of positive evidence in a single validation episode. These 'steps' include the degree to which there are observations bearing upon observational concepts that pertain to all the theoretical concepts in the generalization. A first step is whether there is positive evidence supporting a generalization for some of its component concepts. The second step is whether there is positive evidence for all of the generalization's component concepts. The third step is whether there is evidence that observations are representative. The fourth step is whether there is evidence of temporal order. The fifth step concerns the existence of evidence of production.

'Representativeness' refers to whether the observations have been in some way biased to compromise the sensing of a reality that pertains to a concept. For example, if the concept in use is one of 'people' and observation is made only of males, then the observations are biased towards men and against women. Evidence that is either unrepresentative or not known to be representative is incomplete in the sense that it does not provide observations concerning the reality it is biased against, or it is unknown what it may be biased against. Ethnographers' observations, due to the time demands of participant observation, generally come from small numbers of persons. Hence, their statements to the effect that such and such people have such and such a cultural notion or social practice are particularly open to questions of representativeness.

Evidence about temporal order and production is relevant to causality. Causality has been treated cavalierly in cultural anthropology since the 1970s (see especially Geertz 1973, 1983). The approach used here was formulated in Reyna (2002) and is based upon the work of Miller (1987) and Salmon (1998). A causal generalization proposes that events in reality happen in different spaces and times. First something happens in one space; next something else happens in another space, with the first something being antecedent in time and a cause of the second something, which is a subsequent effect. For example, it is widely accepted that occupation causes resistance. 'Temporal order' is measurements of observations indicating that the antecedents and consequents are in their proper order. First you see the occupation, and then you see the resistance. Additionally, in causal generalizations the causes bring about – that is, 'produce' – the effects. 'Production' is evidence that shows how it is that a cause is able to produce its effect. Perhaps occupation brings about resistance because it provokes feelings of injustice and rage in the resistors toward the occupiers. Production in this case would be evidence of high levels of such emotions after the occupation and before the resistance. To illustrate use of evidential ladders, let us discuss some generalizations showing where they might be placed on the steps of the evidential ladder.

A first step on the evidential ladder would be positive findings concerning some, but not all, of the states of observational concepts and relationships in a generalization. If such evidence exists, and there is no information concerning representativeness, temporality and production, then the confrontation has boosted the generalization one step up on the evidential ladder. For example, I conducted ethnography to explain low fertility among women among the Barma in Chad (Reyna 1972, 1975). This fieldwork was a validation episode, seeking to validate that: A conjunction of a certain type of culture concerning natality and marriage practices caused a high incidence of pelvic inflammatory disease (PID) which, in turn, caused low fertility. This generalization suggested that Barma women had few children because they experienced a high incidence of PID which scarred and closed the fallopian tubes preventing conception. Barma women had a high incidence of PID because their strongly pro-natal culture drove them to want many children. However, men had to pay bridewealth to marry. The costs of bridewealth were high, roughly equivalent to buying a house in the U.S. So men had to postpone marriage for a long time until they acquired the bridewealth. During this time they were not celibate. Rather, they tended to sleep with unmarried women from whom they acquired venereal infections. Then they married much younger women, and passed on their illnesses to their wives. Such women, due to these illnesses, either had no children or only a single child. At this point the cultural pro-natalism again became relevant. Women with no or only one child were failing their culture. This was a ground for divorce. Divorce sent the women back into a population of women with whom young, unmarried men had sexual relations.

The research provided measurements of the states of observational concepts that were relevant to the low fertility, the culture relevant to children, and marriage practices. Barma were highly pro-natalist. They did have high bridewealth. They did have a high age differential between men and women at marriage: men were about eleven years older than their wives. Barma women did have low fertility. However, there was no evidence, one way or the other, because I could not acquire it, of PID. Thus, this research was a first step of the evidential ladder. Let us climb another rung on the ladder.

It is generalized that: In non-state, food producing societies different forms of post marital residence are a cause of different forms of descent groups (Harris 1997: 268–69). The argument is that virilocal and/or patrilocal post-marital residence causes patrilineages or patriclans, while uxorilocal or matrilocal post-marital residence causes matrilineages or matriclans. There are two theoretical concepts in this generalization and one relationship. The theoretical concepts are 'forms of post marital residence' and 'forms of descent groups'. The relationship is one of causation. The observational concept for post-marital residence is, 'in what household of what kin does a married couple live'; while for descent groups the observational concept is, 'what are the married couple's stated clan or lineage memberships'? There are problems validating this generalization because no ethnographer has ever witnessed the emergence of descent groups. Rather, the evidence used to validate it comes from measuring whether, in non-state, food-producing societies, particular forms of post-marital residence are found in association with particular forms of descent groups. This evidence comes from a sample of societies that are included in the Human Relations Area Files (HRAF).

Positive evidence supporting the generalization would be measurements that indicate, firstly, when the married couples go to live with the husband's kin after marriage then there are kin groups based on patrilineal descent; and secondly, when the married couples go to live with the wife's kin after marriage, then there are kin groups based upon matrilineal descent. William Divale and Marvin Harris (1976) provided evidence from the HRAF bearing upon the states of these two concepts. They generally found that when husbands went to live with their wife's kin after marriage, people belonged to kin groups where they said they were descended from a founder of the group through a line of females. They also generally found that where wives went to live with their husband's kin after marriage, people belonged to kin groups where they said they were descended from a founder of the group through a line of males. Such findings indicate that the forms of post-marital residence associated with the forms of descent group are those predicted by the generalization. However, the evidence provided by Divale and Harris provides no measurements as to what came first, descent groups or post-marital residence. Nor does it provide evidence about how post-marital residence brings about – that is, produces – descent groups. Finally, there is no knowledge whether the societies included in the HRAF are representative of all the non-state, food producing societies that have ever existed. Thus, the confrontation of the generalization with the facts was positive, but there is no information concerning temporality, productivity and representativeness. Divale and Harris's validation episode might be said to have moved their generalization a second step up on the evidential ladder. If at some time it was ascertained that the sample of peoples from which the Divale and Harris findings are based is representative of all human populations, then the validation episode would mount to a third step on the evidential ladder. It is time again to be moving on up the ladder.

It is asserted that regressive taxation is related to social inequality. Specifically, it has been generalized: Regressive taxation legislation in advanced capitalist states causes increased social inequality (Phillips 1990). The observational concepts that measure the states of these two theoretical concepts are 'actual votes in the U.S. Congress enacting tax legislation benefiting the rich' and 'actual counts of who gets what amounts of wealth in the U.S.' A confrontation would produce positive evidence if it was observed that there were votes in the U.S. Congress that benefited the wealthy, and that this was followed by a situation where wealthier people become richer and everybody else had the same or less wealth.

Such a confrontation has been made for President Ronald Reagan's administration where it has, indeed, been observed that the U.S. Congress enacted as law various regressive taxation measures. For example, the U.S. top-bracket income tax was 70 per cent of taxable income in 1980, declining during the Reagan presidency to 50 per cent in 1983 and 28 per cent in 1988. It is further observed that afterwards richer people got wealthier, while much of the population had the same or reduced amounts of wealth. For example, it has been shown for representative data samples that average household net worth increased for the wealthiest 1 per cent of households by 42.2 per cent between 1983 and 1998, while average household net worth declined for the poorest 40 per cent of households by 76.3 per cent over the same period (Phillips 1990; Batra 1996). Finally, there is temporality in this evidence. First, the tax laws were voted on; next, inequality rose. Thus, the regressive taxation/social inequality generalization is a fourth step on the evidential ladder.

We will stop ascent of the evidential ladder on the fourth rung because we have already illustrated how the more extensive the observations bearing upon a generalization, the greater the common sense about it and, so, the greater its reliability.

What, then, is a total ladder score? This is the total value of evidential ladder scores for all the validation episodes in a validation history. This can be illustrated if we return to the generalization: A conjunction of a certain type of culture concerning natality and marriage practices caused a high incidence of pelvic inflammatory disease (PID) which, in turn, caused low fertility. Remember that we awarded the research that was the basis of this validation episode an evidential ladder score of one. Let us imagine that a later ethnographer went to the same area, conducted a representative sample survey of Barma women, and was medically able to confirm that, first, men's search for bridewealth led to their gonorrhoea; second, gonorrhoea scarred and closed their partners' fallopian tubes; and, finally, that their partners became infertile. If this were the case, this validation episode would be a five on the evidential ladder, while the total ladder score for the two validation episodes would be a six. The higher the total ladder score, the greater the Peircian common sense and, consequently, the greater the reliability of the generalization. The following section discusses how to establish positivity ratios as a second way of measuring the reliability of all the episodes in a validation history.

Positivity ratios and validation histories

If a validation history is the set of all validation episodes bearing upon a specific generalization, then a positivity ratio may be defined as the ratio of the number of validation episodes in which the confrontation is positive – that is, validates the generalization – considered in terms of the total number of validation episodes in the validation history. Such a ratio might be formally expressed as:

Positivity ratio = number of positive validation episodes/total number of validation episodes (100).

If the positivity ratio of a validation history is positive for its two validation episodes, as is imagined for the generalization concerning Barma women's infertility, then the positivity ratio for that generalizations' validation history is 100 per cent. The generalization looks pretty reliable.

Explicit formulation of positivity ratios is not part of current ethnographic practice, so it is not possible to specify them with any certainty. However, a generalization advanced by certain nineteenth-century unilinear evolutionists concerning whether the 'uncivilized' were lazy may be used to illustrate how such ratios would operate. L.H. Morgan, for example, referring to Native Americans, tied the simplicity of their economies to the absence of a 'passion' that drove those in their 'race' to become 'civilized'. Morgan generalized: 'The great passion [for economic gain] of civilized man ... never crossed the Indian mind. It was doubtless the great reason for his continuance in the hunter state, for the desire for gain is one of the earliest manifestations of the progressive mind. It ... has civilized our race' (Morgan 1851: 57). The generalization here is classic racism: Inferior races are lazy.

Such a generalization might be thought of as a premature ejaculation. After all, as Malinowski said in the early 1920s, concerning economics, 'There is no other aspect of primitive life where our knowledge is more scanty' (Malinowski 1922: 84). Social anthropological research altered this situation. Malinowski's own work on the Trobriand economy in both *Argonauts of the Western Pacific*

(Malinowski 1922) and *Coral Gardens and their Magic* (Malinowski 1935), along with Firth's on Tikopia in *Primitive Polynesian Economy* (Firth 1939) and Audrey Richards's on the Bemba in *Land, Labour, and Diet* (Richards 1939), provided detailed observations on the economies of those said to be of 'inferior races' that might be seen as validation episodes bearing upon Morgan's generalization.

For example, in *Argonauts*, Malinowski (1922) documented that one aspect of Trobriand culture was the belief that certain objects called *vaygu'a* – principally bracelets (*mwali*) and necklaces (*soulava*) – were of immense value and, hence, desirable to possess. He further observed that a particular form of distribution, called the *kula*, in which Trobrianders made long ocean voyages exchanging *vaygu'a*, was an important way by which the Trobrianders could satisfy their goal of acquiring value. In fact, most of *Argonauts* can be read as a documentation of how hard the natives worked (building canoes, sailing canoes, and so on) to acquire value. After reading *Argonauts*, pundits might fault Trobrianders for putting their faith in bangles, but they could not fault them on their work ethic to get those bangles. A tacit criticism in Malinowski's text was that the natives would labour for themselves, not their colonizers. Hence, Malinoswki's findings were negative. Further, Firth's and Richards's findings generally supported those of Malinowski. Accordingly, by the 1940s, a validation history existed that consisted of at least three validation episodes all of which had negative findings concerning the 'inferior races'/laziness generalization. If this were the case, then in three out of four validation episodes bearing upon Morgan's generalization the findings were negative. This meant the positivity ratio would be a low of 25 per cent, suggesting an unreliable generalization whose approximate truth should be viewed as problematic. Finally, let us consider validation universes with duelling generalizations.

Validation universes

Validation up to now has only been concerned with a single generalization. However, it may be desirable to validate two or more generalizations at the same time. This can be done through the creation of 'validation universes'; that is, two or more validation histories, for two or more generalizations, dealing with the same reality. This means that the confrontation is about the reliability of different generalizations confronting the same reality. Judgments about the reliability of such duelling generalizations could be had by making total ladder scores and positivity ratios for the validation histories of the component generalizations in the validation universe. It being understood, assuming the generalizations to be equally accurate, that the generalizations with the lower scores and ratios are the less reliable, and, hence, less approximately true.

The importance of evaluating duelling generalizations in validation universes cannot be underestimated, because it is often argued that there is no single truth to situations and that, in fact, the same reality can be understood in terms of multiple truths. Perhaps this is the case in some instances. Newtonian mechanics certainly holds true for the solar system as does Einsteinian quantum physics, though the latter's physics is true both at the level of the solar system as well as the entire universe. However, there are cases where generalizations that appear to be true on the basis of one or two validation episodes turn out not to be so when the validation universe is enlarged to include more validation episodes per validation history.

To illustrate such a situation reconsider two duelling generalizations concerning laziness. Remember it was Morgan's contention that, 'membership in "inferior races" determines laziness'. Recall further that the Malinowskian riposte to this was that, 'cultural preferences determine value, and that people will be lazy about working for what is unvalued'. These two generalizations deal with roughly the same reality, that of people working. The findings of validation episodes conducted by Morgan, Malinowski, Firth and Richards are fairly anecdotal, and would not be especially high on any evidential ladder; so total ladder scores are likely to be quite low for both generalizations.

However, it is possible to imagine that for Morgan's generalization, as was just suggested, there would be just one positive confrontation (his own) plus three negative ones (of Malinowski, Firth, and Richards); thus, the positivity ratio of Morgan's generalization is 25 per cent. However, for Malinowski's riposte there would be three positive confrontations and only one negative one, a 75 per cent positivity ratio. Hence, in this validation universe the Malinowskian riposte looks pretty reliable when compared to Morgan's undependable original generalization. The point here is that on the basis of a validation universe of only two validation episodes – that of Morgan and Malinowski – the two generalizations look equally true; but when the validation universe is enlarged it is possible to discern that Malinowski's riposte is more reliable and, so, it is the approximately truer generalization. It is time to draw the argument to a conclusion, contemplate crisis, and learn some hard truths.

Hard Truths

This essay revealed two hard truths. The first, exposed by Marcus, was that the chief intellectual product of cultural anthropology, ethnography, was 'often forgotten'. The first section of the chapter explained why this was the case. Ethnographers, wallowing in agnosognosia, are for the most part unaware that they need to reflect upon their statements in order to do things that make them truer. This agnosognosia was encouraged by *Writing Culture*, but it characterized earlier cultural anthropology. It is a hard truth that if ethnographers are indifferent to the truth of their fictions, then their fictions are likely to be 'often forgotten'.

The essay's second section offered an epistemological sketch of how to make approximately truer fictions. The reflexivity of truth-making consists in reflecting upon confrontations between what generalizations say about reality and what reality, in the form of perceptions, says about generalizations. The work involved in such reflection is what it takes to establish the most accurate and reliable generalizations. Blurred concepts were less accurate. Blur was a function of correspondence rules, ambiguity and vagueness, and it was argued that the clearest correspondence rules together with the least ambiguous and vague concepts resulted in the less blurry, more accurate generalizations. Generalizations with blurred concepts can never be true because they can never be validated. Peirce with his very particular version of common sense – what researchers perceive in common – helps us understand reliability. This is because the more thinkers have the same perceptions about generalizations' confrontations with reality, the greater the reliability of the perceptions. Common sense involves establishing validation histories for generalizations and, then, discovering their total ladder scores and positivity ratios. Different generalizations in a validation universe, with concepts at more or less the same level of accuracy, may have different total ladder scores and positivity ratios. Those generalizations that in the common sense of researchers have the highest such scores and ratios are the most reliable. They are the approximate truths in that universe.

So researchers who have worked to make the most accurate and reliable generalizations have laboured to make approximately truer generalizations. Such work is hard. This is the second hard truth revealed in this essay. Approximate truths constructed on the basis of establishing accuracy and reliability are literally hard truths. Finally, this recognition allows us to go beyond *Writing Culture* and, concurrently, to contribute to solving the crisis of ethnography. Going beyond *Writing Culture* and helping to solve the crisis involves doing the work of making hard truths. The alternative is to continue being 'forgotten'.

References

Alston, William. 1996. *A Realist Conception of Truth*. Ithaca, NY: Cornell University Press.

Batra, Ravi. 1996. *The Great American Deception*. New York: Wiley.

Boghossian, Paul. 2006. *Fear of Knowledge: Against Relativism and Constructivism*. Oxford: Oxford University Press.

Carnap, Rudolf. 1953[1936/7]. 'Testability and Meaning', in Herbert Feigl and May Bordbeck (eds), *Readings in the Philosophy of Science*. New York: Appleton-Century-Crofts, 47–93.

———. 1966. *Philosophical Foundations of Physics*. New York: Basic Books.

Clifford, James. 1986. 'Introduction: Partial Truths', in James Clifford and George E. Marcus (eds), *Writing Culture: The Poetics and Politics of Ethnography*. Berkeley: University of California Press, 1–26.

Clifford, James and George E. Marcus (eds). 1986. *Writing Culture: The Poetics and Politics of Ethnography*. Berkeley: University of California Press.

Crapanzano, Vincent. 1986. 'Hermes' Dilemma: The Masking of Subversion in Ethnographic Description', in James Clifford and George E. Marcus (eds), *Writing Culture: The Poetics and Politics of Ethnography*. Berkeley: University of California Press, 51–77.

Deleuze, Gilles and Felix Guattari. 1987. *A Thousand Plateaus*. Minneapolis: University of Minnesota Press.

Derrida, Jacques. 1985. 'Letter to A Japanese Friend', in David Wood and Robert Bernasconi (eds), *Derrida and Différance*. Warwick: Parousia, 1–5.

Divale, William and Marvin Harris. 1976. 'Population, Warfare, and the Male Supremacist Complex', *American Anthropologist* 78(3): 521–38.

Domhoff, G. William. 2006. *Who Rules America?* 5th edn. New York: McGraw Hill.

Ember, Carol, Melvin Ember and Bruce Russett. 1992. 'Peace Between Participatory Polities: A Cross-Cultural Test of the "Democracies Rarely Fight Each Other" Hypothesis', *World Politics* 44: 573–99.

Firth, Raymond. 1965[1939]. *Primitive Polynesian Economy*, 2nd edn. New York: Norton.

Geertz, Clifford. 1973. *The Interpretation of Cultures*. New York: Basic Books.

———. 1983. *Local Knowledge: Further Essays in Interpretive Anthropology*. New York: Basic Books.

Harris, Marvin. 1997. *Culture, People, and Nature*, 7th edn. New York: Addison-Wesley Longman.

Hüwelmeier, Gertrud. 2000. 'When People are Broadcast their Ethnographies: Text, Mass Media, and Voices from the Field', *Social Anthropology* 8(1): 45–51.

James, Allison, Jenny Hockey and Andrew Dawson. 1997. *After Writing Culture: Epistemology and Praxis in Contemporary Anthropology*. London: Routledge.

James, William. 1968[1907]. *Pragmatism*. New York: Meridian Books.

Kant, Immanuel. 1957[1795]. *Perpetual Peace*, Lewis Beck (ed.) New York: Liberal Arts Press.

Kitcher, Philip. 1995. *The Advancement of Science: Science without Legends, Objectivity without Illusions*. Oxford: Oxford University Press.

Lake, David. 1992. 'Powerful Pacificists: Democratic States and War', *American Political Science Review* 86: 24–37.

Laymon, Ronald. 1985. 'Idealizations in the Testing of Theories by Experimentation', in Peter Achtinstein and Owen Hannaway (eds), *Observation, Experiment, and Hypothesis in Modern Physical Science*. Cambridge, MA: MIT Press.

Layne, Christopher. 1992. 'Kant or Cant: The Myth of Democratic Peace', *International Security* 19: 5–49.

McEwan, Ian. 2005. *Saturday*. London: Vintage.

Malinowski, Bronislaw. 1922. *Argonauts of the Western Pacific.* New York: Dutton.
———. 1935. *Coral Gardens and Their Magic,* 2 vols. London: Allen and Unwin.
Marcus, George E. 1986. 'Contemporary Problems of Ethnography in the World System', in James Clifford George E. Marcus (eds), *Writing Culture: The Poetics and Politics of Ethnography.* Berkeley: University of California Press, 165–92.
———. 1994. 'After the Critique of Ethnography: Faith, Hope and Charity. But Greatest of these is Charity', in Robert Borofsky (ed.), *Assessing Cultural Anthropology.* New York: McGraw Hill, 40–52.
———. 2002. 'Beyond Malinowski and After Writing Culture: On the Future of Cultural Anthropology and the Predicament of Ethnography', *Australian Journal of Anthropology* 13: 191–99.
Marcus, George E. and Michael M.J. Fisher. 1986. *Anthropology as Cultural Critique.* Chicago: University of Chicago Press.
Miller, Richard William. 1987. *Fact and Method: Confirmation and Reality in the Natural and Social Sciences.* Princeton, NJ: Princeton University Press.
Mills, C. Wright. 1956. *The Power Elite.* Oxford: Oxford University Press.
Mintz, Alex and Nehemia Geva. 1993. 'Why don't Democracies Fight Each Other?' *Journal of Conflict Resolution* 37(3): 484–503.
Morgan, Lewis Henry. 1851. *League of the Ho-dé-no-sau-nee, or Iroquois.* Rochester, NY: Sage and Brother.
Niiniluoto, Ilkka. 1987. *Truthlikeness.* Dordrecht: Reidel.
Palast, Greg. 2003. *The Best Democracy Money Can Buy.* Harmondsworth: Plume.
Peirce, Charles S. 1902. 'Vague', in James Mark Baldwin (ed.), *Dictionary of Philosophy and Psychology.* New York: Macmillan, 748.
———. 1958a[1871]. 'Critical Review of Berkeley's Idealism', in Charles S. Peirce, *Values in a Universe of Chance: Selected Writings of Charles S. Peirce (1839–1914),* Philip Wiener (ed.), New York: Anchor, 73–88.
———. 1958b[1878]. 'How to Make Our Ideas Clear', in Charles S. Peirce, *Values in a Universe of Chance: Selected Writings of Charles S. Peirce (1839–1914),* Philip Wiener (ed.), New York: Anchor, 113–141.
———. 1958c. *Values in a Universe of Chance: Selected Writings of Charles S. Peirce (1839–1914),* Philip Wiener (ed.), New York: Anchor.
Phillips, Kevin. 1990. *The Politics of Rich and Poor: Wealth and the Reagan Aftermath.* New York: Random House.
Popper, Karl. 1963. *Conjectures and Refutations.* London: Routledge and Kegan Paul.
Rabinow, Paul. 1986. 'Representations are Social Facts: Modernity and Postmodernity in Anthropology', James Clifford and George E. Marcus (eds), *Writing Culture: The Poetics and Politics of Ethnography.* Berkeley: University of California Press, 234–61.
Resnik, David. 1992. 'Convergent Realism and Approximate Truth', *Philosophy of Science Association* 1: 421–34.

Reyna, Stephen. P. 1972. *The Costs of Marriage: A Study of Some Factors Affecting Northwest Barma Fertility.* Ann Arbor, MI: University Microfilms.

———. 1975. 'Age Differential, Marital Instability and Venereal Disease: Factors Affecting Fertility among Northwest Barma', in Moni Nag (ed.), *Population and Social Organization.* Chicago: Aldine, 55–73.

———. 2001. 'Theory Counts: (Discounting) Discourse to the Contrary by Adopting a Confrontational Stance', *Anthropological Theory* 1: 9–29.

———. 2002. *Connections: Brain, Mind, and Culture in a Social Anthropology.* London: Routledge.

———. 2004. 'Hard Truth and Validation: What Zeus Understood', *Max Planck Institute for Social Anthropology Working Papers No. 65.* Halle/Saale: Max Planck Institute for Social Anthropology.

Richards, Audrey.1939. *Land, Labour and Diet in Northern Rhodesia.* London: Oxford University Press.

Runes, Dagobert. 1962. *Dictionary of Philosophy.* Totowa, NJ: Littlefield, Adams and Co.

Salmon, Wesley. 1998. *Causality and Explanation.* Oxford: Oxford University Press.

Tyler, Steven A. 1986. 'Post-modern Ethnography: From Document of the Occult to Occult Document', in James Clifford and George E. Marcus (eds), *Writing Culture: The Poetics and Politics of Ethnography.* Berkeley: University of California Press, 122–41.

Weston, Thomas. 1992. 'Approximate Truth and Scientific Realism', *Philosophy of Science* 59: 53–74.

Zammito, John. H. 2004. *A Nice Derangement of Epistemes: Post-Positivism in the Study of Science from Quine to Latour.* Chicago: University of Chicago Press.

10

The Migration of the 'Culture' Concept from Anthropology to Sociology at the *Fin de siècle*

John H. Zammito

Beyond *Writing Culture* lies a hurly-burly of theoretical and practical reorientation. If one can surmise that this intervention of 1986 opened some doors, it seemed also to essay the closure of others, perhaps most firmly on the 'culture' concept in anthropology. But here we come upon a case of revolving doors, for what seemed to close in anthropology simultaneously flew open in sociology. In this age of ostensible 'interdisciplinarity', it is sometimes fruitful to consider specific disciplines in a comparative light, or better still, to see them not as closed systems but as porous and plural (to perform what I mean to discern). I wish briefly to configure, in a narrative of transfer, the migration of the 'culture' concept from anthropology to sociology at the *fin de siècle*. It is, as we will see, a story of *crise de conscience* in each of the disciplines, and 'culture' figures centrally in the response to that sense of crisis, but in paradoxically disparate ways. Even as anthropologists, the traditional purveyors of the 'culture' concept, seem to have grown deeply disenchanted with it, a battery of sociologists have taken it up with real fervour (Sewell 1999). If anthropologists have been desperately seeking to get out from under the culture construct, the situation in sociology proved just the opposite. Thus we must assess what repelled the anthropologists and what attracted the sociologists.

The *Crise de Conscience* in Anthropology
and the Turn Away from 'Culture'

The *crise de conscience* of American cultural anthropology appears datable to the year 1986. Not that there were not perturbations earlier, or that the rupture was total (they never are, Foucault and Kuhn notwithstanding).[1] Obviously, I am referring to the little tempest created in the discipline by *Writing Culture* and *Anthropology as Cultural Critique* (Clifford and Marcus 1986; Marcus and Fischer 1986). This has been labelled the 'postmodern' moment in cultural anthropology, though mainly by critics hostile to the enterprise.[2] Instead, the protagonists saw themselves carrying through the 'linguistic turn' in their discipline that had occurred earlier in other disciplines – in literary studies, classically, in the 1960s; and in history, as a failed insurrection, with Hayden White's *Metahistory* (1973) – though there is a sense in which Clifford Geertz had already launched it in his 'interpretive' or 'symbolic' anthropology.[3] They preferred to style themselves advocates of 'experimental ethnography'.[4] But the 'postmodern' rubric has stuck in the ensuing controversy.[5]

Two forces converged to occasion the crisis in (American) anthropology in 1986: the reception of the poststructuralist critique of 'representation' in language, and the widespread admission of anthropology's complicity in colonialism and imperialism ... and racism and sexism – in short, all the sins of the West against its many subalterns.[6] In particular, however, I think the most important impact was the rise of feminism, both politically and academically, and, closely associated with it, and deriving its strength primarily from it, the American version of

---

1   For earlier perturbations, see, e.g., Kroeber and Kluckhohn (1963), Boon (1972), Hymes (1972), Schneider (1972), Keesing (1974), Ruby (1982) and Ortner (1984). On Kuhn and Foucault on rupture, see Zammito (2004).

2   But not all: for positive responses, see Coombe (1991), James, Hockey and Dawson (1997) and, after a fashion, Pool (1991) and Linstead (1993).

3   In American literary studies Paul de Man is the exemplary figure, and with him the so-called 'Yale School'. For history, see White (1973). For Geertz's anthropology, see Geertz (1973, 1983, 1988, 1995); the new intervention clearly acknowledged its conflicted filiation from Geertz (see Ortner 1999).

4   Clifford and Marcus (1986); Marcus (1994). The notion of 'experiment' was explicitly drawn from avant-garde modernism: 'We believe that anthropology never self-consciously had a "modernist" moment until the present, when the influences of literary and cultural classic modernism of the late nineteenth and early twentieth centuries are finally being brought to bear by bridging scholars such as Clifford, Rabinow and Crapanzano, who are equally schooled in literary theory and in the history of anthropology' (Tyler and Marcus 1987: 277).

5   'One of the most notable features of the post-modernist/deconstructionist debates in anthropology, as elsewhere, was that it was anti-theory, in the sense that it provided a critique of the exclusionary practices of Western theorizing and explicitly eschewed "grand theories" and "meta-narratives" on the grounds that they homogenized difference' (Moore 1999: 5). See Pool (1991), who seeks to argue that 'postmodern' is just a wrong descriptor, since the properties associated with the 1986 intervention tally with high modernism. What Pool misses is that the new argument is not with modernism (which, as a style of art, may well have been postmodern already), but with modernity, and especially the style of thought associated with the despised 'Enlightenment project' (see Lyotard 1984).

6   The first full indictments were entered by Asad (1973) and Said (1978); the subsequent swell of postcolonial criticism is monumental. For a sampling, see Guha and Spivak (1988), Bhabha (1994) and Ashcroft, Griffiths and Tiffin (1995).

'cultural studies'.[7] The boom of American cultural studies set in during the 1980s as 'questions of ethnicity, gender, sexuality and race ... bec[a]me central largely to the exclusion of class' and method centred round 'representation and textual politics, which followed from an engagement with post-structuralist and deconstructive theory' (Thomas 1999: 268). While Roger Keesing correctly observed that the preponderant sense of 'culture' in American 'cultural studies' was not identical with the anthropological concept, he admitted that 'these alternative approaches to cultural theory being developed in "cultural studies" have much to teach anthropology' (Keesing 1994: 303, 308–09). This was the stance, too, of Renato Rosaldo (1994). But others definitely felt threatened, as when, in 1996, the Group for Debates in Anthropological Theory considered the proposition: 'Cultural studies will be the death of anthropology' (Thomas 1999: 266; see also Borofsky 1994; Nugent and Shore 1997; Wright 1998).

The tenor of things in Britain was, at least initially, different. First of all, the British were convinced that they did something else – 'social' anthropology – and thus were not so invested in the 'culture' concept.[8] Second, 'cultural studies' in Britain had a far more concrete and almost traditional centre and signification – Birmingham neo-Marxism, for which the concept of 'culture' derived from Raymond Williams and a critique of the 'high' cultural tradition from Arnold to Eliot.[9] For British cultural studies, class mattered, and it took some time for feminism to add the other ingredients from the 'new social movements' into the purview of British consideration (Harris 1992). It was British feminists, too, who first took up with interest the 'postmodern' critique within American anthropology after 1986: Marilyn Strathern played a decisive role here.[10] Still, it is fair to say that the *fin de siècle* crisis, in its two-fold political/moral and epistemological form, beset British anthropology as well.

The initial reviews of *Writing Culture* registered a strong sense of outrage and alarm; the reception of *Anthropology as Cultural Critique* I think, somewhat less

---

7   'Second-wave' feminism and its engagement with postmodernism are anthologized in Nicholson (1990). For an early and important feminist intervention in anthropology, see Rosaldo and Lamphere (1974). See the massive anthology of American cultural studies edited by Grossberg, Nelso and Treichler (1992). Nicholas Thomas has written very astutely on the challenge posed to anthropology by American 'cultural studies' in an essay tellingly entitled 'Becoming Undisciplined': 'If there are threats to anthropology from outside the academy, the emergent discipline of cultural studies has appeared to constitute a threat from within ... There can be no doubt that among students, in English, history and in other fields in the humanities as well as in anthropology, cultural studies has far more cachet than the more 'mainstream' and 'conventional' areas of research within those disciplines' (Thomas 1999: 266).

8   Thus, Fox and King observe: 'British anthropologists ... have always been skeptical of the culture concept' (Fox and King 2002: 1). Adam Kuper has insisted on this difference in a set of key works: see Kuper (1994a, 1996, 1999a, 1999b).

9   On British 'cultural studies', see Hall (1980, 1990, 1992); Johnson, (1986/87, 1997); Brantlinger (1990); Harris (1992); and see Williams (1958). For an acute sense of the difference, see Thomas (1999: 266–68).

10   'Whether we are or are not entering a postmodern phase in social anthropology, enough people seem to be speaking as though we were for the idea to be important' (Strathern 1987b: 263). Other feminists have been more cautious about endorsing the shift (Mascia-Lees, Sharpe and Cohen 1989). See generally on the relationship between feminism and anthropology: Ortner (1974), MacCormack and Strathern (1980), Strathern (1987a) and Behar and Gordon (1995).

so (Kapferer 1988; Sangren 1988; Polier and Roseberry 1989; Roth 1989; Spencer 1989; Birth 1990; Reyna 1994). In a measure, that was because the impact of the two challenges was differential: most American anthropologists were prepared to plead their discipline guilty on the political/moral register, but not many were prepared to jettison all claim to 'objectivity'.[11] That is, the epistemological challenge seemed more novel and in some sense more pressing. The combined senses, however, seemed to raise questions about the very 'future of anthropology'.[12] The crisis took on a particularly menacing edge because it seemed that the traditional identification of anthropology with the ethnographic account of a remote (often 'primitive') culture seemed a dubious prospect in a world where 'globalization' both brought the West into every corner of the 'other' world, and at the same time brought the 'other' directly into the metropole, either literally through diaspora or vicariously through media.[13] One response was simply to return 'home' and conduct ethnographies of populations in the metropole – whether elite, ethnic or 'hybrid'. Meanwhile, however, the proliferation of the usage of 'culture' as the self-affirmation of any group interested in posing an 'identity' for political purposes, or as the rubric for an invasive advertising campaign or managerial strategy in the 'global economy', betokened that anthropology had clearly lost control of the 'culture' concept.[14]

As the crisis set in, it appeared perhaps the best expedient for anthropology to ditch the 'culture' concept.[15] Two rather distinct impulses seemed to manifest themselves. First, it appeared that this rejection of the 'culture' concept was a tacit concession to the other purveyors – both academic ('cultural studies') and political-economic (the 'identity' manufacturers) – that they had successfully seized it away.[16] The presumption was that the profession of anthropology would go on crafting its discipline in silence over the purloined term, the claim being

---

11 For a rich exploration of the intensities of these two concerns and their potential conflict, see D'Andrade (1995) and Scheper-Hughes (1995), with comments from others.

12 For two titles that betokened that sense of disciplinary prospects, see Ahmed and Shore (1995) and Moore (1996). An aspect of this anxiety of some note was the concern that anthropology as a discipline was abandoning (social) science to accommodate itself to the humanities. This was more than the longstanding tension between nomothetic social science and interpretive analysis, though it is interesting that for hardcore 'positivists' it seemed hard to tell the difference (see Harris 1999).

13 Arjun Appadurai has been the main theorist, here; see Appadurai (1991, 1996). See also Friedman (1994), Hubinger (1996) and, in a narrower domain, Ginsburg and Rapp (1995).

14 See esp. Wright (1998). The sense that the discipline has lost control of the 'culture' concept pervades the recent literature. Thus, e.g., 'Anthropologists no longer have the influence to determine the "proper" definitions and uses of the term "culture"' Barth (2002: 23); 'Culture's popular success is its own theoretical demise', and 'Culture is out there, and anthropologists have no control over its deployment' (Trouillot 2002: 37, 38). On the whole 'scene', see Kahn (1995).

15 See, e.g., Fox (1991, 1995) and Abu-Lughod (1991). For dismay over this apostasy, see Yengoyan (1986), Sahlins (1993, 1999) and Brumann (1999).

16 'Few people outside anthropology now bother to ask anthropologists what they mean by culture … Even within academe we are losing ground to cultural studies in the debate over the appropriation of the word culture' (Trouillot 2002: 55). And there is a third contender: cognitive science: 'Culture is being usurped by cognitive science' (Brown 2002: 169).

that it didn't need it anyway.[17] 'We need to get on with doing anthropology, and the first step is to reject a "love it or leave it" relationship with the concept of culture' (Fox and King 2002: 2).[18] As Trouillot has put it in a formulation that appears widely congenial: 'There is a conceptual kernel to defend, but that defense need not be tied to a word that the general public now essentialises on the basis of anthropologists' own fetishization. We need to abandon the word while firmly defending the conceptual kernel it once encapsulated' (Trouillot 2002: 56). But the other strain of this impulse to critique the concept and, at the extreme, to abandon it, was an effort to make the discipline more responsible to both the political/moral and epistemological critiques. Here, the concern was both to acknowledge the self-fashioning of the 'natives' in their own right, and to critique the misuse of the 'culture' concept as the vehicle for the old racism or the new ethnic nationalism.[19] Thus, one of the key counter-concepts that became appealing for anthropologists has been 'cosmopolitanism'.[20]

Why did anthropology get scared of the 'culture' concept? The most common objection in the anthropological literature has been to the notion of culture as coherent, as organic unity.[21] 'Contestation, entropy, and chaos have long since displaced coherence and integration as the privileged disciplinary themes.' That is, 'the claim is not only that cultures are internally diverse (vs. homogeneous) but that they are disordered, contradictory, and sometimes disputed' (Brightman 1995: 517). The objection to the coherence of the culture construct is complemented by a rejection of its closure. 'The concept of a fixed, unitary, and bounded culture must give way to a sense of the fluidity and permeability of cultural sets', Eric Wolf (1982: 387) proclaimed (see also Clifford 1992; Gupta and Ferguson 1992). Cultures should not be viewed as 'natural kinds', critics agreed, since they were neither primordial, nor local, nor discrete. Instead, 'criteria of delimitation are multiple, redundant, incongruent, and overlapping' (Brightman 1995: 519). Indeed, Arjun Appadurai resorted to the notion of fractals to claim that there were 'no Euclidean boundaries, structures, or regularities' to culture (Appadurai 1990: 20).

---

17 'Anthropology can prosper without a global concept of culture or without any concept of culture' (Fox and King 2002: 4); 'The vitality of anthropology, with or without a culture concept, was simply assumed by participants at the conference which generated their volume' (ibid.: 13). That confidence was reinforced by the deliberate construction of 'anthropology' to include primatology and cognitive scientific approaches to language. Thus, Christina Toren could write, 'To claim that anthropology is "the whole science of what it is to be human" is not to be merely provocative. Rather, it seems important to draw attention to anthropology as science in this juncture in the history of the discipline, when it would appear to some to have been eclipsed by the rise of cultural studies, on the one hand, and of cognitive science, on the other' (Toren 2002: 105). For a rather different sense, see Ingold (1998). Still, there are signs of a recovery of nerve, e.g., Knauft (1996) and Moore (1997).

18 The 'love it or leave it' rhetoric is in reaction to harsh criticism from Marshall Sahlins (1993, 1999).

19 This was the thrust of Abu-Lughod (1991); see also Hann (2002).

20 See esp. Kuper (1994b, reprinted in 1999a).

21 Thornton (1988). The blame for this heritage is ascribed heavily to Herder and German romanticism and historicism.

Robert Brightman identified no fewer than fifteen different aspersions against the 'culture construct' within current cultural anthropology, observing wryly thereupon: 'When we encounter arguments today that *the* culture construct should be abandoned, we must naturally wonder which of its formulations from among all the possible ones we should be rid of' (Brightman 1995: 527). In 'The Concept(s) of Culture', William Sewell, Jr. discriminates between two 'fundamentally different meanings' of the term culture: as an abstract category for one form of (social) structure, and as a concrete, bounded community of beliefs and practices, as in the ethnographic sense of culture(s). Sewell makes the convincing point that the anthropologists' disillusionment with the second notion need not carry over to an abandonment of the first. Picking up on a left-handed avowal from James Clifford, Sewell insists 'we cannot do without a concept of culture', and therefore 'we need to modify, rearticulate, and revivify the concept' (Sewell 1999: 38).[22] Two aspects that he seeks to rearticulate are culture-as-system and culture-as-practice. Sewell urges that these are 'complementary concepts'; thus, 'system and practice constitute an indissoluble duality or dialectic' (ibid.: 47). The real challenge is to cash out this idea of duality and dialectic: to show how structure (in this case, *cultural* structure) and practice form a mutuality without obfuscating the distinction. Responding to the contradictory or conflictual elements within cultures, Sherry Ortner, in an influential theoretical overview of disciplinary trends in 1984, proposed a 'practice orientation'; that is, the shift from the 'abstraction' of culture as a whole to the 'strategies' and 'interests' in individuated practice or 'agency' (Ortner 1984). This was the line Sewell – and with him the new 'cultural' sociology – took up. We have reached the moment of transfer and must turn to the second discipline, sociology.

The *Crise de Conscience* of Sociology and the Turn to 'Culture'

Since 1970, when Alvin Gouldner published *The Coming Crisis of Western Sociology*, 'at least 150 articles concerning the "crisis of sociology"' have appeared (Steinmetz and Chae 2002: 113). Indeed, the 'sense of disorientation in American sociology ... has never really abated since 1970' (ibid.: 112). It is thus a commonplace to observe that 'since the mid-1960s the discipline has endured a crisis of identity' (Kuklick 1983: 292). Steven Seidman, noting this 'almost permanent sense of crisis', proclaimed, 'sociological theory has gone astray' (Seidman 1991: 131). Even more drastic was Norman Denzin's pronouncement that: 'sociology is dying. The death of the social is upon us' (Denzin 1987: 179). Since the dissolution of the Parsonian orthodox consensus, 'the very idea that sociology has a "core" has become doubtful' (Lynch and Bogen 1997: 484). One adherent of this lapsed orthodoxy lamented in 1993 what he called *The*

---

22 He is picking up on Clifford's avowal: 'culture is a deeply compromised idea I cannot yet do without' (Clifford 1988: 10). Geertz expressed a similarly half-hearted acknowledgment.

Decomposition of Sociology (Horowitz 1993). At the end of the century, Stephen Cole organized a massive inquiry into *What's Wrong with Sociology?* (Cole 2001).[23] Over the discipline there had clearly settled a mood for which several commentators found the nineteenth-century phrase *fin de siècle* of renewed resonance. Anthony Giddens saw sociology beset with 'feelings of disorientation and malaise' (Giddens 1994: 56) identified with the notion of *fin de siècle*, and Jeffrey Alexander entitled a 1995 book *Fin de siècle Social Theory* (Alexander 1995). Stuart Hall, the doyen of British cultural studies, made the point elegantly: 'When I was offered a chair in sociology, I said, "Now that sociology does not exist as a discipline, I am happy to profess it"' (Hall 1990: 11).

John Law penetratingly characterized the situation in 1986 as a 'crisis in the sociology of knowledge'. What had come under attack was 'the idea that there is a backcloth of relatively stable social interests which directs knowledge or ideology' (Law 1986: 2). Such a stable backcloth had allowed sociological explanation of beliefs and actions in terms of structure, but now, especially under the impact of Michel Foucault, 'structure has collapsed into knowledge in the form of discourse, and the sociology of knowledge (if this is still an acceptable title for an inquiry that has so extensively chopped away at its own foundations) has been refocused' on 'the *technique* of power/knowledge' (ibid.: 18). The whole structure of sociological explanation was being undermined. The mid 1980s witnessed the shattering of faith in the categories of causal explanation of orthodox sociology. As Bruno Latour put it in *The Pasteurization of France*, 'the evolution of our field has made the notion of a "social explanation" obsolete' (Latour 1988: 256; see Schaffer 1991: 185). Latour was emphatic: 'notions like "context", "interest", "religious opinion", "class position", are ... part of the problem rather than of the solution' (Latour 1990: 155; see also Latour 1992). Michel Callon explained, 'Since society is no more obvious or less controversial than nature, sociological explanation can find no solid foundation' (Callon 1986: 199). The summary verdict pronounced by Michael Lynch has reverberated widely:

> Sociology's general concepts and methodological strategies are simply overwhelmed by the heterogeneity and technical density of the languages, equipment, and skills through which ... practitioners in many ... fields of activity make their affairs accountable. It is not that their practices are asocial, but that they are more thoroughly and locally social than sociology is prepared to handle. (Lynch 1992: 298)

With the crisis of sociological explanation, with the abandonment of empirical accounts by 'discourse analysis', and, most importantly, with the articulation of 'new literary forms' and radical reflexivity, the whole enterprise of

---

23 This volume is based on a special issue of *Sociological Forum* from 1994 edited by Cole on the same topic. See also Mouzelis (1995).

sociology reached a fatal impasse.[24] The initiative passed to a different disciplinary cadre and to a different theoretical orientation: 'cultural studies'.[25] Cultural studies responded directly to the rise of the so-called 'new social movements' and the restive political dissent associated with the New Left (Laraña, Johnston and Gusfield 1994; Pichardo 1997). The key issues of race, gender and sexuality, as these have become canonized in contemporary discourse, followed out of the rise of the 'new social movements', yet with the ebbing of their wider social efficacy, cultural studies has tended to become increasingly academicized and persists as a radical agenda within (or better, against) the disciplinary structures of academia (Giroux et al. 1985; Morris 1988, 1991; Frow 1991; Ruthven 1991; Grossberg, Nelson and Treichler 1992; Grossberg 1997; McRobbie 1997; Messer-Davidow 1997; Long 1997; Dean 2000; McChesney 2002).

There is a very strong connection between 'cultural studies', as it has evolved in the United States, and adamant advocacy of French poststructuralism.[26] In his contribution to a volume notably entitled *From Sociology to Cultural Studies*, Steven Seidman (1997) wishes to draw upon cultural studies to 'challenge' disciplinary sociology to accept the fundamental poststructuralist epistemological and theoretical positions – the semiotics of Barthes and Foucault, the psychoanalysis of Lacan, and so on – as more socio-politically emancipatory.[27] Seidman abjures any claims to ultimate warrant or even empirical adequacy and pitches his case entirely on 'pragmatic' grounds.[28] On similarly pragmatic

24 Donna Haraway writes of a 'crisis of confidence among many scholars that their very fruitful research programs of the last 10 years are running into dead ends' (Haraway 1992: 336).
25 Mario Biagioli, introducing his key anthology *The Science Studies Reader*, suggested 'contrasting science studies with ethnography' to highlight the major novelty after 1990 (Biagioli 1999: xiii). See Rouse (1993).
26 'Thinkers like Levi-Strauss, Roland Barthes, and the early Michel Foucault created a revolution in the human sciences by insisting on the textuality of institutions and the discursive nature of social action', Jeffrey Alexander observed. Simultaneously or sequentially, the works of Lacan, Derrida and Foucault swept the theoretical world. Swiftly poststructuralism radicalized the scene, both problematizing the epistemological frames of structuralist semiotics and introducing a grim reckoning with the problem of domination: 'Althusser converted texts into ideological state apparatuses. Foucault conflated discourse with dominating power' (Alexander 1996: 4). See Purvis and Hunt (1993) for the endless wrangles of Althusserian vs. Foucauldian terminologies.
27 'Cultural studies seems to parallel French "postmodern" theory in viewing the new role of the mass media, the saturation of daily life by commerce and commodification, the new technologies of information, and the foregrounding of cultural politics as signaling perhaps a second "great transformation" in post-Renaissance Western societies' (Seidman 1997: 45). 'A Foucauldian perspective shifts the ground of social analysis to a focus on the making of bodies, desires, and identities, to power/knowledge regimes and to dynamics of moralizaton, discipline, and surveillance' (ibid.: 46). 'Psychoanalysis offers a language of an intricate, dense, psychic, and intersubjective life, a life of fantasies, wishes, fears, shames, desires, idealizations, identification, that cannot be comprehended by a vocabulary of interests, means-ends rationality, cost-benefit calculations, need dispositions, or values, or by the surface psychologies of behaviorism, cognitivism, or symbolic interactionism' (ibid.: 49). Thus, 'cultural studies departs from these assumptions by imagining an individual as socially produced; as occupying multiple, contradictory psychic and social positions or identities; and by figuring the self as influenced by unconscious processes' (ibid.: 46). And 'cultural studies places struggles over meanings, identities, knowledges, and the control of discursive production and authorization on an equal footing with struggles over the distribution of material resources' (ibid.: 55).
28 'Deconstructing "the empirical" means that we recognize that discursive conflicts, even ones about the social, can never be resolved by appeals to the empirical alone, and that such discourses should acknowledge their own entanglement in power and therefore, at times, when pragmatically useful, bring ethical reflection and political considerations into social discourse' (Seidman 1997: 58).

grounds, however, one may well dispute the benefit of buying into Foucault, Lacan and their brethren at anything like the rate of (cultural) exchange at which American postmodernists have valued them. It seems to me that we are well underway to a decisive deflation of their intellectual value.

If the knowledge(s) in question belong to somehow agglomerated others, how are we to constitute them into groups (or discern what has befallen or been achieved by them)? Above all, what does it mean to talk about 'social construction'? How can the 'social' explain, when we scruple about what (or whether) that can signify, concretely, and we can't even agree on what an explanation should or can do? Paradoxically, sociologists turned to the 'culture' concept for answers. Cultural sociology is that response. The slogan 'from knowledge to culture' suggests that the essential question is not merely about 'ways of knowing' but, more pertinently, about the constitution of communities. Whose knowledge(s) seems as important as the what or how of 'knowing'.[29] Politically, that can insinuate a reflexive anxiety about representation: Is speaking about cultures of others not a matter of speaking for them, suborning them into our discourse?[30] As we have seen, the postmodern crisis of ethnography seems to have revolved around that conundrum (Clifford and Marcus 1986).

Culture had seen 'the weakest analytical development of any key concept in sociology', according to Margaret Archer (1985: 333). Craig Calhoun agrees that 'the study of culture has been strikingly marginalized in sociology, especially in the United States' (Calhoun 1989: 1). In their explicit characterization of 'cultural sociology' as the shift 'from knowledge to culture', Swidler and Arditi note that 'scholars in history, philosophy, anthropology, and the history of science' have played as important a role as sociologists (Swidler and Arditi 1994: 306). Calhoun observes that 'the reformulation of sociological theory depends in large part on a rethinking of the place of culture within it', that is to say, on 'how sociologists relate to other disciplines and to interdisciplinary discourses' (Calhoun 1989: 1). Surveying the development of recent cultural sociology, Michèle Lamont and Robert Wuthnow observe that 'a growing number of American cultural sociologists are increasingly reading outside their discipline, and are becoming more influenced by the interdisciplinary current in which European cultural theorists play a central role' (Lamont and Wuthnow 1990: 306). More specifically, 'as American cultural sociology has begun to flourish again in recent years, it has been increasingly influenced by the work of scholars such as Foucault, Habermas, Douglas, and Bourdieu' (ibid.: 301).

---

29 The question: 'Whose knowledge?' is at issue in two very prominent publications of the recent era (MacIntyre 1988; Harding 1991). See Alcoff (1991) for a thoughtful consideration of the issue.

30 'We have to keep a discomforted eye on the historical pedigrees and current orthodoxies of what is sometimes called "ethnography", a practice of representing the cultures of others. The practice, like the word, already extends social distance and constructs relations of knowledge-as-power' (Johnson 1986/7: 70). Fuller (1996) offers a precise formulation of this logic of representation; Haraway (1992) lays out the same argument.

While there has always been 'sociology of culture', Jeffrey Alexander claims, what is new is the emergence of a 'cultural sociology'. Alexander goes so far as to pirate the slogan of a 'strong program' from science studies to characterize the radical novelty of the agenda of this 'new' cultural sociology (Alexander 1996). For Alexander, 'commitment to ... cultural autonomy is the single most important quality of a strong program'. The second principle is a commitment to interpretive or 'hermeneutic' reconstruction, 'a Geertzian "thick description" of the codes, narratives, and symbols that create the textured webs of social meaning.' The third defining principle is the effort 'to anchor causality in proximate actors and agencies, specifying in detail just how culture interferes with and directs what really happens' (Alexander 2003: 13–14).

Alexander offers a telling anecdote about chatting with sociology colleagues at UCLA in the 1970s who found the very idea of 'cultural sociology' laughable (Alexander 2003: 4–5). That it nonetheless became 'a prominent subfield' by 1988 and 'a major growth industry in the sociological portfolio' for the 1990s therefore requires some explication (Wuthnow and Witten 1988: 49). A variety of impulses led to this surge; it was part of what William Sewell has dubbed 'a kind of academic culture mania' in the 1980s and 1990s (Sewell 1999: 36). One of its domestic American origins lay in the 'production-of-culture' approach led by Diana Crane and Richard Peterson; that is, attention to the concrete institutional context of actual cultural objects (Peterson 1979, 1994; Crane 1994). But decisive for the 'culture mania' of the 1980s and 1990s, of course, was the impact of structuralism and poststructuralism, and with these, the rise of 'cultural studies'. The latter saw its task as overcoming 'a general failure in work on cultural production to analyse historically the sign systems, codes and styles which are available for authorial and audience groups to make meanings with' (Barrett et al. 1979: 23). Within the discipline of sociology, Sewell observes, 'by the late 1980s, the work of cultural sociologists had broken out of the study of culture-producing institutions and moved toward studying the place of meaning in social life more generally' (Sewell 1999: 37).

The new cultural sociologists were no more disposed to accept the holistic notion of culture than their anthropological colleagues, for all the variance of their disciplinary trajectories. Indeed, the dawning of theoretical interest in culture within sociology came with the abandonment of what Margaret Archer called the 'myth of cultural integration' (Archer 1985). Ann Swidler similarly characterized and dismissed 'the older definition of culture as the entire way of life of a people', and instead opted for the 'image of culture as a "tool kit" of symbols, stories, rituals, and world-views, which people may use in varying configurations' (Swidler 1986: 273). As with the anthropologists, the concern that drove the new field was to grasp concrete practices, to reject at one and the same time 'structural' determinism and cultural determinism, to create a more sophisticated theoretical space for agency. But the endeavour was also to grasp the specific contribution – enabling and constraining – that cultural factors made to practices. That entailed a more differentiated notion of culture, breaking it out into more determinate structures of its own, and then finding how, concretely, these affected practices. The core issue was cultural 'causality' and, as its logical prerequisite, cultural 'autonomy' (Kane 1991; Alexander 1992). Culture, the new cultural sociology sought to establish, was at once an autonomous factor (not an outcome or epiphenomenon of social structure) and a component (not a self-sufficient determinant) of the concrete practices of agents who possessed, accordingly, their own element of autonomy. Sociology, such thinking suggests, moved substantially toward 'cultural studies', ethnomethodology and hermeneutics. 'Thick description' and 'local knowledge(s)' appeared more achievable and credible than a 'nomothetic' universalism (Wright 1971). That is, the balance between 'interpretive' and 'positivist' social science has shifted substantially in favour of the former (Hayes 1985). Hence all the talk of 'turns' – rhetorical, interpretive and, of course, cultural (Hiley, Bohman and Shusterman 1991; Chaney 1994; Seidman 1994; Bonnell and Hunt 1999).

The key difference American cultural sociologists claim between their version of 'cultural studies' and the Europeans is that the latter lapsed into determinism, making subjects over into 'cultural dopes', even if in the sophisticated formulations of Bourdieu or Foucault, whereas the new American cultural sociologists seek a better balance between structure and agency (Alexander, Smith and Sherwood 1993: 10–11; Sherwood, Smith and Alexander 1993). American cultural sociology of the late 1980s and the1990s set itself the task of working through the theoretical resources developed in continental structuralism and poststructuralism, above all Foucault and Bourdieu, as well as in the work of theorists in the 'interpretive' tradition of social theory, like Clifford Geertz, Anthony Giddens and Jürgen Habermas, to make clearer sense of the relations among structure, agency and culture. A recent anthology entitled *The New American Cultural Sociology* (Smith 1998b) brings together some of the seminal works in the new field. In his introduction to this volume, Smith both recognizes the diversity of approaches and seeks to construe their commonality (Smith 1998a). Crucial to the American theorists is the effort to elaborate a more effective notion of agency, avoiding the two extremes of structuralist determinism and voluntarist freedom, neither of which seem adequate to the theoretical or empirical task. Thus they endeavour to situate the concept of culture effectively in this force field between structure and agency.

Beyond *Writing Culture?*

What lies beyond *Writing Culture?* One commentator has asserted: 'it is now possible to reread the ethnographic experiments since ... *Writing Culture* ... as more than the vagrant, self-indulgent efforts of a few who were challenging the borders and boundaries of traditional ethnography' (Denzin 1997: 250). In a body of work, Norman Denzin has sought to transpose symbolic interactionism in sociology into postmodern cultural studies (Denzin 1992, 1997). With collaborators he has proposed a diagnosis of the *fin de siècle* crisis in the human sciences (termed the 'fifth moment') and a therapy for the future (the 'sixth moment') (Lincoln and Denzin 1994).[31] While, to be sure, Denzin and his colleagues make all the ritual avowals about the openness of the future and the plurality of positions in the present, they carry on with the conviction that they have established a clear understanding of the crisis and that they know both what is wrong and what is to be done. They discern two crises as constituting the present (the 'fifth moment') – the crisis of representation and the crisis of legitimation. 'If the crisis of representation makes problematic the link between experience and text, the crisis of legitimation or authority makes problematic the link between text and truth' (Lincoln 1995: 39). The sense of fait accompli comes through vividly: 'It is clear that postmodern and poststructural arguments are moving further and further away from postpositivist models of validity and textual authority' (Lincoln and Denzin 1994: 578). Perhaps these arguments may be, but the disciplines of the human sciences cannot be so clearly said to be doing so, nor should we be very content were they to do so. Lincoln and Denzin argue: 'a text is always a site of political struggle over the real and its meanings. Truth is political, and verisimilitude is textual', and thus, 'a good text exposes how race, class, and gender work their ways in the concrete lives of interacting individuals'. As 'validity is gone, values and politics, not objective epistemology, govern science' (ibid.: 579–80). 'The feminist, communitarian ethical model produces a series of norms for ethnographic writing' (Denzin 1997: xiv). 'Poststructural feminism urges the abandonment of any distinction between empirical science and social criticism' (Lincoln and Denzin 1994: 581).

These are bald assertions, wrapped for security in the moral militancy feminism has always provided for cultural studies and postmodernism. But feminism speaks by no means exclusively in a poststructural 'voice' (Alcoff 1988; Mohanty 1988; Fuss 1989; Alway 1999; Bloch 1993a, 1993b; Benhabib et al. 1995). Moreover, the relation between empirical science and social criticism is far more intricate, and Denzin's dismissal of postpositivist theories of empirical inquiry strikes me as unwarranted either as a description of current practice or as an evaluation of cogency (Zammito 2004). Yet, when faced with criticism, Denzin carries out a classic postmodernist/poststructuralist strategy, namely to deny that he or his colleagues ever made hyperbolic claims, and to represent critics as crude oversimplifiers and/or authoritarian bigots (Denzin 1997: 253–264).

---

31 Independently, Lincoln explains the 'moments' succinctly: an original ('first') moment of traditional ethnography, followed by a 'modernist moment' of academic institutionalization, followed by a 'third', the moment of 'blurred genres' associated with Geertz, followed by a 'fourth' moment of 'crisis of representation' – the moment of 1986? – leading to the 'fifth' or current moment, most essentially characterized as a 'crisis of legitimation' (Lincoln 1995: 38–39).

I agree with Denzin that 'the material and ethical practices of an entire discipline are on the line' (ibid.: 251). Indeed, I would say this is so for the whole panoply of disciplines identified as the human sciences. But I think there is much more plausibility to the proposals of Fredrik Barth:

> By all means, let us be prepared – indeed, let us expect – to discover *some* functional imperatives, *some* normative pressures, *some* deep structural patterns, *some* effect of the relations of production on life choices, and *some* shared cultural themes in ranges of local institutions. But let us demand that their presence be demonstrated through a record of extant variation, not asserted by fiat. (Barth 2002: 31)

What Barth aims at, a 'naturalistic', empirical approach, brings together the research ambitions of both self-critically attuned anthropological ethnography and the new 'cultural' sociology of structure and agency. It 'incorporate[s] a pared-down ideational notion of culture as one among many elements in a larger, enveloping class or category of phenomena, human action'. That is, '"social action" is a very differently constituted class of phenomena from that of anthropology's received "culture" … [S]ocial action is conceptualized as composed of distinguishable components, elements that combine in every event or action but can be disaggregated in analysis and indeed studied component by component, sector by sector, if that proves fruitful.' Such an approach 'should enable analysts to lay out linkages and causal connections *in their particularity* without stripping away the qualitative richness of the phenomena' (ibid.: 34–35; see also Barth 1994). I would only add that we need to stop being so frightened of 'structure' in attempting to account for human action. Can scholars think they really have achieved something by electing to write of 'the cultural' but not of 'culture', of 'sociality' but not of 'society', and of 'pattern' but not of 'structure'? [32] 'Essentialism' is not a matter of lexicon but of analytic sophistication, and Marx was right long ago to insist that if we make our own history, we always do it on a stage that is already set.

---

32   See the various contributors to Fox and King (2002), for these manoeuvres.

References

Abu-Lughod, Lila. 1991. 'Writing Against Culture', in Richard Fox (ed.), *Recapturing Anthropology: Working in the Present.* Santa Fe, NM: School of American Research Press, 137–62.

Ahmed, Akbar and Cris Shore (eds). 1995. *The Future of Anthropology: Its Relevance for the Contemporary World.* London: Athlone.

Alcoff, Linda. 1988. 'Cultural Feminism versus Post-Structuralism: The Identity Crisis in Feminist Theory', *Signs* 13: 405–36.

———. 1991. 'The Problem of Speaking for Others', *Cultural Critique* 20: 5–32.

Alexander, Jeffrey. 1992. 'The Promise of a Cultural Sociology', in Richard Münch and Neil Smelser (eds), *Theory of Culture.* Berkeley, CA: University of California Press, 293–323.

———. 1995. *Fin de siècle Social Theory: Relativism, Reduction, and the Problem of Reason.* London: Verso.

———. 1996. 'Cultural Sociology or Sociology of Culture? Towards a Strong Program', *Culture* 10: 1–5.

———. 2003. *The Meanings of Society: A Cultural Sociology.* New York: Oxford University Press.

Alexander, Jeffrey, Philip Smith and Steve Sherwood. 1993. 'Risking Enchantment: Theory and Method in Cultural Studies', *Culture* 8: 10–14.

Alway, Joan. 1999. 'The Trouble with Gender: Tales of the Still-Missing Feminist Revolution in Social Theory', *Sociological Theory* 13: 209–28.

Appadurai, Arjun. 1990. 'Disjuncture and Difference in the Global Cultural Economy', *Public Culture* 2: 1–25.

———. 1991. 'Global Ethnoscapes: Notes and Queries for a Transnational Anthropology', in Richard Fox (ed.), *Recapturing Anthropology: Working in the Present.* Santa Fe, NM: School of American Research Press, 191–210.

———. 1996. *Modernity at Large: Cultural Dimensions of Globalization.* Minneapolis: University of Minnesota Press.

Archer, Margaret. 1985. 'The Myth of Cultural Integration', *British Journal of Sociology* 36: 333–53.

Asad, Talal (ed.). 1973. *Anthropology and the Colonial Encounter.* New York: Humanities Press.

Ashcroft, Bill, Gareth Griffiths and Helen Tiffin (eds). 1995. *The Post-Colonial Studies Reader.* New York: Routledge.

Barrett, Michele, Philip Corrigan, Annette Kuhn and Janet Wolff. 1979. 'Representation and Cultural Production', in Michele Barrett, Philip Corrigan, Annette Kuhn, and Janet Wolff (eds), *Ideology and Cultural Production.* New York: St. Martin's Press, 9–24.

Barth, Fredrik. 1994. 'A Personal View of Present Tasks and Priorities in Cultural and Social Anthropology', in Robert Borofsky (ed.), *Assessing Cultural Anthropology.* New York: McGraw-Hill, 349–61.

———. 2002. 'Toward a Richer Description and Analysis of Cultural Phenomena', in Richard Fox and Barbara King (eds), *Anthropology Beyond Culture*. Oxford: Berg, 23–36.

Behar, Ruth and Deborah Gordon (eds). 1995. *Women Writing Culture*. Berkeley: University of California Press.

Benhabib, Seyla, Judith Butler, Drucilla Cornell and Nancy Fraser. 1995. *Feminist Contentions: A Philosophical Exchange*. New York: Routledge.

Bhabha, Homi. 1994. *The Location of Culture*. London: Routledge.

Biagioli, Mario. 1999. 'Introduction', in Mario Biagioli (ed.), *The Science Studies Reader*. New York: Routledge, xi–xviii.

Birth, Kevin K. 1990. 'Reading and the Righting of Writing Ethnographies', *American Ethnologist* 17(3): 549–57.

Bloch, Ruth. 1993a. 'A Culturalist Critique of Trends in Feminist Theory', *Contention* 2: 79–106.

———. 1993b. 'Response to Sandra Harding and Barbara Laslett', *Contention* 2: 127–32.

Boon, James A. 1972. 'Further Operations of "Culture" in Anthropology: A Synthesis of and for Debate', *Social Science Quarterly* 52: 221–52.

Bonnell, Victoria E. and Lynn Hunt (eds). 1999. *Beyond the Cultural Turn: New Directions in the Study of Society and Culture*. Berkeley, CA: University of California Press.

Borofsky, Robert (ed.). 1994. *Assessing Cultural Anthropology*. New York: McGraw-Hill.

Brantlinger, Patrick. 1990. *Crusoe's Footprint: Cultural Studies in Britain and America*. New York: Routledge.

Brightman, Robert. 1995. 'Forget Culture: Replacement, Transcendence, Relexification', *Cultural Anthropology* 10(4): 509–46.

Brown, Penelope. 2002. 'Language as a Model for Culture: Lessons from the Cognitive Sciences', in Richard Fox and Barbara King (eds), *Anthropology Beyond Culture*. Oxford: Berg, 169–92.

Brumann, Christoph. 1999. 'Writing for Culture: Why a Successful Concept Should Not Be Discarded' (with Comments and Reply), *Current Anthropology* 40(supplement): S1–S27.

Calhoun, Craig. 1989. 'Introduction: Social Issues in the Study of Culture', *Comparative Social Research* 11: 1–29.

Callon, Michel. 1986. 'Some Elements of a Sociology of Translation: Domestication of the Scallops and the Fishermen of St. Brieuc Bay', in John Law (ed.), *Power, Action and Belief*. London: Routledge and Kegan Paul, 196–233.

Chaney, David. 1994. *The Cultural Turn: Scene-Setting Essays on Contemporary Cultural History*. London: Routledge.

Clifford, James. 1992. 'Traveling Cultures', in Lawrence Grossberg, Cary Nelson and Paula Treichler (eds), *Cultural Studies*. New York: Routledge, 96–116.

Clifford, James and George E. Marcus (eds). 1986. *Writing Culture: The Poetics and Politics of Ethnography*. Berkeley: University of California Press.

Cole, Stephen (ed.). 2001. *What's Wrong with Sociology?* New Brunswick, NJ: Transaction.

Coombe, Rosemary. 1991. 'Encountering the Postmodern: New Directions in Cultural Anthropology', *Canadian Review of Sociology and Anthropology* 28: 188–205.

Crane, Diana (ed.). 1994. *The Sociology of Culture: Emerging Theoretical Perspectives*. Oxford: Blackwell.

D'Andrade, Roy. 1995. 'Moral Models in Anthropology', *Current Anthropology* 36(3): 399–408.

Dean, Jodi. 2000. 'Introduction: The Interface of Political Theory and Cultural Studies', in Jodi Dean (ed.), *Cultural Studies and Political Theory*. Ithaca, NY: Cornell University Press, 1–19.

Denzin, Norman. 1987. 'The Death of Sociology in the 1980s: Comment on Collins', *American Journal of Sociology* 93(1): 175–80.

———. 1992. *Symbolic Interactionism and Cultural Studies*. Oxford: Blackwell.

———. 1997. *Interpretive Ethnography: Ethnographic Practices for the Twenty-first Century*. Thousand Oaks, CA: Sage.

Fox, Richard. 1991. *Recapturing Anthropology: Working in the Present*. Santa Fe, NM: School of American Research Press.

———. 1995. 'Editorial: The Breakdown of Culture', *Current Anthropology* 36(1).

Fox, Richard and Barbara King (eds). 2002. *Anthropology Beyond Culture*. Oxford: Berg.

Friedman, Jonathan. 1994. *Cultural Identity and Global Process*. Thousand Oaks, CA: Sage.

Frow, John. 1991. 'Beyond the Disciplines: Cultural Studies', in K. K. Ruthven (ed.), *Beyond the Disciplines: The New Humanities*. Canberra: Australian Academy of the Humanities, 22–28.

Fuller, Steve. 1996. 'Talking Metaphysical Turkey about Epistemological Chicken, or the Poop on Pidgin', in Peter Galison and David Stump (eds), *The Disunity of Science: Boundaries, Contexts, and Power*. Stanford, CA: Stanford University Press, 170–86.

Fuss, Diana. 1989. *Essentially Speaking: Feminism, Nature and Difference*. New York: Routledge.

Geertz, Clifford. 1973. *The Interpretation of Cultures: Selected Essays*. New York: Basic Books.

———. 1983. *Local Knowledge: Further Essays in Interpretive Anthropology*. New York: Basic Books.

———. 1988. *Works and Lives: The Anthropologist as Author*. Stanford, CA: Stanford University Press.

————. 1995. *After the Fact: Two Countries, Four Decades, One Anthropologist.* Cambridge, MA: Harvard University Press.

Giddens, Anthony. 1994. 'Living in a Post-Traditionalist Society', in Ulrich Beck, Anthony Giddens and Scott Lash, *Reflexive Modernization: Politics, Tradition and Aesthetics in the Modern Social Order.* Stanford, CA: Stanford University Press, 56–109.

Ginsburg, Faye and Rayna Rapp (eds). 1995. *Conceiving the New World Order: The Global Politics of Reproduction.* Berkeley: University of California Press.

Giroux, Henry, David Shumway, Paul Smith and James Soskowski. 1985. 'The Need for Cultural Studies: Resisting Intellectuals and Oppositional Public Spheres', *Dalhousie Review* 64: 472–86.

Gouldner, Alvin Ward. 1970. *The Coming Crisis of Western Sociology.* New York: Basic Books.

Grossberg, Lawrence. 1997. 'Cultural Studies, Modern Logics, and Theories of Globalization', in Angela McRobbie (ed.), *Back to Reality: Social Experience and Cultural Studies.* Manchester: Manchester University Press, 7–35.

Grossberg, Lawrence, Cary Nelson and Paula Treichler (eds). 1992. *Cultural Studies.* New York: Routledge.

Guha, Ranajit and Gayatri Chakravorty Spivak (eds). 1988. *Selected Subaltern Studies.* Delhi: Oxford University Press.

Gupta, Akhil and James Ferguson. 1992. 'Beyond "Culture": Space, Identity, and the Politics of Difference', *Cultural Anthropology* 7: 6–23.

Hall, Stuart. 1980. 'Cultural Studies: Two Paradigms', *Media, Culture and Society* 2: 57–72.

————. 1990. 'The Emergence of Cultural Studies and the Crisis of the Humanities', *October* 53: 11–23.

————. 1992. 'Cultural Studies and Its Theoretical Legacies', in Lawrence Grossberg, Cary Nelson and Paula Treichler (eds), *Cultural Studies.* New York: Routledge, 277–86.

Hann, Chris. 2002. 'All "Kulturvölker" Now? Social Anthropological Reflections on the German-American Tradition', in Richard Fox and Barbara King (eds), *Anthropology Beyond Culture.* Oxford: Berg, 259–76.

Haraway, Donna. 1992. 'The Promises of Monsters: A Regenerative Politics for Inappropriate/d Others', in Lawrence Grossberg, Cary Nelson and Paula Treichler (eds), *Cultural Studies.* New York: Routledge, 295–337.

Harding, Sandra. 1991. *Whose Science, Whose Knowledge? Thinking from Women's Lives.* Ithaca, NY: Cornell University Press.

Harris, David. 1992. *From Class Struggle to the Politics of Pleasure: The Effects of Gramscianism on Cultural Studies.* London: Routledge.

Harris, Marvin. 1999. *Theories of Culture in Postmodern Times.* Walnut Creek, CA: AltaMira.

Hayes, Adrian. 1985. 'Causal and Interpretive Analysis in Sociology', *Sociological Theory* 3: 1–10.

Hays, Sharon. 1994. 'Structure and Agency and the Sticky Problem of Culture', *Sociological Theory* 12: 57–72.

Hiley, David R., James F. Bohman and Richard Shusterman (eds). 1991. *The Interpretive Turn: Philosophy, Science, Culture*. Ithaca, NY: Cornell University Press.

Horowitz, Irving L. 1993. *The Decomposition of Sociology*. New York: Oxford University Press.

Hubinger, Václav (ed.). 1996. *Grasping the Changing World: Anthropological Concepts in the Postmodern Era*. London: Routledge.

Hymes, Dell H. (ed.). 1972. *Reinventing Anthropology*. New York: Pantheon.

Ingold, Tim. 1998. 'From Complementarity to Obviation: On Dissolving the Boundaries Between Social and Biological Anthropology, Archaeology and Psychology', *Zeitschrift für Ethnologie* 123: 21–52.

James, Allison, Jenny Hockey and Andrew H. Dawson (eds). 1997. *After Writing Culture: Epistemology and Praxis in Contemporary Anthropology*. London: Routledge.

Johnson, Richard. 1986/7. 'What is Cultural Studies Anyway?' *Social Text* 16: 38–80.

———. 1997. 'Reinventing Cultural Studies', in Elizabeth Long (ed.), *From Sociology to Cultural Studies: New Perspectives*. Oxford: Blackwell, 452–88.

Kahn, Joel S. 1995. *Culture, Multiculture, Postculture*. London: Sage.

Kane, Anne. 1991. 'Cultural Analysis in Historical Sociology: The Analytic and Concrete Forms of the Autonomy of Culture', *Sociological Theory* 9: 53–69.

Kapferer, Bruce. 1988. 'The Anthropologist as Hero: Three Exponents of Post-Modernist Anthropology', *Critique of Anthropology* 8: 77–104.

Keesing, Roger. 1974. 'Theories of Culture', *Annual Review of Anthropology* 3: 73–97.

———. 1994. 'Theories of Culture Revisited', in Robert Borofsky (ed.), *Assessing Cultural Anthropology*. New York: McGraw-Hill, 301–19.

Knauft, Bruce M. 1996. *Genealogies for the Present in Cultural Anthropology*. New York: Routledge.

Kroeber, Alfred and Clyde Kluckhohn. 1963. *Culture: A Critical Review of Concepts and Definitions*. New York: Random House.

Kuklick, Henrika. 1983. 'The Sociology of Knowledge: Retrospect and Prospect', *Annual Review of Sociology* 9: 287–310.

Kuper, Adam. 1994a. 'Anthropological Futures', in Robert Borofsky (ed.), *Assessing Cultural Anthropology*. New York: McGraw-Hill, 113–18.

———. 1994b. 'Culture, Identity and the Project of a Cosmopolitan Anthropology', *Man* 29 (3): 537–54.

———. 1996. *Anthropology and Anthropologists: The Modern British School*, 3rd rev. edn. London: Routledge.

———. 1999a. *Among the Anthropologists: History and Context in Anthropology*. London: Athlone.

————. 1999b. *Culture: The Anthropologists' Account.* Cambridge, MA: Harvard University Press.

Lamont, Michèle and Robert Wuthnow. 1990. 'Betwixt and Between: Recent Cultural Sociology in Europe and the United States', in George Ritzer (ed.), *Frontiers of Social Theory: The New Syntheses.* New York: Columbia University Press, 287–315.

Laraña, Enrique, Hank Johnston and Joseph Gusfield (eds). 1994. *New Social Movements: From Ideology to Identity.* Philadelphia, PA: Temple University Press.

Latour, Bruno. 1988. *The Pasteurization of France.* Cambridge, MA: Harvard University Press.

————. 1990. 'Postmodern? No, Simply Amodern! Steps Towards an Anthropology of Science', *Studies in History and Philosophy of Science* 21: 145–71.

————. 1992. 'One More Turn After the Social Turn', in Ernan McMullin (ed.), *The Social Dimension of Science.* Notre Dame, IN: University of Notre Dame Press, 272–94.

Law, John. 1986. 'Introduction', in John Law (ed.), *Power, Action and Belief: A New Sociology of Knowledge?* London: Routledge and Kegan Paul, 1–19.

Lincoln, Yvonne. 1995. 'The Sixth Moment: Emerging Problems in Qualitative Research', *Studies in Symbolic Interaction* 19: 37–55.

Lincoln, Yvonne and Norman Denzin. 1994. 'The Fifth Moment', in Norman Denzin and Yvonne Lincoln (eds), *The Handbook of Qualitative Research.* Thousand Oaks, CA: Sage, 575–86.

Linstead, Stephen. 1993. 'From Postmodern Anthropology to Deconstructive Ethnography', *Human Relations* 46: 97–120.

Long, Elizabeth (ed.). 1997. *From Sociology to Cultural Studies: New Perspectives.* Oxford: Blackwell.

Lynch, Michael. 1992. 'From the "Will to Theory" to the Discursive Collage', in Andrew Pickering (ed.), *Science as Practice and Culture.* Chicago: University of Chicago Press, 283–300.

Lynch, Michael and David Bogen. 1997. 'Sociology's Asociological "Core": An Examination of Textbook Sociology in Light of the Sociology of Scientific Knowledge', *American Sociological Review* 62: 481–93.

Lyotard, Jean-François. 1984. *The Postmodern Condition: A Report on Knowledge.* Minneapolis: University of Minnesota Press.

MacCormack, Carol P. and Marilyn Strathern (eds). 1980. *Nature, Culture and Gender.* Cambridge: Cambridge University Press.

MacIntyre, Alasdair. 1988. *Whose Justice? Which Rationality?* Notre Dame, IN: University of Notre Dame Press.

Marcus, George E. 1994. 'After the Critique of Ethnography: Faith, Hope, and Charity, but the Greatest of These is Charity', in Robert Borofsky (ed.), *Assessing Cultural Anthropology.* New York: McGraw-Hill, 40–51.

Marcus, George E. and Michael Fischer. 1986. *Anthropology as Cultural Critique: An Experimental Moment in the Human Sciences.* Chicago: University of Chicago Press.

Mascia-Lees, Frances E., Patricia Sharpe and Colleen B. Cohen. 1989. 'The Postmodern Turn in Anthropology: Cautions from a Feminist Perspective', *Signs* 15(1): 7–33.

McChesney, Robert. 2002. 'Whatever Happened to Cultural Studies?' in Catherine Warren and Mary Douglas Vavrus (eds), *American Cultural Studies.* Urbana: University of Illinois Press, 76–93.

McRobbie, Angela (ed.). 1997. *Back to Reality: Social Experience and Cultural Studies.* Manchester: Manchester University Press.

Messer-Davidow, Ellen. 1997. 'Whither Cultural Studies?', in Elizabeth Long (ed.), *From Sociology to Cultural Studies: New Perspectives.* Oxford: Blackwell, 489–522.

Mohanty, Chandra. 1988. 'Under Western Eyes: Feminist Scholarship and Colonial Discourse', *Feminist Review* 30: 61–88.

—. (ed.). 1996. *The Future of Anthropological Knowledge.* London: Routledge.

———. 1997. 'Interior Landscapes and Exterior Worlds: The Return of Grand Theory in Anthropology', *Australian Journal of Anthropology* 8: 125–44.

Moore, Henrietta. (ed.). 1999. *Anthropological Theory Today.* Cambridge: Polity.

Morris, Meaghan. 1988. 'Banality in Cultural Studies', *Discourse* 10(2): 3–29.

———. 1991. 'Cultural Studies', in K.K. Ruthven (ed.), *Beyond the Disciplines: The New Humanities.* Canberra: Australian Academy of the Humanities, 1–21.

Mouzelis, Nicos. 1995. *Sociological Theory: What Went Wrong?* London: Routledge.

Nicholson, Linda J. (ed.). 1990. *Feminism/Postmodernism.* New York: Routledge.

Nugent, Stephen and Cris Shore (eds). 1997. *Anthropology and Cultural Studies.* London: Pluto.

Ortner, Sherry. 1974. 'Is Female to Male as Nature Is to Culture?' in Michelle Rosaldo and Louise Lamphere (eds), *Woman, Culture, and Society.* Stanford, CA: Stanford University Press, 67–88.

———. 1984. 'Theory in Anthropology since the Sixties', *Comparative Studies in Society and History* 26: 126–66.

———. (ed.). 1999. *The Fate of 'Culture': Geertz and Beyond.* Berkeley: University of California Press.

Peterson, Richard. 1979. 'Revitalizing the Culture Concept', *Annual Review of Sociology* 5: 137–66.

———. 1994. 'Culture Studies Through the Production Perspective: Progress and Prospects', in Diana Crane (ed.), *The Sociology of Culture: Emerging Theoretical Perspectives.* Oxford: Blackwell, 163–90.

Pichardo, Nelson A. 1997. 'New Social Movements: A Critical Review', *Annual Review of Sociology* 23: 411–30.

Polier, Nicole and William Roseberry. 1989. '*Tristes tropes*: Postmodern Anthropologists Encounter the Other and Discover Themselves', *Economy and Society* 18(2): 245–64.

Pool, Robert. 1991. 'Postmodern Ethnography?' *Critique of Anthropology* 11(4): 309–31.

Purvis, Trevor and Alan Hunt. 1993. 'Discourse, Ideology, Discourse, Ideology, Discourse, Ideology …', *British Journal of Sociology* 44(3): 474–99.

Reyna, Stephen P. 1994. 'Literary Anthropology and the Case Against Science', *Man* 29(3): 555–81.

Rosaldo, Michelle and Louise Lamphere (eds). 1974. *Woman, Culture, and Society*. Stanford CA: Stanford University Press.

Rosaldo, Renato. 1994. 'Whose Cultural Studies?' *American Anthropologist* 96(3): 524–29.

Roth, Paul A. 1989. 'Ethnography without Tears' (with Comments and Reply), *Current Anthropology* 30(5): 555–69.

Rouse, Joseph. 1993. 'What Are Cultural Studies of Scientific Knowledge?' *Configurations* 1: 1–22.

Ruby, Jay (ed.). 1982. *A Crack in the Mirror: Reflexive Perspectives in Anthropology*. Philadelphia: University of Pennsylvania Press.

Ruthven, K.K. (ed.). 1991. *Beyond the Disciplines: The New Humanities*. Canberra: Australian Academy of the Humanities.

Sahlins, Marshall. 1993. 'Goodbye to *tristes tropes*: Ethnography in the Context of Modern World History', *Journal of Modern History* 65: 1–25.

———. 1999. 'Two or Three Things that I Know About Culture', *Journal of the Royal Anthropological Institute* 5: 399–421.

Said, Edward. 1978. *Orientalism*. New York: Pantheon.

Sangren, Steven. 1988. 'Rhetoric and the Authority of Ethnography: "Postmodernism" and the Social Reproduction of Texts' (with Comments and Reply), *Current Anthropology* 29(3): 405–35.

Schaffer, Simon. 1991. 'The Eighteenth Brumaire of Bruno Latour', *Studies in History and Philosophy of Science* 22(1): 174–92.

Scheper-Hughes, Nancy. 1995. 'The Primacy of the Ethical: Propositions for a Militant Anthropology' (with Comments and Reply), *Current Anthropology* 36(3): 409–40.

Schneider, Louis. 1972. 'Some Disgruntled and Controversial Comments on the Idea of Culture in the Social Sciences', *Social Science Quarterly* 53(2): 377–92.

Seidman, Steven. 1991. 'The End of Sociological Theory: The Postmodern Hope', *Sociological Theory* 9(2): 131–46.

———. (ed.) 1994. *The Postmodern Turn: New Perspectives on Social Theory*. Cambridge: Cambridge University Press.

———. 1997. 'Relativizing Sociology: The Challenge of Cultural Studies', in Elizabeth Long (ed.), *From Sociology to Cultural Studies: New Perspectives*. Oxford: Blackwell, 37–61.

Sewell Jr., William. 1999. 'The Concept(s) of Culture', in Victoria Bonnell and Lynn Hunt (eds), *Beyond the Cultural Turn*. Berkeley, CA: University of California Press, 35–61.

Sherwood, Steven J., Philip Smith and Jeffrey Alexander. 1993. 'The British are Coming– Again! The Hidden Agenda of "Cultural Studies"?' *Contemporary Sociology* 22(3): 370–75.

Smith, Philip. 1998a. 'The New American Cultural Sociology: An Introduction', in Philip Smith (ed.), *The New American Cultural Sociology*, 1–14.

———. (ed.). 1998b. *The New American Cultural Sociology*. Cambridge: Cambridge University Press.

Spencer, Jonathan. 1989. 'Anthropology as a Kind of Writing', *Man* 24(1): 145–64.

Steinmetz, George and Ou-Byung Chae. 2002. 'Sociology in an Era of Fragmentation: From the Sociology of Knowledge to the Philosophy of Science, and Back Again', *Sociological Quarterly* 43(1): 111–37.

Strathern, Marilyn. 1987a. 'An Awkward Relationship: The Case of Feminism and Anthropology', *Signs* 12: 276–92.

———. 1987b. 'Out of Context: The Persuasive Fictions of Anthropology' (with Comments and Reply), *Current Anthropology* 28(3): 251–81.

Swidler, Ann. 1986. 'Culture in Action: Symbols and Strategies', *American Sociological Review* 51(2): 273–86.

Swidler, Ann and Jorge Arditi. 1994. 'The New Sociology of Knowledge', *Annual Review of Sociology* 20(1): 305–29.

Thomas, Nicholas. 1999. 'Becoming Undisciplined: Anthropology and Cultural Studies', in Henrietta Moore (ed.), *Anthropological Theory Today*. Cambridge: Polity, 262–79.

Thornton, Robert. 1988. 'The Rhetoric of Ethnographic Holism', *Cultural Anthropology* 3(3): 285–303.

Toren, Christina. 2002. 'Anthropology as the Whole Science of What It Is To Be Human', in Richard Fox and Barbara King (eds), *Anthropology Beyond Culture*. Oxford: Berg, 105–24.

Trouillot, Michel-Rolph. 2002. 'Adieu, Culture: A New Duty Arises', in Richard Fox and Barbara King (eds), *Anthropology Beyond Culture*. Oxford: Berg, 37–60.

Tyler, Stephen A. and George E. Marcus. 1987. 'Comment', *Current Anthropology* 28(3): 275–77.

White, Hayden. 1973. *Metahistory: The Historical Imagination in Nineteenth-Century Europe*. Baltimore, MD: Johns Hopkins University Press.

Williams, Raymond. 1958. *Culture and Society 1780–1950*. London: Chatto and Windus.

Wolf, Eric. 1982. *Europe and the People without History*. Berkeley: University of California Press.

Wright, Georg Henrik von. 1971. *Explanation and Understanding*. Ithaca, NY: Cornell University Press.

Wright, Susan. 1998. 'The Politicization of "Culture"', *Anthropology Today* 14(1): 7–15.

Wuthnow, Robert and Marsha Witten. 1988. 'New Directions in the Study of Culture', *Annual Review of Sociology* 14: 49–67.

Yengoyan, Aram. 1986. 'Theory in Anthropology: On the Demise of the Concept of Culture', *Comparative Studies in Society and History* 28(2): 368–74.

Zammito, John. H. 2004. *A Nice Derangement of Epistemes: Postpositivism in the Study of Science from Quine to Latour*. Chicago: University of Chicago Press.

11

Epilogue:
How Do Paradigm Shifts Work In Anthropology? On the Relationship of Theory and Experience

Günther Schlee

Examples of Paradigm Shifts in Anthropology

There are a number of turning points in the history of anthropology. Older theories have been discarded *in toto*, or at least characterized as hopelessly antiquated and uninteresting, and have been replaced by supposedly new ideas in publications and curricula. One example of this process is the replacement of evolutionism by Malinowski's functionalism, with Malinowski and his disciples acting with the pathos of a movement and the air of an entirely new beginning. Adam Kuper writes in ironic retrospect that, with the help of his disciples, Malinowski succeeded in creating a myth about himself which – apart from early hardships, revelations and heroic total isolation from other Europeans during his field research in the Trobriand Islands – included the notion that after his return to England, 'in the face of pig-headed opposition from reactionary evolutionists and mad diffusionists he buil[t] up a group of dedicated disciples' (Kuper 1983: 10).

Another example is the demise of the culture history school (*kulturhistorische Schule*). The folk history of anthropology has it that the renowned representative of this school, Josef Haekel of Vienna, renounced it formally in 1956, and that since then it has been dead. Precisely what Haekel said can no longer be ascertained.[1] Murdock

---

1   Personal communication from J.C. Winter, to whom I am grateful for help with many of the ideas presented here and on earlier occasions (Schlee 1990).

writes about the end of the *Kulturkreislehre* of the German-Austrian culture-historical school with the clemency of the victor:

> Despite a genuinely admirable methodology, e.g., in the criteria of form and quantity, this group reached erroneous conclusions in their postulation of a small series of culture complexes which allegedly spread as units over enormous areas of the world's surface. The culture history of the present volume has nothing in common with the approach of this group. A criticism, however, is not in order since the leading exponents of the theory publicly renounced it at a world anthropological congress in 1956, in what was perhaps the most laudable demonstration of scientific integrity in the history of our subject. (Murdock 1959: 41)

A renunciation which has earned so much (although slightly poisoned) praise is hard to revoke or even to qualify. Nevertheless, what precisely Haekel revoked remains an open question: Was it certain *Kulturkreise*, which may have been considered to be too speculative and too far-reaching; or was it, as Murdock reports, the cultural-historical approach as such? The latter can hardly have been the case, for in a methodological overview of anthropology from 1973, Knorr still stressed the basically historical character of the Vienna school, citing recent works by Haekel as examples (Knorr 1973: 295). In the present context, however, this is not a point on which we should dwell too long, for in the end anthropology did turn its back on *Kulturkreise*. Today this line of research is presented in English-language introductory works to anthropology with the sketchiness of a caricature, in a way which makes clear that the authors have never read a single work of this school and that student readers will never do so either because they are told that they do not have to.

Another turning point was marked by the anthology *Writing Culture*, edited by James Clifford and George Marcus, though this 1986 publication is actually the well-developed expression of an extant shift, rather than its cause. Whether the term 'paradigm shift' can be used for this change as well is a contentious issue. Robert Ulin (1991) points out that postmodernism, as epitomized by *Writing Culture* and, even more so, by its sister publication *Anthropology as Cultural Critique* (Marcus and Fischer 1986), does not consider itself to be a paradigm in the Kuhnian sense, though he does not elaborate on that thought. Later in this chapter we have the opportunity to pursue the question of what has changed and why the Kuhnian term paradigm shift may no longer apply here. In the superficial sense of a radical alteration, however, the change to postmodernism was undoubtedly a paradigm shift, and Olaf Zenker and Karsten Kumoll (in this volume) use the term in this context without any inhibitions.

Attitudes about Paradigm Shifts

For some people, paradigm shifts are a serious matter. They do not change their paradigms, and they preserve their convictions until death. Thomas Kuhn cites Max Planck in the following passage: 'A new scientific truth does not triumph by convincing its opponents and making them see the light, but rather because its opponents eventually die, and a new generation grows up that is familiar with it' (Kuhn 1996: 151, citing Planck 1949: 33–34). In other words, we lose a conviction by dying and acquire a new one by getting used to it at an early age. Karl Popper, on the other hand, advises us to let theories die, instead of people. Falsification, he says, opens the way for better theories, which possibly withstand falsification attempts longer until they, too, make way.

For others, abandoning basic concepts seems to work in a rather playful or voluntaristic fashion. Lila Abu-Lughod writes 'against culture' for the following reasons:

> The notion of culture (especially as it functions to distinguish "cultures"), despite a long history of usefulness, may now have become something anthropologists would like to work against in their theories, their ethnographic practice and their ethnographic writings. A helpful way to begin to grasp why is to consider what the shared elements of feminist and halfie anthropology clarify about the self/other distinction central to the paradigm of anthropology. (Abu-Lughod 2006: 466)

I, and many others, are in broad agreement with Abu-Lughod's reservations about the term culture, and particularly cultures as countable units. More problematic, in my view, is the reason she gives for her departure from the concept of culture. Possibly, she claims, we should write against the concept of culture despite having found it useful for a considerable amount of time. For a change, as it were. So, does that mean we should decide on a whim to accept or reject theories and paradigms? And if so, is that good?

In anthropology, for decades there has been a tendency to pluralize and historicize positions – that is, to explain theories by their genesis. Whatever is said is qualified with regard to the person speaking, their social embeddedness and their interests. Critics, therefore, like to speak of relativism and describe where this, in their opinion, goes too far. This type of explanation by genesis has in many cases substituted an examination on the basis of empirical data or the demand for such an examination. The latter, on the other hand, has been largely neglected. In the eyes of different observers, this development had different starting points and different culmination points, and these in turn have different anniversaries. The colloquium on which the present volume is based marked the twentieth anniversary of the publication of *Writing Culture*. Other people detect other markers in time. In 1991, Ulin referred to the publication of *Reinventing*

Anthropology, edited by Dell Hymes (1969) just over twenty years before, in an essay entitled 'Critical Anthropology Twenty Years Later'. According to Ulin, the foothold of anthropologists in hegemonic systems was critically reflected on in Hymes's collection. The volume *Anthropology and the Colonial Encounter* (Asad 1973) might certainly have served as a parallel example. There is a line of development leading from a criticism of hegemonic positions to the relativization of every position and to the abandonment of each and every claim to validity for explanations. This development, however, is not at all logically necessary.

Instead of relativity, we could also speak of historicity; historicization can be seen as a special form of relativization.[2] On the relationship of historicity and truth, Lorraine Daston points out that one cannot infer invalidity from historicity :

First, the historical and cultural specificity of the origins of an idea or a technique – or the very fact that ideas and techniques have origins – in itself implies nothing restrictive about their validity in time and space. Mathematical demonstration seems to have arisen only once in human history, in ancient Greece, although sophisticated mathematics was a far more widely distributed cultural attainment. Yet mathematical demonstration was successfully transmitted, most notably in countless editions of Euclid's *Elements*, to intellectual traditions as different as ninth-century Islam and seventeenth-century China. Hence historicity per se should hold no terrors for those who defend the validity of various forms of rationality. (Daston 2003: 10)[3]

What is said here in a general overview about forms of rationality is, of course, also valid in particular and in detail for every theory and every hypothesis. They can be false or correct, independent of how specific or even how disreputable their origin.

The increased critical effort since anthropology's 'critical' turning point, the disclosure of interests and 'positionalities' which has replaced the question of research bias, which had actually been asked all along, is frequently not used to deduce more plausible hypotheses that better stand up to testing in reality. To pin down the authors of *Writing Culture* to one specific epistemological position is

---

2   Popper (2003: 250) speaks of 'historicism' and 'sociologism' as closely related, almost identical lines of thought. Both follow a relativity principle. He refers to Kant, Hegel and Marx, universal categorical systems, the national spirit and class interests. It is not possible to delve into this debate here. Present debates of this type are about 'culture' and 'power'. I just cite it as an example to show that the type of reasoning I try to employ here has been used for a long time and also by people more knowledgeable than myself, as a disclaimer of originality, so to speak.

3   This English translation has been kindly provided by Daston herself. The original German reads: '[D]ie historische und kulturelle Spezifizität der Ursprünge einer Idee oder Technik – oder die bloße Tatsache, daß Ideen oder Techniken überhaupt Ursprünge haben – bringt noch keine Einschränkung ihrer Gültigkeit in Raum und Zeit mit sich. Das mathematische Beweisen scheint in der Menschheitsgeschichte nur ein einziges Mal entstanden zu sein, im alten Griechenland, obwohl anspruchsvolle Mathematik eine viel weiter verbreitete kulturelle Errungenschaft war. Aber das mathematische Beweisen wurde, vor allem durch zahllose Ausgaben von Euklids *Elementen*, höchst unterschiedlichen geistigen Traditionen vermittelt, so etwa dem Islam des neunten und dem China des siebzehnten Jahrhunderts. Wer auf der Gültigkeit bestimmter Rationalitätsformen beharrt, braucht also vor Historizität nicht zurückzuschrecken'.

not so easy. In our debates at the original workshop from which this volume comes, this issue, among others, was discussed. One of the volume's contributors, Vincent Crapanzano, was present and made it clear that *Writing Culture* was not a book on epistemology. Clearly it is not. There are long passages which deal only with improving ethnography as genre of writing. The excessive relativism, of which opponents accuse the *Writing Culture* crowd and which is said to lead to arbitrariness and to make empirical controls impossible, is not postulated explicitly anywhere in the volume. The most relativist element of the book is indeed its title, if taken literally. But I am not quite sure whether it is meant to be. If it is taken literally, however, then there is no denying the fact that in the title, the word 'culture' serves as a direct object of the verb 'to write'. It can be conjugated: I write culture / you write culture / he/she/it writes culture. Here, culture is the product of an action, of writing. If, however, culture is only constituted by writing, then no false statement can be written about culture. One simply writes culture differently from everybody else and, therefore, writes (an)other culture.

This has implications for the question mentioned above of whether the *Writing Culture* movement is a paradigm shift in the Kuhnian sense or not. A paradigm shift is triggered by the pressure of empirical data contradicting a theory. If contradictions become too many and too significant, then at some point there is no attraction to harmonizing old theories with the data any longer. Instead, preference is given to a new theory which provides better explanations for the data, even if it might at first not have the same explanatory power as the old theory. But the turning point for which the book *Writing Culture* stands is not about data and better or less good explanations of a certain theory. Where there is nothing wrong, there can be nothing right either. The Kuhnian paradigm shift – in which theories either bend under the pressure of empirical data, or break and are replaced – in spite of the paradoxes pointed out by Kuhn, requires an epistemological realism. Although the *Writing Culture* movement cannot be pinned down to one explicit epistemological position, it is, however, in its basic sentiment not realist, but relativist.

Now, 'relativist' is, like 'postmodern', mostly a designation used by others. Nobody really wants to have this laid at their door. Explicitly relativistic positions can be disproved by the bundle very elegantly and briefly. Hartmut Lang (1994), for example, needs no more than ten pages to point out the internal contradictions of five variants of relativist theories and to pluck their most colourful feathers regarding their innovative claims. The best way to avoid such criticism is to remain vague. If you do not think relativism through to the end, it is not really all that bad.

Lila Abu-Lughod's position, detailed above, basically invites us to choose our terms and convictions as we wish. Paul Feyerabend's 'anything goes' can be heard in the background. In her own ethnographic practice, however, she does not write whatever she wishes, according to her respective mood on any given day, but first-rate and empirically, abundantly substantiated ethnography, as exemplified in her book *Veiled Sentiments* (Abu-Lughod 1988).

There is another, rightly much-lauded, monograph, *Purity and Exile* by Liisa Malkki (1995), which greatly profits from its author not truly keeping up her relativist programme and in the end being much more realist than she had originally planned. Repeatedly she emphasizes that it is not her intention to write factual history; only in the historical introductory part does she do so of necessity and for the sake of brevity. Rather, she claims to be concerned with the mythico-histories of Burundian refugees in Tanzania. Although it is possible, she states, to write a real history of the horrors causing the flight of these people, and whoever writes for international organizations has to do exactly that, she herself is interested in something different; namely, the symbolic function of tradition, and for this purpose factual correctness is essentially not very important. But, in fact, what is right and what is wrong become very clear in her account. The described horrors of mass murder and expulsion are obviously in accordance with the facts, even if processes of selection and symbolic reshaping are at work. Another mythico-history, namely, that the Tanzanian authorities unjustly collect taxes from the refugees – because according to international law refugees do not have to pay taxes – is not correct, however, and the author says so, too. There is no international law on tax privileges for refugees. So Malkki does not keep up her own programme of inspecting discourses not for their factual correctness, but only for their effects with regard to the promotion of a sense of community. Fortunately she does not, because in this way we learn more.

What is a little disquieting is that ever since *Writing Culture*, younger authors, who at this time went through a formative phase, seem to be ashamed of using facts to back up arguments, and if they do so they apologize for it. Apparently, reading this book leads some people to have basic epistemological attitudes which make it difficult for them to accept any kind of knowledge as reasonably safe and as potential building blocks for theory-building or even, more modestly, as elements of a description of the world which others might share because they would find the same things. This includes knowledge that they have produced themselves with all the methodological refinement and all the critical self-reflection they can muster. There may be epistemological arguments against this kind of hyper-scepticism. The argument outlined above, following Daston, which proposes that just because something is said from an identifiable position does not mean that it is wrong, may be part of a line of reasoning which leads us back to a somewhat more realist epistemology. If we follow Abu-Lughod's more voluntarist style – if it is good enough for her, why should it not be good enough for us? – we might also simply say something like the following: Despite a long history of extreme scepticism, anthropologists, in their theories, their ethnographic practice and their ethnographic writings, may now wish to move back onto slightly firmer epistemological ground. A helpful way to begin to grasp why is to suggest that they might get tired of just deconstructing knowledge about the world. Surely the desire which once made them take up the study of anthropology was to explain how people tick and how they interact with each other, rather than denying the possibility of any such explanation. It may also dawn on them that their employers and sponsors, public and private, may not be prepared to continue indefinitely financing a discipline which constantly proclaims its own uselessness by disclaiming its potential to produce any useful and reasonably reliable knowledge.

The Deconstructionist Turn in Individual Intellectual Biographies

A better use of *Writing Culture* than deriving epistemological guidance from it, which, according to Crapanzano, was not the intention behind it,[4] is to read it as an invitation to self-reflection. This is what Rozita Dimova does in this volume. She describes her own experience with the deconstructionist turn. She had learned that the *zadruga*, the patrilineal coresident extended family, was a reality in the Balkans. She was a bit worried because in her own experience she had not come across any living examples of such groups. Then the whole concept just vanished under the impact of deconstructionist critique. She sounds as if she experienced this dissolution of an orthodoxy as a kind of liberation.

Allow me to follow Dimova's example and reflect for a while on how I experienced the turn in anthropology for which *Writing Culture* stands. Before, during and after the *Writing Culture* turn, I was either in Kenya, doing research among pastoral nomads, or at least my mind was there. I missed many debates going on in Europe and the United States and could therefore reflect on what they meant for my own work only a little later. In fact, some of this reflection has led to the present essay.

I want to illustrate what *Writing Culture* means for my own work through the example of my book, *Identities on the Move: Clanship and Pastoralism in Northern Kenya* (Schlee 1989). This book, published three years after *Writing Culture*, also has a long history of reception, and one I cannot complain about. It has a clear regional focus and never aimed at being a trendsetter for big theoretical debates. It has mostly been well received among regional specialists and also has been used as a model or an inspiration for similar studies in other parts of the world (see Schlee 2008). *Habent sua fata libelli.* Here, however, I am not going to discuss the different fates of different books. I take up the example of my own work to reflect on some issues raised in the *Writing Culture* debate (subjects and objects in anthropological writing) and earlier in this chapter (paradigm shifts). In this I am assisted by John Galaty, who has written a review of that book (Galaty 1992). So I do also have somebody else's view to reflect on.

---

4   See also the remarks by Olaf Zenker and Karsten Kumoll in the Prologue about Clifford's claim that ethnography, as envisaged by him, would not have to give up claims of factuality.

The study is about interethnic clan relationships: the phenomenon that many of the ethnic groups of northern Kenya and southern Ethiopia – though they are clearly divided by cultural discontinuities and often by rivalries as well, violent conflict and changing alliances – are composed to a considerable extent of clans believed to be the same. Thus, some of the clans found among the Gabra were believed to be the same as certain Rendille, Sakuye or Garre clans. I was not just interested in these beliefs and the uses made of these beliefs – that is, what people can achieve in certain situations by claiming to be clan brothers of one or the other segment of a neighbouring ethnic group. I also wanted to find out to what extent these claims to be related might be based on historical fact. To that end I used the method universally used by historians, namely, source criticism. I tried to find sources which were independent of each other by collecting clan histories in different ethnic groups and in different localities among people who did not know each other or at least had not had an opportunity to harmonize their versions of history and to agree on what they told me.[5] The comparison of these oral testimonies with each other and with the scarce archival sources, and the examination of clan-specific cultural forms present in the representations of certain clans in more than one ethnic group, soon revealed that there were real historical events behind these interethnic clan relationships: clans had split and the products of such splits had ended up in different ethnic groups.

In his review, Galaty notes that comparing cultural forms in order to trace relationships is what an earlier generation of anthropologists did, and although much of the book is about how northern Kenyans instrumentalize these relationships today – that is, their sociological aspect – the *Kulturkreise* part of my analysis, unusual by the 1980s, strikes him as more remarkable and receives his emphasis with an undertone of irony: 'Although he calls for a synthesis of British sociological and continental historical anthropology, Schlee in fact pursues, in grand old style, the comparative study of culture traits, historically reconstructing a "Proto-Rendille-Somali" (PRS) camel complex' (Galaty 1992: 219). This complex of features, regulating what is propitious or unpropitious to do with a camel on which day, is indeed an important part of the results of my analysis and sheds new light on the history of the area, which is dominated by an Oromo/Somali dichotomy. The PRS-derived features of many Oromo speakers of the area, which link them to the Rendille, who speak a Somali-like language without being Somali (for that they would have to be Muslims), shows that there are populations and cultural forms present in the area which (to the dismay of some politicians) do not

---

5   Group interviews have become fashionable in development studies, especially as part of a 'quick assessment' package of methods, and have been adopted by some anthropologists. One of their disadvantages is that they blur the differences between different views. Politically dominant personalities may silence divergent views, or the community might wish to present a harmonious picture to the stranger and agree on a compromise version of (historical or contemporary) self-description. The (degree of) independence of different pieces of information, which adds to their value in confirming each other is lost in this process. After all, truth is not established by political compromise or by majority vote.

fit into the modern ethnic dichotomy. Galaty sees all this and discusses it at some length, taking my results seriously, and can therefore not have rejected my methods completely. How then to explain the element of irony? Galaty and I are friends, cooperate closely and meet fairly often, taking into account that we live on different sides of the Atlantic. Whenever we meet, however, we have more important things to discuss than our feelings. So I never asked him for an explanation. My suspicion is that the irony here hides a degree of sympathy. It is a tribute to the zeitgeist. By 1990 (or even by 1960), one could no longer talk about cultural history and diffusionism without a distancing note, and one could no longer bluntly admit that one finds these approaches quite interesting. A paradigm shift had occurred, or rather, as I argue here, a change of fashion.

Seeing the cyclical nature of anthropological fashions, I never worried about getting out of fashion, because I was always sure that fashion would come back to me. There has been evolutionism and functionalism and then neo-evolutionism and neo-functionalism. Let us wait for the neo-neo versions. Neo-diffusionism has come under the name of globalization theory. Because of the limitations of their reading, globalization theorists claim a greater degree of originality than is due to them. They are not aware of older schools which emphasized intercontinental cultural exchanges; they believe globalization to be both a new phenomenon and a new theory. I think that the time has come to reconsider diffusion and to call it unashamedly by its name. Think of the proverbial bathwater. Diffusionism was discarded and rather summarily became a textbook example of the errors of the past. If we examine the bathwater more closely, we might find more and more babies in it and a correspondingly smaller proportion of dirty water.

Diffusionism observes spatial distributions in order to reconstruct temporal sequences. It is a method to reconstruct the past which I applied to clan-specific cultural features in order to shed light on the historical relationships between these clans. Other parts of the evidence I present are based not on cultural comparisons but on oral traditions. Here I applied the ordinary method of source criticism. The assessment of the biases of sources is an important element of source criticism. Divergent interpretations of what happened might be based on different interests, mostly consisting broadly of trying to enhance the prestige or the status of one's own group. Such interests must be taken into account and their influence on the presentation of history discounted if in the comparison of partly agreeing and partly divergent accounts one wishes to get closer to what might actually have happened. My sources did not agree with each other on everything, and my own reconstruction of history is also in partial agreement, partial disagreement with my sources. Nevertheless I cite my sources by name, discuss their positions and then, to a greater or lesser extent, disagree with them. This is what one does in a scholarly debate. What would have given me the right to treat my conversation partners among the pastoral nomads of northern Kenya differently from colleagues in Germany? Is it the fact that they are illiterate? That they have never undergone any formal education in the Western sense? To me all that mattered little in comparison to their right to intellectual acknowledgement.

Generally, however, in the relationship between an anthropologist and their 'field', the conventions are different. Some handbooks of method prescribe that all data need to be anonymized and even place-names fictionalized, so as to be sure not to harm any interlocutor. This position, like anything that has to do with ethics in anthropological debates, tends to be put forward with a heavy moral undertone. But there are other considerations, equally having an ethical dimension, which also need to be taken into account and which might lead to the conclusion that in certain cases the right of the sources of one's information to be mentioned by name carries more weight than the harm possibly done thereby. They have intellectual property rights. It goes without saying that any scholar must cite a colleague to whom he owes information or an idea. Many of the persons I interviewed were historians of their respective social environments. They had vast knowledge and were able to discuss this knowledge critically, in one or two cases on an intellectual level above that of one or two colleagues I have come across at European universities. Would I have been allowed or even obliged to treat them anonymously as native informants? Whatever merits my book has is to a substantial part owed to them, and therefore they merit being mentioned by name.[6] Many of my interlocutors were old men who have since died and it is the memory of them rather than themselves which is honoured. Never have I been criticized for disagreeing with parts of what they have said or for exposing them to criticism. Even where I disagree with them, readers seem to sense my seriousness and my respect towards my interlocutors, which allows me to disagree without causing hurt. I have often heard about Kenyans who were proud to find their late father or grandfather mentioned by name and cited at great length in a book. So in the end I managed to pay for the intellectual property that these people entrusted to me by according some posthumous prestige to them. I would feel ashamed if I had deprived them of this by changing their names.

Galaty finds it difficult to localize me in time. 'Schlee is both conscientious and creative in lending "personal context" to his informants' accounts, and in considering his informants as virtual co-authors he adds to his marvellously archaic method a dialogical postmodern scent' (Galaty 1992: 220). When I wrote *Identities on the Move*, I was not aware of being postmodern in any sense. I had spent much of the 1970s and 1980s driving, walking or riding through northern Kenya, learning three different Cushitic languages and trying to disentangle clan histories and interethnic relations among Rendille, Oromo and Somali, far away

---

6 Certain conditions, of course, must be met. If historical views are hotly contested for political reasons, one might value the safety of one's interlocutors more than the moral obligation to give credit to them. Of course, my informants were aware that I was going to use the information that they gave me for my scholarly work, and had neither requested nor been promised anonymity. It also goes without saying that I did change or omit names wherever I reported illegal activities or might have put members of the groups that I studied at risk in any other way.

from the hot-spots of fast-changing intellectual fashions.[7] So I felt flattered by this characterization, which made me look up to date. What I actually had been doing was to apply what I had learned when I studied anthropology in Hamburg in the 1970s. I had learned that in order to enable the reader to assess from which position an account is written, the anthropologist must reveal some information about themselves. The possible biases of the author need to be brought to light. I applied this approach to the accounts of others as well, which I used in synthesizing my own. I simply used the tools of the craft I had learned.

The Question of Objectivity

Unlike Malkki, who contributes to factual history but claims not to do so, in my case it was an avowed ambition not just to compare different views of history (in the ways they are guided by interests, respond to each other, and so on) but to add my own reconstruction of history as I thought things might actually have happened as a further element of comparison. The mistrust of any claims to present anything as factual history is deep and old in anthropology. From a Malinowskian perspective, it is not the factuality of history that is the issue but its function as a 'mythical charter' that serves one group or another. Radcliffe-Brown (1929: 53) not only denounced all attempts by anthropologists of his time to reconstruct history in the absence of written sources as 'conjectural history' but generally shifted the interest from history, conjectural or not, to sociology, a position which implies that history is not of interest to sociologists.

It is not just the possibility of writing factual history that is questioned by anthropologists but even its desirability. I have repeatedly been asked by students why I think a reconstruction of historical facts matters if indeed the main problem we are dealing with from a more sociological perspective is what effects the different views that actors hold of their histories have – such as symbolic identification, moral lesson, enemy stereotypes. I return to this question at the very end of this chapter. The brief version of my answer, which must suffice here, is that facts add an important element to our understanding of history, something which any down-to-earth realist would find so obvious that they would wonder why such a point needs to be made. But before coming back to the question of the desirability of factual knowledge we might clarify the question of its possibility.

A possible reaction to a call to care more about facts is to say: Of course it would be nice if anthropologists could make harder statements of a more testable

---

7   This includes even Barth's seminal introduction to *Ethnic Groups and Boundaries* (Barth 1969), of which I only became aware twenty years later. No one drew my attention to it because my approach was so similar to Barth's that everyone assumed I knew about it. Of course I had heard Barthian concepts floating about in debates and had read some of his earlier work, with *Nomads of South Persia* (Barth 1961) having a prominent place in my memory, so I was influenced by his theory about ethnicity in unconscious ways. Still, I could have saved myself much trouble figuring out things by myself if I had read more of the relevant theoretical literature at the right time.

kind. We also see the danger that our sponsors, the state and other funding bodies, might in the long run get tired of financing an academic discipline which disclaims the ability to explain anything. But what can we do about it if our carefully considered epistemological positions do not permit any 'harder' form of being scientific? Should we then pretend to have 'factual' knowledge although we know we do not? Of course not. Far be it for me to try to persuade anyone to give up their intellectual sincerity. The possibility of 'factual' knowledge and the question of how real our 'reality' can be therefore needs to be considered a bit more closely.

'Realism', 'positivism' and 'objectivism' have often been connected with the name Karl Popper, the prototypical 'positivist' for all those for whom positivism is a swearword. A closer reading of Popper, however, reveals that for him there is no objectivity in the sense of objects having characteristics which are totally independent of subjects looking at them. On the contrary, he defines objectivity as a result of intersubjective agreement on a proposition. Such agreement can be reached if a plurality of persons agree on the conditions under which they accept or reject a proposition. A proposition can be corroborated by repeated testing against observational data, but is considered valid only until one such test reveals irreconcilable differences from these observational data. Then it would be considered false. Thus, in a Popperian understanding, a statement can be true only in a very weak sense, in the sense of being considered valid until further testing, but it can be considered false in a very definite sense. Falsification, however, is not considered to be a setback but a step in the progress of knowledge: the elimination of an error.

The accusation of postitivism against Popper can therefore be rejected. There is nothing 'positive' in his epistemology. His whole emphasis is on falsification, on negative evidence. Another criticism is directed at the implications that Popperian epistemology is thought to have for the motivations of researchers. Ethnographies of scientific research have shown that scientists are not motivated by the desire to falsify their hypotheses, a point made abundantly clear by Knorr Cetina (1999). This work comprises ethnographies of two 'tribes' of scientists; namely, high-energy physicists at CERN in Geneva and molecular biologists in Heidelberg and Göttingen. The physicists at CERN, the site of a huge particle accelerator, work in large, multinational teams on experiments which are expensive in terms of time, labour and money. They try to find the traces of particles on screens, signs of events that have lasted fractions of a second. In order to distinguish these traces from thousands of other traces of events which are not part of the theory to be tested – in other words, to distinguish the message from the background noise – the background noise also needs to be analysed in detail, and every little change in the experimental set-up needs to be recorded with all its intended and unintended consequences. All the efforts of the physicists are directed at making things work, of getting the results out of the noise. Their nightmares are about being responsible for messing something up. They are interested in finding what they look for: the traces of certain particles which should emerge under just the specified experimental conditions. On the motivational level this is a far cry from regarding the negative outcome of an experiment as a step in the acquisition of knowledge, as falsification theory seems to suggest. Failure can result from thousands of different reasons and in itself is not very interesting, just failure and frustration.

The other tribe Knorr Cetina looks at is made up of molecular biologists at the Max Planck Institutes in Heidelberg and Göttingen. They work individually or in small teams, and their experiments are not as expensive; this means that they can afford to try lots and lots of variations in their experimental set-up. In this they seem to be inspired by the nature they study, applying an evolutionary model of variation and selection. After many tries, they may come across what they are looking for or perhaps something else which is of interest. Here, too, the many failed attempts are not very interesting and not really joyful events. Still, their way of proceeding has some basic similarities with Popper's falsification theory. Both are based on the principles of variation and selection.

Scientists do not open bottles of champagne when their assumptions have been falsified. They do so when they have been corroborated. I suppose Popper knew that. It might therefore be unfair to criticize him for the fact that his epistemology, in which falsification is a fortunate event, is not reflected in the motivations of the researchers. After all, he wanted to explain the basic conditions of knowledge. Popper's falsification theory is about epistemology, not about the psychology of research.

The emphasis of Knorr Cetina's research is on the construction of knowledge in communities of scientists, in 'epistemic cultures'. The factors which intervene and lead to the failure of a high-energy physics experiment, expensive as it may be, are outside factors beyond these construction processes. Likewise, the fact that many cell cultures just die, in Göttingen or elsewhere, and that experiments do not have the expected results shows that the outside world interferes. At the risk of being called naive empiricists, we might call this the reality principle. I do not think Knorr Cetina would deny the existence of this ultimate corrective, which comes in from outside the construction process and which we might call reality. After all, her argument is not really affected by such a philosophical question. What she is interested in is the sociology of knowledge (or the anthropology of science). She does not intend to write a new epistemology (realist or subjectivist or whatever) of her own and therefore should not be excessively interpreted in terms of the epistemological implications of her findings. In discussions, I have heard people say that Knorr Cetina has proved that even in the hard sciences the assumption of reality interfering in the selection of explanations has been abandoned and that all kinds of knowledge are just constructed according to rules of internal consistency. People cite Knorr Cetina against Popper. I do not think that this does justice to either of them.

We may conclude at this point that Knorr Cetina's description of epistemic cultures does not affect the 'objectivity' of science postulated by Popper. There is even some overlap between these authors. Popper himself explains 'objectivity' as a social, supra-individual phenomenon resulting from public debate and mutual criticism – that is, in a very sociological manner for a philosopher. Both authors lead us to the question of the supra-individual epistemic subject,[8] which is perhaps more interesting than the old question of objectivity discussed here. The extent of any contradiction construed between Popper and Knorr Cetina is further reduced by the different foci of the two scholars. Popper's focus is on improving science and liberating it from epistemological errors. Knorr Cetina is an ethnographer who observes how two different communities of scientists, high-energy physicists and molecular biologists, in rather different ways arrive at what they perceive as scientific knowledge. She does not argue for a different epistemology, nor does she propose a better version of physics or biology as the result of her ethnography. She argues on a different, less normative and more specific and descriptive level. All this would make it difficult for anyone to use her against Popper.

Some of these observations may be helpful in answering the opposite question: Can Popper be used against Knorr Cetina? This too appears difficult to me, because there is little direct contradiction between the two authors. Popper devotes a whole chapter (Popper 2003: 248–61) to his argument against the sociology of knowledge, but this criticism is clearly directed at a different type of sociology of knowledge that which Knorr Cetina exemplifies. Earlier sociologists of knowledge aimed to arrive at a purer or higher kind of knowledge by making the social and historical formative forces – such as national and class interests, ideologies – conscious and in this way eliminating them. Popper describes this effort as futile and ironically applies a kind of class analysis to these sociologists themselves. Knorr Cetina clearly does not claim to be able to arrive at a purified and truer version of physics or biology by making us aware of the social processes

---

8   For Popper science is a supra-individual process, with control and mutual criticism being essential components. He carries out two thought experiments. In one of them he shows that a revealed truth which by some coincidence is identical with a scientific truth discovered later is not a scientific truth, because it has not passed the test of criticism by the scientific community. In the other, he poses the question of the status of the findings of Robinson Crusoe, if Robinson Crusoe had been a scientist and had carried out experiments in isolation. Here he comes to the same result (Popper 2003: 255–57). Knorr Cetina discusses the collective nature of research in high-energy physics as it is reflected in conventions about authorship under the heading 'The Erasure of the Individual as an Epistemic Subject' (Knorr Cetina 1999: 166–71). A fuller discussion of supra-individual epistemic subjects should also examine the phenomenon of 'distributed cognition' (Hutchins 2006; see also Heintz, this volume), the phenomenon that cognitive processes can involve many people and machines and would be impossible both without sensors which perceive things in a way that our natural senses cannot and without computers which arrange the data in a way beyond the calculating capacity of our brains. We may need a satellite in order to look at the Earth from space and confirm a certain hypothesis. There is no individual being who has all the skills and all the knowledge required for launching one alone. To achieve the desired viewpoint, we need an organization comprising many persons and many machines. The same, of course, applies for many technological gadgets that we use every day in our homes.

The quest for supra-individual epistemic subjects may be inspired by modern technology, but we can find such subjects also in settings where modern technology plays no role at all. Take plurispecies symbiotic systems such as pastoralism: a plurality of human beings with different tasks, their dogs, their reindeer, camels or cattle. Their measure of distance is how far the animals can walk in a day; the direction of their movements is determined by where pasture smells sweetest to the ungulates. Multiple and complex cognitive processes comprise steps which make use of the senses of the (non-human) animals. Kirill Istomin is currently working on such complex forms of cognition.

under which physical and biological knowledge is generated. Nor have I found any claim in her work that, as an anthropologist or sociologist, she is to a lesser degree a part of a supra-individual system or bound any less by conventions than the physicists or biologists whom she describes. There are no claims to superiority, purity or a higher degree of intellectual freedom in her work; Popper's criticism of sociologists of knowledge therefore clearly does not pertain to her. What she does is provide a detailed ethnographic description of how scientific knowledge is actually generated in specific laboratories. I can think of no objection that Popper or a Popperian could have against such an exercise.

A Plea for Realism

The main result of this excursion into philosophy and the sociology of knowledge is that there is no contradiction between the awareness of belonging to an epistemic culture and the striving for 'objectivity' in a Popperian sense. I hope to have shown that there are no hard obstacles to anthropologists who want to make use of a higher dose of realism. The social reality described by an anthropologist is of course influenced by the anthropologist. The anthropologist interacts with the field. But even that is not specific to anthropology and is therefore no reason to be less scientific than other sciences. If the Göttingen molecular biologists look at the object of their study through an electron microscope, they shoot at it with particles and destroy it in the process.[9] So they need to examine their own influence on what they study as well. And the Geneva high-energy physicists spend more time on measuring the effects of their instruments and excluding side effects than on observing what they actually want to see. A complicated relationship between subject and object is not a peculiarity of anthropology, but only anthropology allows itself to be paralysed by it, in extreme cases to the extent of disclaiming the possibility of knowledge as such.

Anthropologists have often internalized the fundamental scepticism characteristic of their discipline to such an extent that they reconcile themselves with the presumed impossibility of statements about reality by disclaiming their desirability if they were possible. We now return to a question raised earlier, the question I have been asked by students: Why do you want to find out what really has taken place? Is it not more important to study what people think of it? Is it not perceptions of history which guide our behaviour rather than history itself?

I have explained above that in order to write a history that we can assume to be closer to the facts, we need to take biases, ambitions and interests into account and discount their effects on the presentation of history. If the topic is not history but the social forces at work in the presentation of history, then these effects

---

9   The 'anthropological gaze', by contrast, is believed just to distort, but not to destroy.

should, of course, not be discounted. On the contrary, for such a study they would be the focus of attention. The study of these social forces would, however, not be very satisfactory without having also made at least a serious attempt to reconstruct factual history. Without a skeleton of facts, one would not be able to state what rival interpretations refer to, or describe in which direction a given view of history diverges from the facts and for which reasons. It is good to know about the object behind the lens in order to study the effects of the lens, although we might arrive at knowledge about the object only by looking at it through many different lenses.

References

Abu-Lughod, Lila. 1988. *Veiled Sentiments: Honor and Poetry in a Bedouin Society.* Berkeley, CA: University of California Press.

———. 2006[1991]. 'Writing Against Culture', in Henrietta L. Moore and Todd Sanders (eds), *Anthropology in Theory: Issues in Epistemology.* Oxford: Blackwell, 446–79.

Asad, Talal (ed.). 1973. *Anthropology and the Colonial Encounter.* London: Ithaca Press.

Barth, Fredrik. 1961. *Nomads of South Persia: The Basseri Tribe of Khamseh Confederacy.* Boston: Little Brown.

———. (ed.). 1969. *Ethnic Groups and Boundaries: The Social Organization of Culture Difference.* Boston: Little Brown.

Clifford, James and George E. Marcus (eds). 1986. *Writing Culture: The Poetics and Politics of Ethnography.* Berkeley: University of California Press.

Daston, Lorraine. 2003. *Wunder, Beweise, Tatsachen: Zur Geschichte der Rationalität.* Frankfurt am Main: Fischer.

Galaty, John. 1992. 'Review of Günther Schlee, *Identities on the Move: Clanship and Pastoralism in Northern Kenya*', *Man* 27(1): 219–20.

Hutchins, Edwin. 2006. 'The Distributed Cognition Perspective on Human Interaction', in N. J. Enfield and Stephen C. Levinson (eds), *Roots of Human Sociality: Culture, Cognition and Interaction.* Oxford: Berg, 375–98.

Hymes, Dell (ed.). 1969. *Reinventing Anthropology.* New York: Random House.

Knorr, Karin D. 1973. 'Methodik der Völkerkunde', in *Enzyklopädie der geisteswissenschaftlichen Arbeitsmethoden*, vol 9. Munich: Oldenbourg, 295–345.

Knorr Cetina, Karin. 1999. *Epistemic Cultures: How the Sciences Make Knowledge.* Cambridge, MA: Harvard University Press.

Kuhn, Thomas S. 1996[1962]. *The Structure of Scientific Revolutions.* Chicago: University of Chicago Press.

Kuper, Adam. 1983. *Anthropology and Anthropologists: The Modern British School,* 2nd edn. London: Routledge and Kegan Paul.

Lang, Hartmut. 1994. *Wissenschaftstheorie für die ethnologische Praxis.* Berlin: Reimer.

Malkki, Liisa. 1995. *Purity and Exile: Violence, Memory and National Cosmology among Hutu Refugees in Tanzania.* Chicago: University of Chicago Press.

Marcus, George E. and Michael M.J. Fischer. 1986. *Anthropology as Cultural Critique.* Chicago: University of Chicago Press.

Murdock, George Peter. 1959. *Africa: Its Peoples and Their Culture History.* New York: McGraw-Hill.

Planck, Max. 1949. *Scientific Autobiography, and Other Papers,* trans. Frank Gaynor. New York: Philosophical Library.

Popper, Karl. 2003[1945]. *Die offene Gesellschaft und ihre Feinde, 2: Falsche Propheten: Hegel, Marx und die Folgen.* Tübingen: Mohr Siebeck.

Radcliffe-Brown, Alfred R. 1929. 'A Further Note on Ambrym', *Man* 29: 50–53.

Schlee, Günther. 1989. *Identities on the Move: Clanship and Pastoralism in Northern Kenya.* Edinburgh: Edinburgh University Press.

———. 1990. 'Das Fach Sozialanthropologie/Ethnologie seit dem Zweiten Weltkrieg', in Wolfgang Prinz and Peter Weingart (eds), *Die sogenannten Geisteswissenschaften: Innenansichten.* Frankfurt am Main: Suhrkamp, 306–12.

———. 2008. 'The "Five Drums," Proto-Rendille-Somali, and Oromo Nationalism: A Response to Aneesa Kassam', *Ethnohistory* 55: 141–83.

Ulin, Robert C. 1991. 'Critical Anthropology Twenty Years Later: Modernism and Postmodernism in Anthropology', *Critique of Anthropology* 11(1): 63–89.

Notes on Contributors

Vincent Crapanzano is Distinguished Professor of Comparative Literature and Anthropology at the City University of New York Graduate Center. He received an A.B. from Harvard University and his Ph.D. from Columbia University. Among his books are *The Fifth World of Forster Bennett: A Portrait of a Navaho* (1972), *The Hamadsha: An Essay in Moroccan Ethnopsychiatry* (1973), *Tuhami: A Portrait of a Moroccan* (1980), *Waiting: The Whites of South Africa* (1985), *Hermes' Dilemma and Hamlet's Desire: On the Epistemology of Interpretation* (1992), *Serving the Word: From the Pulpit to the Bench* (2000), *Imaginative Horizons: An Essay in Literary-Philosophical Anthropology* (2004) and *The Harkis: the Wound That Never Heals* (2011). He is currently finishing a philosophical-reflective memoir.

Rozita Dimova completed her Ph.D. in 2004 in Anthropology at Stanford University. She also holds an M.A. in History from the Central European University, Budapest and an M.Phil. in Social Anthropology from the University of Cambridge. From 2004–2006 she was a postdoctoral research fellow at the Max Planck Institute for Social Anthropology in Halle/Saale. Since 2006 she has been a project coordinator at the Institute for Eastern European Studies at the Free University, Berlin. She has published academic articles in the journals *Nationalities Papers, Ethnologia Balkanica, Zeitschrift für Ethnologie* and *Ethno-Anthropo Zoom*. She is an editor of the book *The Echo of the Nation: Historical-anthropological Perspectives on Macedonian National Identity* (2009).

Christophe Heintz is assistant professor of cognitive science at the Central European University, Budapest. He studied mathematics and philosophy in Paris and Cambridge (U.K.), and holds a Ph.D. from the Ecole des Hautes Etudes en Science Sociales, Paris. His work attempts to bridge cognitive and social sciences, and he has been exploring the prospects, through case studies, of theoretical frameworks such as distributed cognition and cultural epidemiology. In particular, he has worked on the relevance of results drawn from cognitive psychology for the history and sociology of mathematics. His journal articles include 'Institutions as Mechanisms of Cultural Evolution' (*Biological Theory*, 2007), 'Web Search Engines and Distributed Assessment Systems' (*Pragmatics and Cognition*, 2006) and 'The Ecological Rationality of Strategic Cognition' (*Behavioral and Brain Science*, 2005). He edited the volume *Studies in Cognitive Anthropology of Science* (2004).

Thomas G. Kirsch is professor and chair of social and cultural anthropology at the University of Konstanz. He received his Ph.D. from the European University Viadrina, Germany, in 2002 and taught at the Department of Anthropology in Halle and then at the Department of Anthropology at Goldsmiths College, University of London, before coming to Konstanz in 2009. Between 1993 and 2001, he conducted fieldwork in Zambia. He has published two monographs on African Christianity and articles in the journals *American Anthropologist* (2004), *Visual Anthropology* (2006) and *American Ethnologist* (2007). Since 2003, he has also conducted fieldwork on issues of security and crime prevention in South Africa.

Karsten Kumoll is programme manager at the German Council of Science and Humanities in Köln. He has a Ph.D. in sociology from the Albert Ludwigs University, Freiburg, Germany, and holds master's degrees in sociology from the Albert-Ludwigs University, Freiburg, and in social anthropology from the London School of Economics. During his doctoral studies, he was a visiting fellow at Harvard University. His publications include *'From the Native's Point of View'? Kulturelle Globalisierung nach Clifford Geertz und Pierre Bourdieu* ('Cultural Globalisation after Clifford Geertz and Pierre Bourdieu', 2005) and *Kultur, Geschichte und die Indigenisierung der Moderne: Eine Analyse des Gesamtwerks von Marshall Sahlins* ('Culture, History and the Indigenization of Modernity: An Analysis of the Complete Works of Marshall Sahlins', 2007).

Stephen P. Reyna is an associate of the Max Planck Institute for Social Anthropology and a member of the Core Staff of the Humanitarian and Conflict Response Institute at the University of Manchester. He is interested in social epistemology and theory and was the founder and first editor of *Anthropological Theory*. He authored 'Literary Anthropology and the Case against Science' (*Man*, 1994), 'Theory in Anthropology in the Nineties' (*Cultural Dynamics*, 1997) and 'Force, Power, and the Problem of Order: An Anthropological Approach?' (*Sociologus*, 2003). He has authored, among other works, *Wars Without End: A Political Economy of a Precolonial African State* (1990), *Connections: Brain, Mind, and Culture in a Social Anthropology* (2002) and *Crude Domination: Towards an Anthropology of Oil* (2011, co-edited with Andrea Behrends and Günther Schlee). He is currently finishing a book tentatively entitled *Deadly Contradictions: The*

New American Empire and Global Warring, 1945-2012.

Günther Schlee is a Director at the Max Planck Institute for Social Anthropology at Halle. Until 1999 he was a Professor at Bielefeld. His habilitation thesis (Bayreuth, 1986) was published as *Identities on the Move: Clanship and Pastoralism in Northern Kenya* (1989). In his department, Integration and Conflict, he directs research on Africa, Central Asia and Europe. Among his recent publications are *Imagined Differences: Hatred and the Construction of Identity* (2002), *How Enemies are Made: Towards a Theory of Ethnic and Religious Conflicts* (2008) and two volumes, co-edited with E.E. Watson, entitled *Changing Identifications and Alliances in North-East Africa* (2009).

Steffen Strohmenger is a social anthropologist and visiting research fellow at the Graduate School programme 'Society and Culture in Motion' at the Martin Luther University, Halle-Wittenberg, Germany. He received an M.A. from the Free University, Berlin and his Ph.D. from the Martin Luther University, Halle-Wittenberg. He is currently conducting research on the afterlife in everyday discourses of Muslims in Egypt and is working on a book on the Jabaliya Bedouins of the south Sinai. His publications include *Kairo: Gespräche über Liebe. Eine ethnographische Collage in 12 Szenen* ('Cairo: Conversations About Love. An Ethnographic Collage', 1996) and *Sachfragen und Glücksfragen: Von der Asymmetrie zur Re-Symmetrisierung ihrer Wahrheitsfähigkeit* ('On the Symmetry of Non-Value and Value Judgements', 2006).

John H. Zammito is John Antony Weir Professor of History at Rice University, Texas. He received his B.A. from the University of Texas at Austin and his Ph.D. from the University of California, Berkeley. His research focuses on Enlightenment, idealism and romanticism in Germany, and on the history and philosophy of science. His key publications are *The Genesis of Kant's Critique of Judgment* (1992), *Kant, Herder, and the Birth of Anthropology* (2002) and *A Nice Derangement of Epistemes: Post-Positivism in the Study of Science from Quine to Latour* (2004). He is currently working on the 'pre-history' of biology as a special science in eighteenth-century Germany.

Olaf Zenker is Ambizione Research Fellow (SNSF) at the Institute of Social Anthropology at the University of Bern, Switzerland, where he previously worked as assistant professor. He received a M.Sc. in social anthropology from the London School of Economics and an M.A. in linguistics and literature from the University of Hamburg. While doing his Ph.D. at the Martin Luther University, Halle-Wittenberg, he was a doctoral student at the Max Planck Institute for Social Anthropology, where he also became a postdoctoral research fellow in the project group 'Law, Organization, Science & Technology (LOST)'. His publications include *Irish/ness Is All Around Us: Language Revivalism and the*

Culture of Ethnic Identity in Northern Ireland (2013) as well as articles in the journals *Paideuma, Zeitschrift für Ethnologie, Nations and Nationalism, Social Science & Medicine* and *Critique of Anthropology.*

Index

www.ingramcontent.com/pod-product-compliance
Lightning Source LLC
Chambersburg PA
CBHW060033030426
42334CB00019B/2302